PRAISE FOR

*Evening in the Palace of Reason*

"Gaines writes with admirable erudition. . . . No author could want a more promising pair of antagonists."
—*New York Times Book Review*

"An eloquent and fascinating study, highly debatable at points yet all the more stimulating for that. . . . Accessible and entertaining."
—*Time*

"Gaines maps sweeping cultural history onto his dual biography with dazzling virtuosity. . . . If you've ever wondered about the metaphysics of Bach's music, you won't find a more lucid and engaging guide."
—*Entertainment Weekly*

"Gaines has a deep understanding of music and an infectious zeal for narrative history. . . . He has created a moving portrait of genius and human failure."
—*People* (four stars)

"Lively . . . with a delicious cast of characters. . . . Gaines shows himself a deft writer."
—*Denver Post*

"Gaines writes very accessibly. . . . Clever without being frivolous and explanatory without being effete . . . [*Evening in the Palace of Reason*] is a marvelous story that will captivate the classical music audience."
—*Booklist*

"Highly entertaining. . . . Gaines masterfully weaves parallel narratives of the lives of Bach and Frederick leading up to their momentous meeting. . . . Lovers of music, European history, and Western philosophy will find this book an enormous pleasure."

—*Library Journal* (starred review)

"The questions Bach raises are so urgent that it feels as though Gaines had no choice but to write this book. He writes superbly, too—he is a first-rate communicator of ideas. Even when they thrill him, he manages to avoid indulgence; he draws on the knowledge he has given the reader as if sharing an in-joke, and makes us feel at home with things that would have sounded arcane otherwise."

—*Daily Telegraph*

"Intelligent, stylish, wryly witty, serious yet never solemn, and, above all, passionate in its celebration of a great composer."

—*Guardian*

"Impossible to put down when one is dancing, swerving, [and] stumbling through the extraordinary brilliance, blood-thirst cruelty, fecundity, and religious and other feuds of the society that helped to inspire Bach and sustain Frederick. . . . A wonderfully engaging tale."

—*Sunday Independent*

"Articulate, well-informed, and rigorous. . . . Gaines makes this dauntingly technical subject accessible."

—*Sunday Telegraph*

MICHAEL CROUSER

---

*About the Author*

---

A longtime journalist and the former editor of several magazines, including *Time* and *People*, JAMES R. GAINES lives with his family in Paris.

EVENING IN THE PALACE OF REASON

*Also by James R. Gaines*

Wit's End: Days and Nights of the
Algonquin Round Table

The Lives of the Piano

# Evening in the Palace of Reason

BACH *meets* FREDERICK THE GREAT

*in the* AGE OF ENLIGHTENMENT

JAMES R. GAINES

HARPER PERENNIAL

NEW YORK • LONDON • TORONTO • SYDNEY

HARPER ● PERENNIAL

A hardcover edition of this book was published in 2005 by
Fourth Estate, an imprint of HarperCollins Publishers.

P.S.™ is a trademark of HarperCollins Publishers.

HarperCollins books may be purchased for educational,
business, or sales promotional use. For information please
write: Special Markets Department, HarperCollins Publishers,
10 East 53rd Street, New York, NY 10022.

First Harper Perennial edition published 2006.

*Designed by Barbara M. Bachman*

*Map by Paul J. Pugliese*

Library of Congress Cataloging-in-Publication Data has been
applied for.

ISBN 0-00-715658-8
ISBN-10: 0-00-715661-8 (pbk.)
ISBN-13: 978-0-00-715661-0 (pbk.)

07 08 09 10 ❖/RRD 10 9 8 7 6 5 4

*FOR ALLISON, NICK,*

*WILLIAM, AND LILLIAN*

# CONTENTS

..

**Germany 1747**
during the time of
Bach and Frederick the Great

EVENING IN THE PALACE OF REASON

## THEME FOR A PAS DE DEUX

FREDERICK THE GREAT HAD ALWAYS LOVED TO PLAY the flute, which was one of the qualities in him that his father most despised. Throughout his youth, Frederick had to play in secret. Among his fondest memories were evenings at his mother's palace, where he was free to dress up in French clothes, curl and puff his hair in the French style, and play duets with his soulmate sister Wilhelmina—he on the flute he called *Principe*, she on her lute *Principessa*. When Frederick's father once happened unexpectedly on this scene, he flew into a rage. Even more than his son's flute playing, Frederick William I hated everything French—French clothes, French food, French mannerisms, French civilization, all of which he dismissed as "effeminate." He had of course been educated in French, like most German princes (he could not even spell *Deutschland* but habitually wrote *Deusland*), so he had to speak French, but he hated himself for it. He dressed convicts for their executions in French clothes as his own sort of fashion statement.

In this regard and others, Frederick's father was at least half mad. Flagrantly manic-depressive and violently abusive, he also suffered from porphyria, a disease common among descendants of Mary Queen of Scots (which he was, on his mother's side). Its afflictions included migraines, abscesses, boils, paranoia, and mind- engulfing stomach pains. The rages of Frederick William were frequent, infamous, and knew no rank: He hit servants, family members (no one more than Frederick), even visiting diplomats. Racked by gout, he lashed out with crutches, and if the pain was bad enough to put him in his wheelchair, he chased people down in it brandishing a cane. He was infamous for his canings—he left canes in various rooms of the castle so they would always be close at hand—but he also threw plates at people, pulled their hair, slapped them, knocked them down, and kicked them. A famous story has him walking down the street in Potsdam and noticing one of his subjects darting away. He ordered the man to stop and tell him why he ran. Because he was afraid, the man said. "Afraid?! Afraid?! You're supposed to love me!" Out came the cane and down went the subject, the king screaming, "Love me, scum!" Such a rage could be sparked by the very word *France*.

Not until his father died when Frederick was twenty-eight could he play his flute free from the threat of censure or attack, so naturally it was among his most beloved and time-consuming pastimes as king. With the musicians in his court Kapelle, who were not only the best in Prussia but the best he could buy away from Saxony and Hanover and every other German territory, he played concerts virtually every evening from seven to nine o'clock, sometimes even on the battlefield. He cared as much about music as he cared about anything, except perhaps for war.

Having had both a love of the military and a cynical, self-protective ruthlessness literally beaten into him by his father, Frederick had already been dubbed "the Great" after only five years on the throne, by which time he had greatly enlarged his kingdom with a campaign of outrageously deceitful diplomacy and equally incredible military strokes that proved him a brilliant antagonist and made Prussia, for the first time, a top-rank power in Europe. A diligent amateur of the arts and literature—avid student of the Greek and Roman classics, composer and patron of the opera, writer of poetry and political theory (mediocre poetry and wildly hypocritical political theory, but never mind)—he had managed also to make himself known as the very model of the newly heralded "philosopher-king," so certified by none less than Voltaire, who described young Frederick as "a man who gives battle as readily as he writes an opera. . . . He has written more books than any of his contemporary princes has sired bastards; and he has won more victories than he has written books." Frederick's court in Potsdam fast became one of the most glamorous in Europe, no small thanks to himself, who worked tirelessly to draw around him celebrities (like Voltaire) from every corner of the arts and sciences.

One Sunday evening in the spring of his seventh year as king, as his musicians were gathering for the evening concert, a courtier brought Frederick his usual list of arrivals at the town gate. As he looked down the list of names, he gave a start.

"Gentlemen," he said, "old Bach is here." Those who heard him said there was "a kind of agitation" in his voice.

§

JOHANN SEBASTIAN BACH was sixty-two years old in 1747, only three years from his death, and making the long trip from Leipzig, which would be his last journey, was surely more a concession than a wish. An emphatically self-directed, even stubborn man, Bach took a dim view of this particular king, the Prussian army having overrun Leipzig less than two years before, and at his advanced age he could not have relished spending two days and a night being jostled about in a coach to meet the bitter enemy of his own royal patron, the elector of Saxony. Even more problematic than the political and physical difficulties of such a journey, though, the meeting represented something of a confrontation for the aging composer—a confrontation, one might say, with his age. In music and virtually every other sphere of life in mid-eighteenth-century Germany, Frederick represented all that was new and fashionable, while Bach's music had come to stand for everything ancient and outmoded. His musical language, teaching, and tradition had been rejected and denounced by young composers and theorists, even by his own sons, and Bach had every reason to fear that he and his music were to be forgotten entirely after his death, had indeed been all but forgotten already. For this reason and others, his encounter with Prussia's young king threatened to bring into question some of the most important qualities by which he defined himself, as a musician and as a man. It would also present him the opportunity for one of the most powerful and eloquent assertions of principle he had ever made, but that would have been anything but clear to him at the time.

Bach came despite the challenges involved because Frederick was the employer of his son Carl Philipp Emanuel Bach, the chief harpsichordist in Prussia's royal Kapelle. Carl had been hired on when Frederick was still crown prince, hiding from his father the fact that he had any musicians and paying their salaries by borrowing secretly from foreign governments and padding his expenses. It was even then an extraordinary group, including the best composers and musicians of the "modern" generation, most of them well known to—but a good deal younger than—Carl's father. Frederick had been hinting broadly that he would like to meet "old Bach" ever since Carl had come to work for him, and Carl's letters home had reflected a growing concern that at some point the king's wish would become his command. But no one knew better than Carl just what a collision of worlds a meeting between his flashy, self-regarding employer and his irascible, deeply principled father would be.

There were very few similarities indeed between the young king and the old composer, but there was this one: They stood firm in their respective roles, their fields of work having been determined by long ancestry. The Hohenzollern dynasty had ruled in Germany for three hundred years before Frederick was born and would rule for two hundred more, to the end of World War I. The Bach line stretched from Luther across three centuries, and theirs too was a family business; more than five dozen Bachs held important musical positions in German towns, courts, and churches between the sixteenth and eighteenth centuries.

Such strong ancestral lines made the journey to Potsdam even more pointedly a foray into enemy territory for Bach, of course, not only literally, as a proud son of Saxony standing against the aggressive Prussian neighbor, but figuratively as well: The king and the composer faced each other as the embodiments of warring values. Bach was a devout Lutheran householder who had had twenty children with two wives; one left him a widower, the second was waiting for him at home. Frederick, a bisexual misanthrope in a childless, political marriage, was a lapsed Calvinist whose reputation for religious tolerance arose from the fact that he held all religions equally in contempt. Bach wrote and spoke German. Frederick boasted that he had "never read a German book."

Nowhere were they more different, though, than in their attitudes toward music. Bach represented church music and especially the "learned counterpoint" of canon and fugue, a centuries-old craft that by now had developed such esoteric theories and procedures that some of its practitioners saw themselves as the custodians of a quasi-divine art, even as weavers of the cosmic tapestry itself. Frederick and his generation were having none of that. They denigrated counterpoint as the vestige of an outworn aesthetic, extolling instead the "natural and delightful" in music, by which they meant the easier pleasure of song, the harmonic ornamentation of a single line of melody. For Bach this new, so-called *galant* style, with all its lovely figures and stylish grace, was full of emptiness. Bach's cosmos was one in which the planets themselves played the ultimate harmony, a tenet that had been unquestioned since the "sacred science" of Pythagoras; composing and performing music was for him and his musical ancestors a deeply spiritual enterprise whose sole purpose, as his works were inscribed, was "for the glory of God." For Frederick the goal of music was simply to be "agreeable," an entertainment and a diversion, easy work for performer and audience alike. He despised music that, as he put it, "smells of the church" and called Bach's chorales specifically "dumb stuff." Cosmic notions like the "music of the spheres" were for him so much dark-age mumbo jumbo.

In short, Bach was a father of the late Baroque, and Frederick was a son of the early Enlightenment, and no father-son conflict has ever been more pointed. Put all too simply, as any one-sentence description of the Enlightenment must be, myth and mysticism were giving way to empiricism and reason, the belief in the necessity of divine grace to a confidence in human perfectibility, the descendants of Pythagoras and Plato to those of Newton. In music, as in virtually every other intellectual pursuit, the intuitions, attitudes, and ideas of a thousand years were being exchanged for principles and habits of thought that are still evolving and in question three centuries later. Frederick the Great and Johann Sebastian Bach met at the tipping point between ancient and modern culture, and what flowed from their meeting would be a more than musical expression of that historic moment.

§

WHEN FREDERICK SAW "old Bach's" name on the visitors' list, he called for the composer to be brought to the palace immediately. Bach no doubt was looking forward to settling in at Carl's house for the evening—he would have been exhausted—but this was a summons, not an invitation. What followed was reported in a palace press release that was picked up by newspapers in Prussia, Saxony, and other German territories.

One hears from Potsdam that last Sunday the famous Kapellmeister from Leipzig, Herr Bach, arrived [at the castle]. . . . His August self [Frederick] went, at [Bach's] entrance, to the so-called *Forte et Piano*, condescending also to play, in His Most August Person and without any preparation, a theme for the Kapellmeister Bach, which he should execute in a fugue. This was done so happily by the aforementioned Kapellmeister that not only His Majesty was pleased to show his satisfaction thereat, but also all those present were seized with astonishment. Herr Bach found the theme propounded to him so exceedingly beautiful that he intends to set it down on paper as a regular fugue and have it engraved on copper. . . .

The account is incomplete, and the blur of Baroque rhetoric somewhat obscures the story. The facts are these: Frederick gave Bach an impossibly long and complex musical figure and asked the old master to make a three-part fugue of it, which was a bit like giving word salad to a poet and asking for a sonnet. So difficult was the figure Bach was given that the twentieth century's foremost composer of counterpoint, Arnold Schoenberg, marveled at the fact that it had been so cleverly contrived that it "did not admit one single canonic imitation"—in other words, that the Royal Theme, as it has come to be known, was constructed to be as resistant to counterpoint as possible. Still, Bach managed, with almost unimaginable ingenuity, to do it, even alluding to the king's taste by setting off his intricate counterpoint with a few *galant* flourishes.

When Bach had finished the three-part fugue, while his audience of virtuosi was still "seized with astonishment," Frederick asked Bach if he could go himself one better, this time making the theme into a fugue for *six* voices. Knowing instantly that he had no hope of doing such a vastly more complex improvisation (Bach had never even *written* a six-part fugue for keyboard), he demurred with the observation that not every subject is suitable for improvisation in six voices; he said he would have to work it out on paper and send it to Frederick later. Clearly no one would have faulted him for turning aside Frederick's challenge—every musician and especially the composers in the room would have realized just how ridiculously demanding it was—but there is no other recorded instance in Bach's life when he had had to concede such a defeat, and this was an exceedingly proud man, the age's acknowledged master of both fugue and improvisation, before an audience of fellow virtuosi as well as his two oldest sons.

Bach's embarrassment may have been the reason he was invited to Frederick's court in the first place. Writing two hundred years later, Arnold Schoenberg found in the Royal Theme's uncanny complexity the evidence of a malicious scheme to humiliate Bach, to beat him at his own game. Schoenberg's even darker conclusion, based on the belief that Frederick could never have written such an insidiously difficult theme by himself, was that the author could have been none other than Bach's son Carl, the only person in Frederick's court with a knowledge of counterpoint sufficient to trump his father's. "Whether malice of his own induced [Carl], or whether the 'joke' was ordered by the king, can probably be proved only psychologically," Schoenberg wrote, concluding from Frederick's sadistic personality and bellicose martial history that his motive was "to enjoy the helplessness of the victim of his . . . well-prepared trap."

"Johann Sebastian must have recognized the bad trick," Schoenberg continued. "That he calls his 'Offering' a *Musikalisches Opfer* is very peculiar, because the German word *Opfer* has a double meaning: 'offering,' or rather 'sacrifice,' and 'victim'— Johann Sebastian knew that he had become the victim of a grand seigneur's 'joke.' "

Schoenberg's theory that Frederick wished to embarrass Bach cannot be proved or disproved, but some unfortunate facts support it. The Prussian king was infamous for mean-spiritedly baiting even (or perhaps especially) those for whom he had the greatest respect. As Voltaire put it at one of the many low points in their relationship, when Frederick said you were his friend, "he means 'my slave.' *My dear friend* means 'you mean less than nothing to me.' . . . *Come to dinner* means, 'I feel like making fun of you tonight.' " Schoenberg's theory that the author of the theme was actually Bach's son Carl, though equally impossible to prove, is also at least plausible. More than once Carl seemed to feel that his respect and affection for his father was in some measure unrequited, a sense of filial injury that often afflicts second sons. There would have been an Oedipal aspect to such a "victory" over Bach for Frederick as well. When they met, Bach was roughly the age Frederick's father would have been, a father at whose hands Frederick had suffered the worst kind of abuse, including the greatest trauma of his young life.

Whoever the author of the Royal Theme may have been, the nature of it leaves no doubt that Frederick meant to give history's greatest master of counterpoint the most taxing possible challenge to his art, and it is easy to imagine that, as his carriage rattled over the rutted roads from Potsdam back to Leipzig, Bach was already working out the puzzle Frederick had presented to him. Certainly he lost no time working on it once he was back in Leipzig. At his composing desk in the southwest corner of the second floor of the St. Thomas School—the noise of the student dormitory barely muffled by a thin wall and the ad hoc insulation of bookshelves heaped with music—he finished his *Musical Offering* to Frederick within a fortnight, turning the king's "joke," if that is what it was, back upon him with all the force at his command.

At the end of a long life spent practicing the art of conveying words in music, this was a great deal of force indeed, and the very quickness of Bach's work suggests how urgent the project was to him. In the end, it implicated the most dissonant themes in his life and in the king's as well: among others, the proper relations between art and power, and the competition between fathers and sons. Perhaps most important, the work addresses the point of greatest conflict between these two men and one of the thorniest of all the issues raised by the Enlightenment, for the eighteenth century and for its latter-day descendants: the role of belief in a world of reason. A work that may be read as a kind of last will and testament, Bach's *Musical Offering* leaves us, among other things, a compelling case for the following proposition: that a world without a sense of the transcendent and mysterious, a universe ultimately discoverable through reason alone, can only be a barren place; and that the music sounding forth from such a world might be very pretty, but it can never be beautiful.

We may be grateful that Bach had spent a lifetime developing a musical language in which to say all that without fear of discovery or retribution, because his *Musical Offering* to Frederick represents as stark a rebuke of his beliefs and worldview as an absolute monarch has ever received. Not incidentally, it is also one of the great works of art in the history of music.

## II

## BIOGRAPHY OF A TEMPERAMENT

J. S. BACH WAS THE FIFTEENTH PERSON TO BE NAMED Johann in his family. Seven of his uncles were Johanns, his father was Johann, and his great-grandfather was Johann. Four of his five brothers were Johanns, the other was for some reason named Johannes, and there was a sister Johanna. As his parents must have done, if only for their sanity, we will call him Sebastian.

There had never been a Sebastian in the Bach family. The name belonged to one of his godfathers, who was the town piper of Gotha. On March 23, 1685, Sebastian Nagel had the honor of holding his two-day-old namesake at the baptismal font of St. George's Church on the market square in Eisenach, a walled, many-spired town that like Gotha was tucked away in the thick forest of Thuringia. The rector of St. George's Latin School, a friend of the family, performed the rite.

Nagel had a professional as well as personal relationship with Sebastian's father, Ambrosius Bach, who was the town piper here in Eisenach: They helped each other musically on occasion, and they had common roots in nearby Gotha. The Bachs had been there for as long as any of them knew. The first Bach to make music his profession had learned his trade from the town piper of Gotha a hundred years before this (though he had kept his day job running his father's bakery as well). Since then there had been Bachs in nearly all the courts, organ lofts, and town bands of Thuringia.

We do not know whether or not there was music at Sebastian's christening, but given that it took place on a Saturday, when church musicians were off, it could have been supplied by all sorts of people: His "uncle" Christoph (actually a second cousin) was the organist at St. George's; his father had not only the members of his band to choose from but even closer to hand all the assistants and journeymen who lived under his roof; and Sebastian Nagel might even have brought some of his musicians from Gotha. Professional musicians were brethren in the late seventeenth century, banded together in part by their campaign against the "beer-fiddlers" (i.e., "will play for beer") who were forever trying to undercut their prices for playing funerals and weddings, fees that were more than incidental to their salaries. The guild worked as well to protect its members' ability to bring sons into the business, as Ambrosius Bach managed to do with all of his Johanns, eventually including Sebastian. Even at St. George's baptismal fount, Johann Sebastian Bach was being held in the arms of his future.

§

HE GREW UP also in the embrace of the Wartburg, a dark, imposing castle on a hill that had already been looming over Eisenach and St. George's for five hundred years. Monument to an earlier, glorious era of German knighthood, it was more recently, like Eisenach itself, at the core of Lutheran myth and history. In the year that Sebastian Bach was born, the citizens of Eisenach did not care, if they knew, about Newton's discovery of gravity, not to mention Brahe's new star or Boyle's air pump, which were right now turning the orderly, Aristotelian world of the past few thousand years on its ear. But the story of Luther's time in Eisenach almost two hundred years before—he had attended St. George's Latin School, sung in its choir, preached from this very pulpit before his climactic appearance at the inquisitorial convocation of imperial princes in 1521 that came to be known as the Diet of Worms—was alive among them. So was the infamous edict that the emperor, in the name of the Diet, had issued against Luther, which set the stage for so much heartbreak and bloodshed:

> He has sullied marriage, disparaged confession and denied the body and blood of Our Lord. He makes the sacraments depend on the faith of the recipient. He is pagan in his denial of free will. This devil in the habit of a monk has brought together ancient errors into one stinking puddle. . . . Luther is to be regarded as a convicted heretic. . . . No one is to harbor him. His followers also are to be condemned. His books are to be eradicated from the memory of man. . . . Where you can get him, seize him and overpower him [and] send him to us under tightest security.

It was widely believed that Luther had been murdered on his way back to Thuringia from Worms, but fortunately for Luther, by this time the power of the emperor was not what it used to be. The Holy Roman Empire was a remnant, theoretically comprising the greater part of Europe but actually confined largely to modern-day Austria, Hungary, the Czech Republic, the former Yugoslavia, and Germany—except that there was no Germany; there were just hundreds of independent princedoms, dukedoms, and bishoprics, the largest of which were Brandenburg (later to become the seat of Prussia) and Saxony. The imperial electors in particular—the most powerful Germanic princes, who had been given the right to elect the emperor—had as much freedom as they dared to take, absolute rulers in their own domains.

Still, Luther's elector, Frederick III of Saxony, "Frederick the Wise," took more liberty than any of the others would have done in Luther's case: He ordered that Luther be closely guarded after the Diet ruled against him and that he be taken into hiding at the Wartburg. There, costumed as a knight and camouflaged by a long black beard, Luther spent the better part of a year: long months of insomniac nights spent beating back satanic visitations in the form of bats careening about his bedchamber, and days spent teaching himself Greek and writing his world-shifting German translation of the New Testament. In this part of the world, Luther was a great deal more compelling than gravity.

In contrast to the precision and rigor of his theology, the world inhabited by Martin Luther, and even the world of Sebastian Bach, was inhabited by wood nymphs, mermaids, and goblins, which had lived in the lakes, forests, minds, and hearts of Thuringia for centuries. Luther's mother believed that evil spirits stole food from her kitchen. Luther himself told the story of a lake near his home into which, "if a stone be thrown, tempests will arise over the whole region, because the waters are the abode of captive demons." Thuringians were famous for being superstitious, though of course they were not alone in that, only somewhat extreme examples. Combined with the desperate fear of God and therefore of hell, rampant superstition helps to explain the credulity of sixteenth-century Christians in Europe—or, to put it more charitably, their great capacity for the suspension of disbelief.

Every year on the eve of All Saints' Day, in a display that in retrospect seems appropriate for Halloween, Frederick the Wise put his relics on display for his people. Over the years he had accumulated a collection rivaled only by Rome's. Among his many thousands of sacred mementos were a piece of straw from the manger, three pieces of myrrh from the wise men, a strand of Jesus' beard, one of the nails driven into His hands, a piece of bread left over from the Last Supper, and a branch of Moses' burning bush. There were also nineteen thousand holy bones. The most potent piece in the collection was a thorn from the crown of Christ that was certified to have drawn His blood. Visiting these particular relics on this particular day would move the pope to grant you or your favorite departed loved one an "indulgence" good for the suspension of exactly 1,902,202 years and 270 days in purgatory. Of course, there was a certain financial price associated with such largesse, but who could possibly resist the argument of a man like Johannes Tetzel, personal pitchman for the Cardinal of Mainz (a Hohenzollern ancestor of Frederick the Great, incidentally, but we will come to that), who was completely without shame in parting the faithful from their ducats. "[Whoever] has put alms in the box . . . will have all his sins forgiven," he pleaded,

> so why are you standing about idly? Run, all of you, for the salvation of your souls. . . . Do you not hear the voices of your dead parents and other people, screaming and saying, "Have pity on me, have pity on me. . . . We are suffering severe punishments and pain, from which you could rescue us with a few alms, if only you would." Open your ears, because the father is calling to the son and the mother to the daughter.

When Martin Luther, still an Augustinian monk, had the temerity to point out that nowhere in Scripture did it say the pope could move people around in the afterlife, that in fact "indulgences" were spiritually dangerous because they tempted people to believe they could sin now and pay their way out of it later, there was, you might say, hell to pay. Proceeds from indulgences had by then become a fiscal addiction, not only to the pope but also to the likes of Frederick the Wise, who needed the money to fund the University of Wittenberg, among other uses.

Frederick's unhesitating and unwavering support of Martin
Luther had several motives—among others, he resented a Hohenzollern cardinal raising money from his people—but one of
them was principle. Frederick was a devout man in the best tradition of Christian princes, who considered themselves responsible
for the spiritual as well as the practical welfare of their subjects.
He actually believed in the power of his relics and in the pope's
ability to relieve souls from purgatory, but he would not allow
Luther to be sacrificed for a contrary belief, and so kept him safe.
In a letter to Frederick on behalf of himself and the emperor, the
pope exploded:

> We have you to thank that the Churches are without peo-
> ple, the people without priests, the priests without honor,
> and Christians without Christ. The veil of the temple is
> rent. Separate yourself from Martin Luther and put a muz-
> zle on his blasphemous tongue [or] in the name of
> Almighty God and Jesus Christ our Lord, whom we rep-
> resent on earth, we tell you that you will not escape pun-
> ishment on earth and eternal fire hereafter. Pope Hadrian
> and Emperor Charles are in accord. Repent therefore be-
> fore you feel the two swords.

Frederick wrote back simply, "I have never and do not now
act other than as a Christian man." Without such a friend—a
prince and elector whom he continued to criticize harshly and
publicly whenever he thought it right to do so—Martin Luther
would long since have been burned at the stake.

§

WHAT LUTHER'S GREAT and wise biographer Roland Bainton
said of Luther's courage before the pope could help explain that

of Frederick the Wise as well: "The most intrepid revolutionary is the one who has a fear greater than anything his opponents can inflict upon him." What was the fury of the pope or the emperor to that of God? For Luther, for Frederick the Wise, for their time and place and Sebastian's as well, the fear of God was beyond palpable, it was physical. Hell was not a metaphor. It was a place you went to, body and soul, where you would burn in actual, unquenchable fire, in unimaginable agony, forever and ever. The devil had form and face. He wanted your immortal soul desperately, and he was smarter and more clever than you could ever be. The world was a great battlefield, life an unending contest between him and Him, in which you were caught squarely in the middle, your eternal safety at stake, your only protection an amorphous wraith called belief.

Small wonder people believed. Horrifying examples of the devil's work were appearing every day in the here and now of the sixteenth century—in the bubonic plague that wiped out half the population of Eisenach in one year, in the floods that surged through Thuringia, "the water [running] with so mighty a force, and such a stream, that it bare the bodies of the dead before it out of their graves in the Church-yard," and in the frequent, widespread fires that sought out the timber of their homes.

And for all that, there was no horror to compare to what rained down during the wars that began in 1618, which fed themselves on belief. For thirty unimaginably long years, all the powers of Europe ruthlessly exploited the forces unleashed by the Reformation and Counter-Reformation to inspire and poison allegiances meant to serve nothing so much as expansionist ambitions. The play of shifting alliances and political treacheries was wanton, and in such a tangle of snakes Germans high and low were as powerless as souls on the battlefield of God and Satan. Using religion as a blunt diplomatic instrument proved so devastatingly successful that all the major combatants—Spain, France, England, Sweden, the Dutch, and the Hapsburgs—chronically ran short of money to pay their mercenary generals for their mercenary soldiers, who thereupon began to take what they could not earn through pillage the likes of which had never been seen before. Rural peasant families were the easiest prey, but even walled towns would fall to sieges that lasted long enough. Eventually the towns devised a crude bell-and-bonfire warning system that allowed some chance of escape from the various crisscrossing armies, but as often as not the soldiers would just take the time to hunt the escapees down, take their valuables, and murder them where they hid. Rape and massacre became the soldiers' recreation, and revenge was terrible when peasants with pitchforks found themselves in a position to exact it. When all the animals were dead and the fields lay gleaned and fallow, epidemic famine caused soldiers and civilians alike to eat the unimaginable. They ate grass and twigs and the skins of dead rats. They ate bodies from gallows, corpses from graveyards, even babies from their cribs. Thirty years later, a third of the population was dead, and the people who remained on the battlefield of Germany—or rather of Germanies, the loose collation of a few thousand now bankrupt dukedoms and princelings—were consigned by the Treaty of Westphalia to an indefinite future of encirclement by Europe's great powers and left to a deranged and hopeless peace.

§

EVERY ARMY HAD its camp followers of prostitutes, hustlers, procurers, and freelance impresarios, ready to whip up a party for their restive military clientele, and so among the followers of every camp were musicians. This was not a time when one could be fussy about jobs. As a result, among the less significant casualties of the Thirty Years War was the reputation of musicians, who had, as it were, accompanied the mayhem and, as the coarseness of what they saw took its toll on them, had taken their share in it. Thus was born the College or Union of Instrumental Musicians of the District of Upper and Lower Saxony and Other Interested Places, a formal musicians' guild, whose bylaws give some hint of just how disreputable musicians were then held to be. The member was enjoined to "conduct himself decently . . . abstain from all blasphemous talk, profane cursing and swearing" and *not* to "divert himself by singing or performing coarse obscenities" or "give attendance with jugglers, hangmen, bailiffs, gaolers, conjurors, rogues or any other such low company." The drafters further felt the need to say that at private parties "nothing shall be stolen from the invited guests."

Sebastian Bach's grandfather, born in 1613, lived through the worst of the Thirty Years War as an adult. After serving for a time "waiting on the Prince" in Weimar, he married the daughter of a town musician. (Such marriages inside the trade were common. Guild rules specified eight years' training before a musician could hire himself out as a master, but marrying a master's daughter cut two years from the mandatory time.) He no doubt suffered from the generally low opinion of musicians in his role as a town musician in Erfurt and later in Arnstadt, where his younger brother had secured the coveted post of chief organist to the court and churches. The brother too had married by then, a step that was a precarious act of faith, as Philipp Spitta pointed out in his magisterial nineteenth-century biography of Bach: During the war, men could guarantee neither the safety of their wives and children nor the security of their income. Despite his distinguished position in Arnstadt, which he held for fifty years, this Bach remembered that during the privations of the war, all the salary he received from the war-bankrupted court he had "to sue for, almost with tears."

Spitta reported of Sebastian's grandfather, perhaps diplomatically, that he found "no record to show that [he] stood forth as a pattern of moral worth," but said he was pretty sure about his brother, since the preacher at his funeral praised his piety. "There may be conditions under which it seems to be no particular merit to be called a pious man," Spitta observed,

> but there are times, too, when piety is the . . . sole guarantee for a sound core of human nature. The German nation was living through such a period. . . . The mass of people vegetated in dull indifference or gave themselves up to a life of coarse and immoral enjoyment; the few superior souls who had not lost all courage to live, when a fearful fate had crushed all the real joys of life around them, fixed their gaze above and beyond the common desolation, on what they hoped in as eternal and imperishable.

§

THREE YEARS BEFORE the end of the war, in the winter of 1645, Sebastian's father Johann Ambrosius and his twin brother Johann Christoph were born in Erfurt, the largest city in Thuringia. According to a note made by Carl Philipp Emanuel Bach in the family genealogy, Ambrosius and his brother were "perhaps the only [twins] of their kind ever known. They loved each other extremely [and] looked so much alike that even their wives could not tell them apart. . . . They were an object of wonder on the part of great gentlemen and everyone who saw them. Their speech, their way of thinking—everything was the same." This is good to know, because while little is known directly about the character of Ambrosius, his twin left a trail.

When the boys were eight or nine, the family moved from Erfurt eleven miles south to Arnstadt, where their father joined the town band and began to concentrate in earnest on the musical training of his sons. He died when they were in their teens, however, and their education was undertaken by his brother, who by then had been the Arnstadt organist for a dozen years. After their apprenticeship and years as an assistant were over, the twins moved back to Erfurt, where they had secured jobs in the town band (thanks to their cousin, its new director).

Ambrosius soon married, and married well, into the family of Valentin Lämmerhirt, an affluent furrier and an influential citizen. The Lämmerhirts were a devout Anabaptist family, which was saying something. The Anabaptists were zealous even by the standards of their onetime leader Zwingli, who espoused a Christianity more ascetic than Luther's but finally denounced the Anabaptists for extremism. The Anabaptists were best known for denouncing infant baptism (at a time when theology had become so narrow and poisonous that baptizing an adult who had been christened in childhood was a capital offense), but their differences with mainstream Protestantism were comprehensive. They renounced all physical adornments, they refused to swear oaths or bear arms, and each member was expected at a moment's notice to give up home and family to take up the life of a missionary. The Lämmerhirts did not live by every tenet of this faith, but merely to remain identified with it in orthodox Lutheran Erfurt was a sign of great commitment. In the bizarrely charged atmosphere of dueling Protestant sects that pitted Lutheran against Lutheran, not to mention Lutheran against Calvinist, both Lutherans and Calvinists had sentenced Anabaptists to the stake. Sebastian Bach's mother came from strong-minded people who were dead serious about religion.

A bit less serious about religion perhaps (most of the Bachs before Sebastian were secular musicians for the courts and towns rather than the churches), the Bachs were no less strong-minded.

After Ambrosius's marriage, his twin Christoph moved back to Arnstadt, where we find him in the records of the town consistory fighting off a young woman named Anna Cunigunda Wieneren, who came before them, with her mother, to accuse Christoph of breaking his promise to marry her. The consistory was the ecclesiastical body responsible for hearing such disputes, among other supervisory duties, and given the clerk's matter-of-fact record of the hearing, it was not the first of its kind.

Both parties appeared before the Consistory, and Anna Cunigunda confessed that she had promised to marry Bach, and he her. . . . They had done no less than give each other rings in pledge of marriage, which they still had . . . and it was now on Bach's conscience whether he thought he could withdraw from her under these circumstances without injuring her. . . .

Christoph Bach confessed, indeed, that he had offered marriage to Anna Cunigunda, but they had merely considered the matter provisionally, and he had not in any way considered himself bound. . . . He had given her a ring . . . but not in pledge of marriage. . . . Besides, Anna Cunigunda has asked for her ring back again. . . .

After Bach had withdrawn from her and his affection had died out, she had desired to have her ring back, on these conditions: she put it to his conscience that if she were not good enough for him, and if he only meant to make a fool of her, he should return her the ring and answer for it in his conscience before God. . . . He, in answer, had sent her word that he had no fear of punishment from God on that account.

The dispute went on for more than a year, when finally the consistory ruled that Bach should marry the girl. That was predictable, given current practice. What was not predictable was that Christoph Bach promptly took the matter over the heads of officials in Arnstadt by appealing to the authorities in Weimar. At this point, according to the records, he "hated the Wieneren so that he could not bear the sight of her." After more weeks and months of appeals, the officials of Weimar overruled Arnstadt and lifted his obligation to marry.

By the time it was over, the affair had lasted more than two years, Christoph Bach had made enemies of his hometown con- sistory, which comprised its most influential citizens, and he had indeed made a fool of Anna Cunigunda Wieneren, who had be- come the talk of Arnstadt. But he had done what it took to get his way, and when we try later to interpret some of the more intem- perate behavior of his nephew Sebastian, including his own even more severe problems with the consistory of Arnstadt, this an- tecedent will be worth remembering.

§

IN THE FALL OF 1671, Ambrosius and Maria Elisabeth Bach moved their belongings out of their rooming house, "The Silver Pocket," and hauled them twenty miles west to Eisenach, where he had rented an apartment in the home of the duke's head forester. His position placed him among the town's most visible and affluent figures. In a few years he became a citizen, bought a home on the market square, and joined the town council, an hon- orific body that met rarely and served mainly as the local duke's rubber stamp but was at least a democratic bunch, including not only a doctor and the town organist, his cousin Christoph, but also a butcher, several keepers of the town clocks and watchtow- ers, a gravedigger, and three shepherds. The Bach household was large from the very beginning in Eisenach, including his three ap- prentices and a journeyman as well as his widowed mother-in-law and his nineteen-year-old sister, who was profoundly impaired both physically and psychologically. (When she died a few years later, the preacher at her graveside called her "a simple creature, not knowing her right hand from her left . . . like a child.") Given the size of his household, Ambrosius must have been grateful for his generous starting salary and housing supplement of fifty florins, and with the promise he could double that with fees for weddings and funerals and for playing in the court Kapelle. By way of comparison, with that much money, roughly four times the town barber's salary, he could have bought several harpsichords every year, or a dozen good lutes. Of course, he had more pressing uses for the money. Ambrosius and Maria Elisabeth brought their first baby Bach with them to Eisenach, and during the next fourteen years there they christened seven more, little imagining that the last of them, their one and only Sebastian, would someday make St. George's baptismal font a music lovers' site of pilgrimage.

## III

# THE HOHENZOLLERN

# REAL ESTATE COMPANY

THE CHRISTENING TWENTY-SEVEN YEARS LATER OF the infant who would become Frederick the Great lacked nothing in pomp. The infant Frederick of Brandenburg-Hohenzollern, Prince de Prusse et d'Orange, Count of Hohenzollern, Lord of Ravenstein, and so on, was dressed in a baptismal gown made of silver cloth studded with diamonds, and he was carried to the fount of the Chapel Royal at Potsdam by two margraves and a margravine. No fewer than six countesses carried the train. The godmothers were all dowagers of this and duchesses of that, and among the five godfathers were Czar Peter the Great, and the elector of Hanover, soon to be King George I of England. We know there was music at this christening but only because the baby's father was not yet king. When he took the throne a year later, one of his first acts was to fire the musicians.

The royal Kapelle of Prussia's king at the time, baby Frederick's grandfather, Frederick I, included some of the best musicians of their day, so although the program does not survive we can be sure the music was entirely equal to the grandeur of the occasion. All the bells of the city rang out to announce the baptism of the crown prince, and we know from Thomas Carlyle (who produced his eight-volume *History of Frederick the Great* after thirteen years that he grimly described to Ralph Waldo

Emerson as "the valley of the shadow of Frederick") that the christening "spared no cannon-volleyings [and] kettle-drummings."
Happily, they appear to have kept the cannons at a distance. According to Carlyle, one previous heir to the Prussian throne had
been killed by the shock of a triumphal volley fired too close to
his crib. Another had died shortly after his christening because
the infant crown had been forced onto his head. Possibly more reliable, certainly more conventional accounts lay the cause of
death of both previous crown princes to trouble with teething. In
any case, the baby's grandfather, Frederick I, had cause to be delighted when at six months the infant crown prince Frederick had
six teeth and was still alive.

A year later, Frederick I died, the victim of a mad third wife,
who somehow eluded her custodians one morning wearing only
a white shift and petticoat. She made straight for the bedchamber
of the king, who mistook her for the apparition that was said always to herald death in the Hohenzollern family—"the White
Lady"—and the shock killed him. Every account holds this story
to be true.

§

THE HOHENZOLLERNS were a funny bunch, but Brandenburg
was lucky to get them, which says something about its earlier history. A hill fortress town, it was taken by siege in the twelfth century by a prince of the Ascanian family, whose name, like many
in the Brandenburg line, was pointed: Albert the Bear. The emperor had given Albert the task of protecting Germany's North
Mark from the heathen hordes to the east, and in time Albert
found himself with the means to expand his territories, which
eventually came to be a scattered patchwork collectively known
as the Mark of Brandenburg.

After the Ascanian family died out, Brandenburg changed
hands several times, and for a couple of centuries things went

from bad to worse. First it went to the Wittelsbachs of Bavaria, whose contest with the Hapsburgs for primacy in the empire inspired in them exactly no interest in an unimportant sandy wasteland to the north except as a source of taxes and whatever else they could grab from a distance. Their complete negligence of Brandenburg would have been a gift, but in the event, having soaked it for what they could and being unwilling even to visit the territory, the Wittelsbach elector sold it to Luxembourg, whose monarch simply gave it to a man named Frederick. This Frederick had fought beside him against the Turks, had become his good friend, and Frederick's family had already acquired a few lands scattered around Germany over the past two centuries by marriage, by purchase, and by force. These were the Hohenzollerns, and the man named Frederick now became Frederick I of Brandenburg.

Understandably surly after the treatment it had received from its various overlords, Brandenburg's snubbed, pickpocketed nobles gave this Frederick a very hard time. His successor beat them down, though, with a strategy whose subtlety can be deduced from his nickname, "Iron Tooth."

The names of Iron Tooth's successors seem less descriptive than ironic. In any case, Albert Achilles really had no notable weak point. In fact, it was Achilles who finally figured out the obvious virtues of primogeniture: that if you did not spread your inheritance among all of your descendants but gave it all to the first son, your lands and your power would be consolidated rather than fractionated. This sounds rather obvious, but the former policy made for a thousand tiny dukedoms and principalities and centuries of complicated, self-defeating German politics. The Hohenzollern policy of primogeniture would become one of their most important advantages.

Unfortunately, Achilles' successor, John Cicero, was no Cicero either, being what historian Sidney Fay called "innocent of

any interest in the new Renaissance movement that was beginning to transform the intellectual life of South Germany."

§

THIS BRINGS US, roughly, to the reign of Frederick the Wise
and the Hohenzollern cardinal Albert of Mainz, whose enthusias-
tic salesman Johann Tetzel did so much to color Martin Luther's
already jaundiced view of indulgences. We enter as well into
some of the same historical territory passed through by the ancestors of Sebastian Bach, but to Albert and his descendant Hohenzollerns, the history of Germany in the sixteenth and seventeenth
centuries, particularly during the Reformation and the Thirty
Years War, looked very different from the way it looked to the senior Bachs, rather like the difference in perspective between war-
den and prisoner.

The Hohenzollern Cardinal of Mainz was a ravenously ambitious and entirely secular figure who had bought two important
bishoprics at the ridiculous age of twenty-three. At twenty-five he
set out to buy the archbishopric of Mainz, which would make him
primate of all Germany. Fine, said the pope's man, that will be
twelve thousand ducats for the Twelve Apostles. Albert said he
thought maybe seven thousand ducats for the Seven Deadly Sins
would be more appropriate. Thanks to the Ten Commandments,
Albert got his red hat, but having already laid out cash for his
other two bishoprics, he had to borrow the money.

To help him pay off the loan and to help with expenses for St.
Peter's in Rome (like Michelangelo's fee), for which he would
take half the receipts, the pope gave Albert a ten-year license to
sell indulgences of unprecedented potency. These indulgences
could actually work on future sins, so that, having paid the right
price for a particular sin, you were preemptively absolved and
presumably could feel at ease sinning likewise for the rest of your
life. The pope authorized Albert to promise, seriously, that even

violating the Mother of God Herself could be forgiven by these indulgences. It was the prospective-absolution feature of these indulgences, a patent encouragement to sin, that made Luther especially furious.

Albert clearly had chosen the right man for the job. When Tetzel came into a city he arrived in procession, holding a huge red cross, fronted by flags and drums and a herald proclaiming, "The Grace of God and of the Holy Father is at the gates!" Making straight for the cathedral, he would plant his cross by the high altar and set his strongbox up beside it. Taking the pulpit, he gave his pitch: "At the very instant that the money rattles at the bottom of the chest, the soul escapes from purgatory and flies liberated to heaven. . . . I declare to you, though you have but a single coat, you ought to strip it off and sell it." Then he would stand by the strongbox, examining each supplicant in turn to determine the amount due. Kings and princes were good for twenty-five ducats, barons ten, etc. The various sins had prices too. Witchcraft was forgiven for two ducats, polygamy for six, murder for eight, and the sin of all sins, stealing money from the church, cost nine. (It is hard to believe that this one could be forgiven indefinitely, however expensive the indulgence.)

Just as Albert and Tetzel had got started with their new indulgences, on the eve of All Saints' Day 1517, when Frederick the Wise would have put out his relics and indulgence fever would be at a pitch, Luther pinned to the door of the Castle Church in Wittenberg his "95 Theses," which took off directly from the promises in Tetzel's latest spiel. For example:

27. They preach man who say that so soon as the penny jingles into the money-box, the soul flies out [of purgatory].
28. It is certain that when the penny jingles into the money-box, gain and avarice can be increased, but the re-

sult of the intercession of the Church is in the power of
God alone. . . .

46. Christians are to be taught that unless they have
more than they need, they are bound to keep back what is
necessary for their own families, and by no means to
squander it on pardons. . . .

75. To think the papal pardons so great that they could
absolve a man even if he had committed an impossible sin
and violated the Mother of God—this is madness! . . .

Drawing to a close, he posed a series of statements from
which he diplomatically distanced himself by characterizing them
as "shrewd questions from the laity":

84. ". . . What is this new piety of God and the pope,
that for money they allow a man who is impious and their
enemy to buy out of purgatory the pious soul of a friend
of God, and do not rather, because of that pious and
beloved soul's own need, free it for pure love's sake?"

86. Again: — "Why does not the pope, whose wealth
is to-day greater than the riches of the richest, build just
this one church of St. Peter with his own money, rather
than with the money of poor believers?"

The rest, as they say, is history, one of whose most wonderful
ironies is that we have a Hohenzollern to thank, if only indirectly,
for the Protestant Reformation.

§

A FEW YEARS LATER another Hohenzollern named Albert had
an encounter with Martin Luther of a very different sort. This Albert was the cardinal's cousin, who had managed to get himself
elected grandmaster of the Order of Teutonic Knights, a once-

powerful group of German nobles who had taken over Prussia by putting down its heathen locals, which involved pretty much exterminating them. They prospered for a time, but that was centuries ago. Now, despised by their subjects and beaten repeatedly on the battlefield when they attempted to expand into Poland and Lithuania, they had been reduced to a small Polish fiefdom. They kept their dreams of independence alive by electing ever richer grandmasters to fill their treasury for more doomed military exploits. That was the reason they elected Albert of Hohenzollern. It was a bad mistake.

Despite the fact that the Hohenzollerns at this point supported the pope and the emperor, Albert was a secret admirer of Luther and an early convert. At the point when he had come to realize that the Teutonic Knights were hopeless, he asked the reformer for advice. Luther, with a pragmatic political sense for which he is not well known, advised Albert to dissolve the Knights and ask Poland in return to let him convert Prussia into a hereditary duchy. Startled by the thought—or perhaps by its source—he sat quiet with the idea for a moment, then erupted in laughter. It was a wonderful idea. All it would require was the betrayal of the order that had been entrusted to his care.

So ended the reign of the Teutonic Knights in Prussia, and thus did the Hohenzollerns add another major holding to Brandenburg and the other Albert's bishoprics.

The son of the new duke of Prussia was clinically insane, but even he managed to expand the Hohenzollern territories. The family arranged for him to marry the eldest daughter of one William the Rich, ruler of five small territories on the Rhine. (She found out he was mad after she was already on her way to Prussia but decided to go anyway, two previous fiancés having left the field.) One of the daughters from this union married the new elector of Brandenburg, Johann Sigismund, who happily converted to Calvinism in order to placate these new Hohenzollern provinces. Since he could not conceivably impose Calvinism on Brandenburg or his subjects in East Prussia, he waived his right to do so. Like most other things Hohenzollern, their tradition of "religious toleration" was all about real estate.

At the death of their crazy Prussian duke, the family agreed that Sigismund should take over Prussia as well, at which point a single branch of the family could lay credible claim to territories from the Rhine to the far side of the Elbe—

Just in time for the Thirty Years War. Sigismund's son had watch over the worst of it, and he was not equal even to a lesser task. His great-great-grandson, our baby crown prince Frederick, would write many years later:

> All the plagues of the world broke over this ill-fated Elec-
> torate—a prince incapable of governing, a traitor for his
> Minister, a war or rather a universal cataclysm, invasion
> by friendly and enemy troops equally thievish and bar-
> barous. . . . Though [the elector] cannot be held responsible
> for all the misfortunes which befell his territories, his . . .
> weakness only left him a choice of errors. . . . Powerless
> and in continual uncertainty he always changed over to the
> strongest side; but he could offer too little to his allies to se-
> cure their protection against their common enemies.

§

LUCKY FOR THE Hohenzollerns, the heir of this ill-starred elector proved to be the savior of the dynasty. Without Freder- ick William I of Brandenburg, known as the Great Elector, it is entirely possible that, for all their earlier success, there would have been no Hohenzollerns ruling in Germany after the war, and no way for the Great Elector's great-grandson to become Great himself.

Thanks to his father's ineptitude, when the Great Elector came to power in the last decade of the war, all of his scattered lands were desolate and occupied. East of the Elbe, Prussia was overrun by Polish troops. To the west, Cleves-Mark was beset by a warring mix of Dutch, imperial, and Hessian forces. Brandenburg itself was occupied in the north by Sweden, which was everywhere else fighting imperial troops in the attempt to occupy the rest. Still not connected at any point, the Hohenzollern patchwork was difficult to defend at the best of times, and these were the worst. The electorate had lost nine hundred thousand people—two-thirds of the entire population—to war and murder. Its fields had been barren for years, and what commerce remained was undercut by plunder and counterfeit currency. The elector had lost virtually all of his power. His treasury was gone, and since most of his troops were mercenary, that meant he was all but defenseless.

Almost miraculously, through drastic military reform and the exercise of a diplomacy no less frenetic but a good deal more effective than that of his father, he managed to get his country, very much scathed but dynastically whole, through the last years of the war to an armistice that led to the Treaty of Westphalia. In the negotiations leading up to that treaty, he managed not only to hold on to all of his occupied lands but to gain some more as well. The treaty left France at war with Spain, and the standoff between Poland and Sweden would lead to the first Northern War, so the Great Elector's diplomatic finesse and military might continued to be tested; at various times he was allied with virtually all of the combatants—Holland, Denmark, Sweden, Austria, Spain, and England, not to mention a variety of German territories. But by the time he died in 1688, the population of his territories had almost tripled, he had won Prussia's independence from Poland, he had created an efficient civil service, and by diligent effort and imaginative reforms he had brought a measure of prosperity to his lands, which came increasingly to be called by the collective name of "Prussia."

He had also created one of the largest, most disciplined and battle-hardened armies in Europe. In advice written to his son and heir long after the first Northern War was over, he credited not his diplomacy but his reform and expansion of the military for his success in aggrandizing his emerging nation. "Alliances, to be sure, are good," he wrote,

> but a force of one's own on which one can rely better. A ruler is treated with no consideration if he does not have troops and means of his own. It is these, Thank God! which have made me *considerable* since the time that I began to have them.

It was this advice that would, for better and worse, become his most important legacy to the Hohenzollerns, to Germany, and to the history of the Western world.

§

THE GREAT ELECTOR'S SON, grandfather to baby Frederick, was not Great, not even good for much, but despite a spinal deformity that kept him in bad health all of his life and despite living in the shadow of a beloved father, he seems to have been quite taken with himself, in a neurotic sort of way. Thanks to the steadily rising revenues that were his father's gift to him, he spent wildly, multiplying by twenty the costs of his father's household and court. Like many princes of his time, but with greater industry and commitment of resources, he loved all things French. He modeled his court on Versailles and himself on the Sun King, even to the point of taking a mistress despite the fact that he preferred his wife. The affection was not returned (which perhaps explains the mistress). His queen Sophie Charlotte, sister of England's George I,* was a knowing and educated woman who sensibly preferred the company of her court philosopher Leibniz to that of her husband. "Leibniz talked to me today about the infinitesimally small," she cracked to a courtier one day, "as if I don't know enough about that here."

Where his father's diplomacy was treacherous but artful, the son's was simply inept. As crown prince he had secretly solicited Austria for a loan to pay for his already outrageous expenses, promising to give back one of his father's provinces upon his accession to the throne. As soon as he was king, he repudiated the deal, saying he could not be bound by the promise of someone who could not speak for the state (meaning himself as crown prince). It hardly needs to be said that his argument got him exactly nowhere, so that among his first acts was the surrender of territory. Among his proudest accomplishments was dreaming up the Order of the Black Eagle, his country's highest honor, for which he came up with the thrilling motto "To each his own."

The greatest achievements of Frederick I were accidents that followed from his faults. He doubled the size of his military because loaning them out was the best way to support his extravagance. Green-eyed at the prospect of fellow electors becoming kings—his brother-in-law the Hanoverian elector was becoming king of England, the Saxon elector had already become king of Poland—he managed, for the loan of a few thousand soldiers, to get the emperor's promise to recognize him as a king should he so proclaim himself in his eastern (nonimperial) province of Prussia. So of course he did. A procession of eighteen hundred car-

---

* George was the son of another Sophie, this one the electress of Hanover and granddaughter of James I. The throne of England passed to her line after Queen Anne, daughter of the last Stuart king, James II, died without a successor.

riages involving thirty thousand post horses (stationed at intervals to draw the carriages and carry supplies for a cast of thousands) accompanied him from Berlin during a stately progress of fourteen days to the capital of Königsberg. There, before the forcibly assembled nobility, he placed a crown on his own head and another on his wife's. The trip and festivities cost him upward of five million thalers, his budget for several years' expenses at home.

All that said, by the time the White Lady came to take him away, he had created for his son and heir a redoubled military and a Prussian monarchy. In deference to that fact and filial obligation, if not respect, Frederick William I threw his father the kind of funeral that Frederick I would have thrown himself. For eight days the king lay in state on a bed of diamond-dotted red velvet, a crown on his head, an ermine-and-purple mantle over his shoulders, the Order of the Black Eagle on his chest, his scepter to his left and sword to his right. Finally, draped in a gown of gold, he was carried in solemn procession to the palace chapel through a guard comprising virtually the entire Prussian army. The new king wore long mourning robes whose train was carried by his father's grand equerry, and the entire court of Frederick I marched behind him. Frederick William I would never appear in such splendor again.

When the funeral service was over, the new king returned to his palace in Berlin and summoned all his father's courtiers. "Gentlemen, our good master is dead," said the father of little Frederick. "The new king bids you all go to hell."

## IV

## A SMALL, UNREADY ALCHEMIST

FOR ALL ITS SPIRES AND WATCHTOWERS AND RED-roofed houses, its cobblestoned market square bordered by church, town hall, and castle, the residents of Eisenach would not have called their hometown charming. To get a sense of Eisenach as it was when Sebastian Bach was a boy, one must conjure up the scent of animal dung from the livestock that shared its streets and walkways, the putrid breeze that wafted from the fish market and slaughterhouse in the square, and, under those red-tiled roofs, a general atmosphere strongly redolent of life before plumbing. The homes of all but Eisenach's wealthiest residents were small—close and hot in the summer, frigid and smoky in winter—and crowded. At one point in the Bach household, Sebastian lived with seven siblings as well as two cousins (orphans from Ambrosius's family whose parents had died of the plague) and his father's apprentices. Death being the family's constant visitor, Sebastian lost a brother when he was two months old, a sister died when he had just turned one, and his childhood continued to be punctuated, repeatedly and intimately, by death. In addition to the loss of numerous more distant relatives, his eighteen-year-old brother Balthasar died when he was six, and the next year one of the cousins who had been in the house his whole life died at sixteen. Both had been apprentices for his father, and Sebastian would have followed them about his father's daily rounds, learning as he saw them learn and helping them with what small chores he could. These deaths, as difficult as they may have been, would not be the most painful losses to mark his youth and his character. Of the deaths in his adult life, it is enough for now to say that he buried twelve of his twenty children. Against this backdrop, the elaborately formal topiary gardens of the Baroque, inspired by the idea that nature needs to be tamed and improved, seem entirely understandable.

What Eisenach had in great abundance, the solace and balm of its six thousand souls, was music. In the villages of Thuringia, by an account that dates from the year of Bach's birth, "farmers . . . know their instruments [and] make all sorts of string music in the villages with violins, violas, viola da gambas, harpsichords, spinets and small zithers, and often we also find in the most modest church music some works for the organ with arrangements and variations that are astonishing." Among the Bachs especially, music was a powerful tonic, and it helped to keep the extended family together. Once a year, as Carl told Bach's first biographer, Johann Nikolaus Forkel, they gathered at one or another Thuringian town for a day of festivities at which music of a sort not meant for the church was the main event. "They sang popular songs, the contents of which were partly comic and partly naughty, all together and extempore, but in such a manner that the several parts thus extemporized made a kind of harmony together, the words, however, in every part being different. They called this kind of extemporary harmony a *Quodlibet*, and not only laughed heartily at it themselves, but excited an equally hearty and irresistible laughter in everybody that heard them."

Every day of Sebastian's childhood was filled with music. His father, as director of town music and the town band, was chief dispenser of all the instrumental music in town, and his house was as busy with it as a conservatory's practice rooms. Every morning at ten and afternoon at five, looking over the marketplace from the balcony of the town hall, Ambrosius Bach's band played dances and folk tunes and the chorales that Luther and Lutheranism had made the most cherished of popular songs. The ensemble for such "tower pieces" included violin, viola da gamba, and other strings, brass, flutes, oboes and other reeds, and various percussion instruments. The town band numbered only five, but each member was trained on several instruments, and there were the apprentices and journeymen to call on.

Ambrosius also played regularly at St. George's and in the duke's court Kapelle, as did his older cousin Christoph, organist for the court as well as for the city's three main churches. Sebastian's "uncle" Christoph appears to have been a bit of a crank. He complained chronically of being short of funds and badly kept (he was finally given a home and stable at the Prince's Mint, a rather grand establishment for an organist), but despite having more than sufficient skill and reputation to better himself, he complained about the same job for sixty years. Having a family member under his watch whom he could not quite control would have been an embarrassment for Ambrosius, and in fact, whether for this reason or another, the two men did not get along. But for Sebastian, having Uncle Christoph around was very good luck. Ambrosius gave the boy his first instruction on stringed instruments, but it was Uncle Christoph who would have given him his first inside view of the bellows, action, and pipes of the church organ, which with the possible exception of the clock was the most complicated mechanism of the seventeenth century. Perhaps the family's greatest musician before Sebastian and the only person writing serious new music in Eisenach, a musician even more accomplished than Ambrosius, Christoph was also the boy's first model as a composer. One of Sebastian's favorite works by Christoph was an elaborate piece for choir and orchestra in which the archangel Michael and his celestial host take on Satan in the form of a dragon along with his cohort of dark angels, a story taken from *Revelations* 12:7–12:

> And there was war in heaven: Michael and his angels fought against the dragon; and the dragon fought and his angels. . . . The great dragon was cast out, that old serpent, called the Devil, and Satan, which deceiveth the whole world: he was cast out into the earth, and his angels were cast out with him.

Scored for two choirs, eight stringed instruments, organ, trumpets, and timpani, it must have been a sensation in its first performance on St. Michael's Day, but we do not know whether young Sebastian was struck more by the beauty of the work or by the thrilling story of an archangel fighting a fire-breathing monster.

Childhood then being an unprivileged state, in which children were considered simply small, unready adults, Ambrosius would have pressed Sebastian into service as soon as he was able, just as he had pressed all his sons into such menial tasks as cleaning brass and stringing violins. Sebastian's boyhood was anything but carefree. Infractions were severely punished, at home and at St. George's School, where the eighty-one children in Sebastian's *quinta** class were packed into one small room whose high Gothic windows were filled not with sunlight and sky but the gray stone walls of the church. The school day ran in two sessions, mornings from seven to ten and afternoons from one to three, which left time for midday and late-afternoon work at home. The only

---

* In the Latin school system there were six grades for students ranging in age from seven to the early twenties—sixth grade *(sexta)* to first *(prima)*, the last grade before university.

vacation they had during the twelve-month school year was at harvesttime, which was no vacation. Choristers like Sebastian had longer hours than others to accommodate music classes and rehearsals; they had performances every Sunday and feast day and at weddings and funerals. A few times a year Sebastian would also join some of his fellow choristers to sing in the streets of Eisenach and nearby villages for small donations, called *Chorgeld,* a source of income for Sebastian throughout his school years.

Martin Luther had done the same thing early in the previous century, an experience that helped to seal his love of music and its place in the Lutheran liturgy. Music had had a somewhat ambiguous history in the church before the Reformation; some of the early church fathers, even Saint Augustine, were suspicious of its emotional power, but Luther put an end to that too.

You will find that from the beginning of the world [music] has been instilled and implanted in all creatures, individually and collectively. For nothing is without sound or harmony. . . . Music is a gift and largesse of God, not a human gift. Praise through word and music is a sermon in sound.

Sebastian had Luther to thank that his youth had at least the light of music in it.

§

ALL OTHER LIGHT was shut off abruptly in his ninth year. In the spring, his mother died. In the fall, his father, having quickly remarried, died as well, leaving his second wife a widow and Sebastian, suddenly, an orphan. Though more common in those days, losing both parents was just as disorienting as it has ever been. Like all newly orphaned children, Sebastian would have felt abandoned, hurt, angry; and if he had had any wish to stay in Eisenach with Uncle Christoph or his new stepmother, it was not fulfilled. He was sent to Ohrdruf, a nearby town, to live with a brother he barely knew.

This brother, also named Christoph, the oldest child of Sebastian's parents, had left home when Sebastian was an infant to apprentice himself to the composer and family friend Johann Pachelbel. Now he was the organist in Ohrdruf, a town much smaller than Eisenach but, in spiritual terms at least, a great deal more intense. While Eisenach was orthodox Lutheran to the core, Ohrdruf was riven, a center of the fierce rivalry between orthodoxy and a more ascetic, devotional form of Protestantism known as Pietism. Over the past century and a half of the Reformation, orthodox Lutheranism had gradually allowed itself to be ground into doctrinal minutiae by constant intersectarian brawling. Lutheran pastors were reduced to giving long-winded sermons on petty theological issues useful mainly for showing how important it was not to be Calvinist or Anabaptist. Pietism, drawing inspiration from such Christian mystics as Thomas à Kempis, Johannes Tauler, and Bernard of Clairvaux, set out to reclaim some of the spiritual energy of the early Reformation by stressing the inner, spiritual life, the daily struggle for meaning, and in doing so they drew sympathizers from all Protestant sects. The Calvinist king of Prussia, Frederick William I, father of Frederick the Great, was one. His Lutheran contemporary Sebastian Bach was another. Though he remained in the camp of the orthodox Lutheran church all his life, Sebastian's sense of vocation as a church musician was rooted in the mystic spirituality of Pietism, an influence that took hold of him here, in Ohrdruf, and in the deepest grief of his childhood.

His commitment to religious studies at the Ohrdruf Lyceum, where the Pietist-orthodox struggle was played out every day, is plain to see in his class standing. When he left Eisenach he was twenty-third in his class at St. George's (he had missed weeks of school during his parents' illnesses, so he did well to keep his standing that high). Despite Ohrdruf's more rigorous standards, he finished his first year of *tertia* in fourth place, and the next year, at age twelve the youngest in his class, he finished first.

There is something melancholy about this academic success, however, the suspicion that his redoubled focus on his work was more than anything else a distraction from his pain—that he was drawn to theology, as he would be drawn to the cold logic of counterpoint, out of a wish for order in his life. The death of both parents is not easily overcome in an adult, not to mention a small, unready adult. Maybe it is never overcome. In any case, from this time forward and for the rest of his life, Sebastian would pursue order, perfection, and spiritual meaning in his music, and never more movingly so than on the theme of triumph over death.

§

ONE OF THE MOST vivid stories of Sebastian's years in his brother's house in Ohrdruf concerns a collection of music Christoph had got from Pachelbel. He kept it locked in a cabinet, but one whose door was a grille through which ten-year-old Sebastian could just barely squeeze a hand. At night, when his brother was asleep, he would reach in, roll up the book of music, pull it out, and since he had no lamp, so the story goes, he would copy it by moonlight. Six months later, just about the time he had finished copying the manuscript, his brother discovered what he had done and took his copy of the book away. Sebastian himself had to have perpetuated this story, perhaps to demonstrate his youthful defiance, a quality that would have been healing for him at such a time. Increasingly that quality would come to the foreground of his character, and naturally so: Martin Luther was his model, after all, a man whose entire career was a heroic act of defiance.

The meaning taken from the story of the "moonlight manuscript" is usually the drive with which Sebastian undertook his own musical education, a drive sufficient to keep him up all night copying music, but the oddest part of the story is his brother's role in it. Why would he have taken away the copy Sebastian had made, and why did he forbid its use in the first place? This part of the story would make no sense if there were not other stories like it. The organist and Bach scholar David Yearsley cites a letter from the composer and theorist J. G. Walther to the well-known cantor Heinrich Bokemeyer—both of whom were renowned for their knowledge of counterpoint—in which Walther complains that his teacher had made him pay to see a musical treatise, then stood over him as he read it and only allowed him to copy a little at any one time. Finally, Walther resorted to bribing his teacher's son to smuggle the work to him at night, when he was able to copy it in one sitting.

Yearsley cited Walther's letter to demonstrate the connection between the practice of learned counterpoint and that of alchemy, the then still-active search for the elusive "philosopher's stone" that could mediate the transformation of base metal into gold, and the connections he found are indeed intriguing. Like alchemy, the roots of counterpoint were centuries old. Ever since the early Middle Ages, when the single chanted line of Gregorian plain-song gave way grudgingly to the presence of another voice, the rich acoustic medium of the medieval stone church had encouraged composers' experiments writing note against note (*punctus contra punctum*) and eventually of braiding related vocal lines through one another to form increasingly rich weaves of melody. The most rigorous such part writing, such as canon and fugue, came to be known collectively as learned counterpoint, and its elaborated codes and principles were handed down as carefully and discreetly as the secrets of alchemy, from *artifex* to *artifex* (the Latin term for alchemist, which Bokemeyer used to describe the composer of counterpoint as well).

Just as the alchemist's ambition was to discover God's laws for "perfecting" iron into gold, the learned composer's job was to attempt to replicate in earthly music the celestial harmony with which God had joined and imbued the universe, and so in a way to take part in the act of Creation itself. Understanding what possessed young Sebastian to spend his nights trying to steal his brother's notebook (after very long days at school and more daily hours at his music practice) requires understanding how the practice of threading musical voices into the fabric of counterpoint could have been endowed with such metaphysical power.

The key is music's relation to number, a connection that was as old as Plato and as new as Newton, dating from the mythic day in the sixth century B.C. when Pythagoras heard a hammer strike an anvil. In his *Textbook of Harmony* of the second century A.D., Nichomachus of Gerasa recorded the moment:

> One day he was out walking, lost in his reflections [when he] happened by a providential coincidence to pass by a blacksmith's workshop . . . and heard there quite clearly the iron hammers . . . giving forth confusedly intervals which, with the exception of one, were perfect consonances. He recognized among these sounds the consonances of the diapason (octave), diapente (fifth) and diatessaron (fourth). . . . Thrilled, he entered the shop as if a god were aiding his plans. . . .

It is a lovely and dubious story that later gets a bit loopy, perhaps through centuries of retelling. As a historical figure, Pythagoras is irretrievably lost in myth, in part because he forbade his disciples to write down anything he said. There is little reason to believe he did not exist, but it may have been someone else, perhaps one of his followers, who figured out Euclid's "Theorem of Pythagoras," which states that the square of the hy-

potenuse of a right triangle is equal to the sum of the squares of
the other two sides. That was one of the Pythagoreans' more useful ideas. They also posited the existence of a "counter-earth" because they could make out only nine planetary bodies and there
had to be ten because ten was the perfect number.

For Western music, the most important discovery attributed
to Pythagoras was that halving a string doubles its frequency,
creating an octave with the full string in the proportion of 1:2. A
little further experimentation showed that the interval of a fifth
was sounded when string lengths were in the proportion of 2:3,
the fourth in that of 3:4, and so on. This congruence was taken to
have great cosmic significance. As elaborated over a few centuries
around the time B.C. became A.D., the thinking (much oversimpli-
fied) was that such a sign of order had to be reflective of a larger,
universal design—and sure enough, the same musical proportions were found in the distances between the orbits of the planets. Further, since such enormous bodies could not possibly orbit
in complete silence, they must be sounding out these intervals together, playing a constant celestial harmony. Certified by Plato's
*Republic* and *Timaeus,* where the celestial music is said to be sung
by sirens seated aboard their respective planets, the mathematical-
cosmic nature of music was transmitted to Baroque composers
and their predecessors by the Roman scholar Ancius Manlius
Severinus Boethius, whose sixth-century writings constituted the
most widely read treatise on music theory for the next thousand
years.

Of course such a perfectly ordered universe could only be the
work of God, the all-encompassing One (represented by the unison in the proportion 1:1), and the unswerving reliability of this
order was taken as proof of His continuing presence in the world.
Despite that, the early church fathers continued to oppose anything but plainsong in the liturgy, hearing the work of the devil in

more elaborate music. Saint Augustine finally resolved the question in favor of liberating music to glorify God, but not without torment.

> I waver between the danger that lies in gratifying the senses and the benefits which, as I know from experience, can accrue from singing. Without committing myself to an irrevocable opinion, I am inclined to approve the custom of singing in church, in order that by indulging the ears weaker spirits may be inspired with feelings of devotion. Yet when I find the singing itself more moving than the truth which it conveys, I confess that this is a grievous sin, and at those times I would prefer not to hear the singer.

Of critical importance for Bach and his time, Martin Luther sided with the Platonic idea of music as evidence of divine order, and he set out to rehabilitate Pythagoras as a servant of God. In his commentary on Genesis he laments the fact that "we have become deaf toward what Pythagoras aptly terms this wonderful and most lovely music coming from the harmony of the spheres." No less than the seventeenth-century astronomer Johannes Kepler gave Luther's position the stamp of scientific certainty in his great work, *Harmonices Mundi*, where he correlates the orbits of the planets to the intervals of the scale and finds them to be "nothing other than a continuous, many voiced music (grasped by the understanding, not the ear)." This last point was debated: Some thought the celestial music was abstract, an ephemeral spiritual object, but others insisted it was real, inaudible to us only because it had been sounding constantly in the background from the time of our birth. In either case music was a manifestation of the cosmic order. "Now one will no longer be surprised," Kepler wrote, "that man has formed this most excellent order of notes or steps into the musical system or scale, since one can see that in this matter he acts as nothing but the ape of God the Creator, playing, as it were, a drama about the order of celestial motions." One of his chapters is titled "There Are Universal Harmonies of All Six Planets, Similar to Common Four-Part Counterpoint."

Never were allegories packed into music more enthusiastically than in Bach's time. Andreas Werckmeister was far from alone in attaching specific integers, for example, to the Trinity: 1 stood for the Father, 2 for the Son, 3 for the Holy Spirit, the last being the sum and proportion of Father and Son (1:2, a unison at the octave). Elsewhere we find that 4 represented the four elements of matter and the four seasons, that 5 meant justice (because it stands at the center of the first ten numbers) and humanity (five senses and the five appendages of arms, legs, and head). Saint Augustine favored the number 6 (creation took six days, so God must have found 6 to be a perfect number), 7 stood for the planets, virtues, liberal arts, deadly sins, and ages of man (although sometimes it is said not to stand for anything, since on the seventh day God rested). Twelve covered apostles, months, prophets, etc. Then there were the combinations, for example: 7 being 3 (the Trinity) plus 4 (elements of matter), and 12 being 3 (ditto) *times* 4 (ditto), it followed (trust me) that 7 and 12 were perfect numbers. And so on. All this from Pythagoras, whose followers thought the best number was 10 because it was the sum of 1, 2, 3, and 4, elemental components of the "figured number" known as the Pythagorean Tetraktys:

It is easy to have fun with number theory, and some of the best such fun is in the distant reaches of the Bach literature, where one can read, for example, that he left a prophecy in musical code of the date of his death on the Rosicrucian calendar. On the other hand, it is only the extent to which Bach's music contains meanings coded in numbers that is hotly debated. The fact that it contains such coded meanings is not.

Cosmological harmony was actually one of the few ideas on which the philosophers, scientists, and theologians of Bach's time were agreed. Newton, for example, could not imagine that a world as orderly as this one could have occurred by "natural Cause alone." A "powerful, ever-living Agent . . . governs all things," he concluded, "not as the soul of the world, but as Lord over all." Newton's Agent was Luther's Celestial Contrapuntist, whose woven voices were like so many planetary orbits.

> We marvel when we hear music in which one voice sings a simple melody, while three, four, or five other voices play and trip lustily around . . . reminding us of a heavenly dance.

This heavenly dance was nowhere more sublime than in canon, the strictest form of contrapuntal writing, in which an entire piece of music is built from a single melodic phrase playing over itself at different intervals of time and key, in varying rhythms and tempi, sometimes appearing backward, inside out, or upside down, and sometimes continuing, at least theoretically, forever. Andreas Werckmeister drew the analogy of cosmos to counterpoint even more explicitly than Luther had done:

> The heavens are now revolving and circulating steadily so that one [body] now goes up but in another time it changes again and comes down. . . . We also have these mirrors of

heaven and nature in musical harmony, because a certain
voice can be the highest voice, but can become the lowest
or middle voice, and the lowest and middle can again become the highest. . . . [In the case of canon] one voice can
become all the other voices and no other voice must be
added. . . .

Another of Bach's contemporaries imagined the moment
when the first contrapuntist, stumbling on a perpetual canon,
found "the beginning and end bound together" and discovered
"the eternal unending origins as well as the harmony of all eternity."

From such a celestial height, perhaps it is possible to look
again at a young boy copying music from his brother's notebook
on a moonlit night and see what he is doing a bit more clearly.
The composers in the "moonlight manuscript"—Kerll, Froberger,
Pachelbel—were the reigning masters of counterpoint, men who
knew about the great design, who plied its strings and levers. To a
boy so recently an orphan, simply the belief that there was such a
design—that God was present in an orderly universe—must
have been as comforting as it was elusive. His brother's notebook
was the closest Sebastian had ever come to such an idea of life and
music, and the gesture of putting his hand through the grille of
that cupboard was about more than the desire for a musical education: He was reaching for answers. Christoph had been Pachelbel's (the sorcerer's) apprentice, so the secrets in his notebook
were worth any amount of lost sleep to Sebastian. But in this
light, Christoph's attitude is no less understandable: What gave
his little brother, a *schoolboy*, the right to such precious and hard-
won knowledge? Of course his brother took away Sebastian's
copy of the notebook, and of course he would have forbidden
anyone to copy it in the first place.

Such a reading of this anecdote requires no great psychoanalytic reach. Sebastian's worldview was profoundly allegorical, like that of his time and culture. The favored allegories at the time were Lutheran, of course, but not exclusively so. After all, Kepler had read horoscopes, and both Newton and Leibniz still had hopes for alchemy. Efforts to advance the education of Sebastian's day could hardly be called enlightened, confounded as they still were by ignorance and superstition. The seventeenth-century educational reformer Jan Amos Comenius, for example, introduced physics into the curriculum, but it was a physics in which the world's qualities were exactly three: "consistence, oleosity and aquasity," the attributes of salt, sulfur, and mercury, a decidedly medieval stew. So Sebastian's education was as thoroughly theological, or, more broadly, mythological, as his father's and grandfather's had been.

In *tertia*, where Sebastian began his Lyceum studies in Ohrdruf, there was some reading of classics and history, but it was carefully edited for religious content; most of his class time was spent on Scripture and the catechism. In *secunda* and the first part of *prima*, he got lots of Latin—especially rhetoric and oratory—as well as some Greek, math, history and science, but his hardest work was on Leonhard Hutter's exhaustive and exhausting exegesis on Lutheran doctrine, the *Compendium locorum theologicorum*, hundreds and hundreds of pages in Latin, great chunks of which he was expected to memorize.

Given his class standing, he obviously mastered it, but it is difficult to see how, even for someone trying to throw himself into work. Outside of class, the lovely singing voice that got him his scholarship made him an anchor not only of the *chorus musicus* but also of a smaller group that did advanced works for the church as well as weddings and funerals. At the same time he must have been practicing the organ and harpsichord for long hours every day. He credited his brother Christoph with giving him his first keyboard lessons, but by the time he left Ohrdruf, after only five years, his technical mastery was already prodigious.

The transformation of a novice into a budding virtuoso in five years would have been a remarkable feat even without all his other work, an accomplishment for which even the best teacher could not take credit.

§

TEN DAYS BEFORE his fifteenth birthday, Sebastian put his clothes in a bag, strung a violin over his shoulder, and set out, on foot, for a new school more than two hundred miles away. Nobody in his family had ventured so far from their Thuringian heartland, but of course Sebastian was not anybody else. The move was forced on him. Christoph's home was becoming overcrowded as his family grew, and Sebastian could no longer pay for his keep because for unknown reasons he had lost his job as a tutor to the children of wealthy citizens. He may have felt he was being orphaned yet again, but in fact the offer of a choral scholarship to St. Michael's Lyceum in Lüneburg, a town almost four times the size of Ohrdruf, was providential. His brother would probably have told him not to go there but to apprentice himself to a master as Christoph had done at this age. None of Sebastian's siblings or ancestors had gone as far in school as he had gone already. But there was a wonderful library at St. Michael's, with a famous collection of all the contrapuntal art of Europe; and Lüneburg was not far from Hamburg, the largest and most musical city in Germany.

For a boy who had known only Eisenach and Ohrdruf, Lüneburg was another country, with large open public squares, Renaissance architecture, and a distractingly robust musical life. We know that Sebastian graduated St. Michael's, but there are no claims for his academic excellence there. When his voice changed soon after he arrived, he kept his music scholarship by singing bass and playing keyboards and violin, but apart from choral service the plainest trail he left in Lüneburg was extravagantly extracurricular.

While St. Michael's tried to teach him yet more Latin, Sebastian taught himself French and Italian, which he needed to make his way through the music library. As Leo Schrade noted in his deceptively small book, *Bach: The Conflict Between the Sacred and the Secular,* the richness of the library at St. Michael's must have been dazzling to Sebastian but also somewhat disorienting: There was a great deal of German church music in the collection, but none of it was as German as it was the work of German composers writing in French or English or Italian or Dutch, the problem that sent Handel off to Italy and Telemann into the opera. After serving as a battleground for the great powers, Germany had not developed its own musical (or any other) traditions since the Thirty Years War so much as it absorbed them, a fact which Bach's foremost predecessor, the great composer Heinrich Schütz, bemoaned in his late life even as he continued to write in the style of Monteverdi. German princes spoke French. The best music came to Germany from Venice or Amsterdam—by sea, to the port of Hamburg.

Hamburg thus became the seedbed of change for German music, and in search of Germany's musical future and his own, Sebastian more than once made the arduous several days' walk to Hamburg and back, taking on the role of journeyman musician. Hamburg had not only a robust, distinctly German school of organists but also an opera. Astride both was the octogenarian Johann Adam Reinken, organist at St. Catherine's Church and one of the opera's founders. Reinken's magnificent organ, with its four keyboards, fifty-eight stops, and full pedal keyboard, had enormous range and power—from the great thirty-two-foot pipes and their thunderous bass to the tiniest whistles, for piccolo and flute. Reinken's was the largest organ Bach had ever seen and became the measure by which he would judge all others. Perhaps first at Reinken's Hamburg apartment, he came under the influence of the great Dietrich Buxtehude, organist at St. Mary's in

Lübeck and a composer of outsize ambition and ability who was working with all the styles and traditions of Europe. Buxtehude would have a more than musical influence on Sebastian in his first job, and it was in him perhaps more than anywhere else that Sebastian would find the inspiration for what was perhaps his greatest gift to Western culture: forging from a multinational babel a single language of European music.

§

SIXTY MILES OF very bad roads from St. Michael's school in Lüneburg, in another direction entirely from the road to Hamburg, lay one of Germany's many mini-Versailles, the very fashionable dukedom of Celle, where, according to his son Carl, Sebastian was exposed to the latest in French culture and music, including the works of Lebègue, Marais, Marchand, Couperin, and especially Jean-Baptiste Lully, the Sun King's own composer and so the paragon of French music (himself however a Florentine, an embarrassment Louis was persuaded to overlook only by the richness of Lully's sycophancy).

Though he learned and adopted a great deal from French music, Sebastian must have been mystified by the French attitude toward it. Like everything else at Versailles and in seventeenth-century France, music was a slave to the narcissism and power of Louis XIV. Its purpose was, simply, to serve the king: as background to his clavecin or lute playing, as accompaniment to the ballets he danced in, and to cover for the noise of the brilliant new machines that allowed whales to belch fireworks and permitted Louis himself to fly as Jupiter on the back of an eagle and as various other deities to float along on clouds in the ostentatious theatricals staged to reinforce his myth. Bach certainly would write flattering music to and for kings and princes, but his music always had a higher goal in mind, the glory of which royal power was but a pale shadow. In France, though, music had only one purpose more important than the glorification of

Louis. The palace gossip sheet *Mercure galant* prattled on about how music mirrored the harmony of the universe and was therefore the king's handmaiden as the arbiter and source of all good order, etc., but the fact was that Louis needed music and musical spectacles to keep his nobles occupied. Dukes with time on their hands had been no end of trouble to his father and Cardinal Richelieu, and Louis knew that a rich court life would keep them distracted and keep them where he could see them. He learned that from his own Cardinal Mazarin, who imported Italian singers, composers, and instrumentalists to distract Louis himself from the notion of meddling in state affairs as a boy king.

In time the Italian composers began to experiment with chromaticism and dissonance, to introduce passion into their music. This was controversial, and so the Italians were banished. Louis then put his imprimatur on Lully's elaborately ornamented, courtly pleasantries, whose halting, ceremonial rhythms were difficult enough to walk much less dance to, a kind of musical Stump the Nobles. (There were other, similarly hobbling fashions; ladies were forced to kneel in their coaches, for example, to compete in that heyday of *haute coiffure*.) Lully's Florentine background was inconvenient, but the *Mercure galant*, which commented frequently and with great assurance on matters of music theory, reported that Lully

> knew perfectly well the necessity of renouncing the taste of his nation in order to accommodate himself to ours; he found that the French judged some things more sanely than the Italians; and he knew that music had no other end than to titillate the ear; it was unnecessary to charge it with affected dissonances.

One of Lully's jobs was to rationalize, in just so many words, Louis's various religious and territorial wars. In *Amadis*, as

French armies marched on the Netherlands and Luxembourg in 1683, Lully put this operatic encomium to Louis in the mouth of his heroine Urgande:

> This hero triumphs so that everything will be peaceful. In vain, thousands of the envious arm themselves on all sides. With one word, with one of his glances he knows how to bend their useful fury to his will. It is for him to teach the great Art of war to the Masters of the Earth. . . . The whole universe admires his exploits; let us go to live happily under his laws.

Pleased, Louis gave Lully a state monopoly on the staging of operas, and Lully became filthy rich. Scandal attached to him now and then. People were given to having sex in the upper galleries at the opera, Lully himself was upbraided by Louis more than once for outrageously gay behavior in public, and the nobles kept getting his singers pregnant. Fiercely disliked and openly opposed by many, including Molière and Boileau (who called Lully an "odious buffoon"), he hung on, getting richer and richer, until finally he made them all happy by impaling himself in the foot with his baton and dying of gangrene. In one of the many satires at his death, an Italian composer attempts to turn him back at the gates of Parnassus, arguing that he had played upon the French weakness for the merely fashionable in order to line his pockets. Lully replies loftily, "I declare quite frankly . . . that I have worked usefully for the corruption of my country, but they [the French] are no less deserving of the glory, because they have followed the composer's intentions."

It hardly needs to be said that nothing could be further from Bach's exalted sense of purpose for music than Louis's utilitarian or Lully's mercenary one, but this early exposure to French music turns up in his earliest compositions and clearly left a deep impression on him.

Attached to St. Michael's was a school for young nobles, called a Knights' Academy, and probably through a friendly sponsor there he had access to the recently completed castle in Lüneburg of Duke Georg Wilhelm, where he also heard the latest music of France. The Knights' Academy also exposed him to a less pleasant aspect of his future. The curriculum of these cadet princelings included not only the usual Latin, history, and science but also French, dancing, heraldry, and other prerequisites for the life of a francophone German noble. Bach and the other choral scholars slept every night in a dormitory just next to that of the Knights' Academy, and some of them served the young princes as valets or tutors. Whether as valet, tutor, or just another invisible spectator among the scholarship boys, Sebastian would have witnessed every day the worst aspects of the petty nobles then living off Germany's fractured territories, and he had every reason to be sobered by the thought that one of them might someday be his patron.

## V.

*GIANTS, SPIES, AND THE LASH:*

*LIFE WITH "FATTY"*

At about the same age Bach had been when he walked the two hundred miles to Lüneburg, Crown Prince Frederick could be found in his favorite red-and-gold embroidered robe and slippers, his hair curled and puffed, playing flute-and-lute duets with his sister Wilhelmina. Usually a lookout was posted at the door because of the intensity with which his father despised this scene. Frederick William had set himself the task of eradicating Frederick's "effeminate" (read: French) tastes, and in that entirely fruitless effort he employed a degree of violence perhaps unique in the annals of kings and their crown princes. What his son endured at his hands explains almost everything about the sort of man and king Frederick would become, but before getting into that we should give the father his due.

Unlike most of his aristocratic peers, Frederick William was a devoted (not devout) Protestant, a faithful husband, hardworking, plain in his tastes, and thrifty. For two years before taking the throne he had investigated the spending habits and ministers of his father, and upon his accession he got rid of both, slashing the royal budget by three quarters, sacking virtually the entire court (including the musicians), selling off most of his father's horses, the royal silver, and the crown jewels. When he made the obligatory trip to Königsberg to receive Prussia's homage to its new king, he took fifty horses and four days (to his father's thirty thousand horses and two weeks), and instead of five million he spent exactly 2,547 thalers on the trip. From the first days of his reign, he made it plain that this would not be his father's monarchy. The Saxon ambassador reported to Dresden:

> Every day his majesty gives new proofs of his justice. Walking recently at Potsdam at 6 in the morning, he saw a post coach arrive with several passengers who knocked for a long time at the post house which was still closed. The King, seeing that no one opened the door, joined them in knocking and even knocked in some window-panes. The master of the post then opened the door and scolded the travelers, for no one recognized the King. But His Majesty let himself be known by giving the official some good blows of his cane and drove him from his house and his job after apologizing to the travelers for his laziness. Examples of this sort, of which I could relate several others, make everybody alert and exact.

Very much in contrast to the contemporary German princes Bach knew at the Knights' Academy, a bunch of narcissistic, free-spending little Sun Kings, Frederick William built a model orphanage, provided for poor widows, recovered large tracts of wetlands for agriculture, and helped to elevate the craft of administration to the level of science, creating in his two universities the first chairs in cameralism, a theoretical approach to managing a centralized economy. In service to his almost obsessive attention to his kingdom's finances—he was forever telling his son about the virtues of *ein Plus machen*, making a profit—he radically reorganized his administration with a remarkable "In-

struction" to his ministers that covered everything from punctu-
ality to trade policy. The structure he created became a fairly efficient bureaucracy, but the Instruction itself betrayed its
autocratic (not to mention compulsive) author. For example, he
was determined not to let Prussian goods get away by allowing
his people to export wool, so he decreed that all of it would be
used—and how:

> The General Directory shall compare the total of the wool
> manufactured with the total of the wool produced. Let us
> suppose the first total to be inferior to the second, and that
> 2,000 pounds of the wool at first quality and 1,000 pounds
> of medium quality will not find buyers. The General Di-
> rectory shall establish in a city nine drapers, each of which
> will use 300 pounds of good wool, and employ one hun-
> dred operatives in the stocking manufactories, each of
> which will work up at least 10 pounds of medium wool.
> The evil is remedied.

After he published this Instruction, the penalty for anyone caught
exporting wool was strangulation.

"A king needs to be strong," he said. "In order to be strong he
must have a good army. In order to maintain a good army he must
pay it. In order to pay it he must raise the money." His ideas were
few and those borrowed—this one was the advice of his grandfather, the Great Elector—but he lived by them. During his reign
he would build up *ein Plus* of no less than eight million thalers, he
would double the size of his army, and through drill, discipline,
and innovation, he would make them the envy of the great powers of Europe. Powerful nations, he told his son, "will always be
obliged to seek a prince who has a hundred thousand men ready
for action and twenty-five million crowns to sustain them. . . . All

the most imposing powers seek me, and emulate each other in fondling me, as they would a bride."

Really it was beyond fondling, they were all over him, but most of the time he had no clue they were taking advantage of him. His two closest ministers were employed as spies by the Hapsburgs. Their code name for the him was "Fatty." "Have no fears," one of them wrote in a dispatch. "Fatty's heart is in my hands, I can do with him as I like. . . ." Frederick William would have called this man one of his best friends.

The result was a foreign policy that could only be described as a mess. At a time when diplomacy was as shadowy and filled with intrigue as it would ever be, Prussia had a king who did not deal well with ambiguity, and no one was more aware of this weakness than himself, one of the reasons he was frequently in a rage. The French ambassador wrote to Versailles: "The variable moods of the King of Prussia and his profound dissimulation are infinitely above all that Your Majesty can imagine." In fact, though, he was less deceitful than simply confused most of the time, acting on the advice of spies, always stumbling out of the trouble they made for him and that he made for himself. He had witnessed and resented how his father and grandfather had been undercut and cheated by a variety of powers, including the Hapsburgs, but he was powerless to avenge them. "Follow the example of your father in finance and military affairs," he told Frederick one day. "Take care not to imitate him in what is called ministerial affairs, for he understands nothing about that."

Frederick William's chief consolations in life were getting drunk and kidnapping giants (not at the same time). He had stolen hundreds and thousands of very large, mostly moronic men for his ornamental guard, the Potsdam Grenadiers, from their homes and fields and from the armies of enemies and friends alike (another diplomatic blooper). At one point kidnapping the giants got a little expensive for him, so he tried breeding them instead, insisting that every large citizen of the realm marry an equally large person, but mixed results sent him back to kidnapping. His methods were varied and no-nonsense. A priest was taken from the altar of his church during mass. "Prussian recruiters hover about barracks, parade-grounds, in Foreign Countries," Carlyle reports, adding that they "hunt with some vigor."

> For example, in the town of Jülich there lived and worked a tall young carpenter: one day a well-dressed, positive-looking gentleman . . . enters the shop; wants "a stout chest, with lock on it [and] . . . must be six feet six in length . . . an indispensable point,—in fact it will be longer than yourself, Herr Zimmerman." . . . At the appointed day he reappears; the chest is ready. . . . "Too short, as I dreaded!" says the positive gentleman. "Nay, your Honor," says the carpenter. . . . "Well, it is."—"No, it isn't!" The carpenter, to end the matter, gets into the chest [and] the positive gentleman, a Prussian recruiting officer in disguise, slams down the lid upon him; locks it; whistles in three stout fellows, who pick up the chest [and go].

In most cases these stories had unhappy endings, and this one was unhappier than most. When the coffin was opened the carpenter was found to have suffocated, and the positive gentleman, one Baron von Hompesch, spent the rest of his life in prison. Obviously, given the lengths to which the baron was willing to go, Frederick William's gratitude for his giants was extreme. When he was in one of his melancholy moods, which were frequent, having a few hundred of them file past him was known to be a reliable pick-me-up.

The other was beer. At night, almost every night, he took his place with his fellows—one hesitates to call anyone in his life a friend—on a wooden bench around a wooden table set with clay pipes, tobacco, wine, and beer. Here in the so-called Tobacco College, he and his closest advisers, most of them senior military officers, consulted, at least briefly, until they muzzily transitioned into song, loud toasts, and curses at the French. (It was in the Tobacco College, later rather than earlier in the evening, that the spies did their best work.) The unwitting jester at these revels was a man named Gundling, a university-educated drunk who had been found near destitution in a tavern by one of the spies and brought into the court to read the newspaper to the family at meals. He was the master of a thousand odd facts of geography, history, and other subjects, about all of which, being credulous as well as besotted, he was easily persuaded to speak. He was the easiest and most appealing kind of target for the king, who loved nothing more than to humiliate the pompous, and Gundling bore the brunt of jokes that became more brutal the more they all drank. Frederick's biographer Nancy Mitford reports that the group once set him on fire. He objected to their taunts (especially, one imagines, to being set ablaze), but he always came back. To reward his loyalty, to keep him around, and most of all to show how little the king thought of scholars and scholarship, Gundling was appointed to succeed Leibniz, the most profound philosopher of his generation, as head of the Berlin Academy of Sciences.

§

THE EGREGIOUS FLAWS of Frederick William would simply be of academic interest or entertainment value were it not for the remarkable fact that his son, a man so different from him in so many ways, would unconsciously incorporate so many of the qualities in his father that he most despised.

Of course, Frederick William carefully presided over his

crown prince's growth and education. *Presided* is in fact a small word for what he did. Frederick's days and lessons were prescribed minutely by another obsessive-compulsive "Instruction" from the king to his tutors. This is Sunday:

> [Frederick] is to rise at seven; and as soon as he has got his slippers on, shall kneel at his bedside, and pray to God so as all the room shall hear it . . . in these words: Lord God, blessed Father, I thank thee from my heart that thou hast so graciously preserved me through this night. Fit me for what thy holy will is; and grant that I do nothing this day, or all the days of my life, which can divide me from thee. For the Lord Jesus my Redeemer's sake. Amen. After which the Lord's prayer. Then rapidly and vigorously wash himself clean, dress and powder and comb himself. . . . Prayer, with washing, breakfast, and the rest, to be done pointedly [by] a quarter-past seven.

That was the first fifteen minutes of a schedule that took him minute by minute up to early evening, and Sunday was his easy day.

What is most notable about the education his father set out for Frederick is what was not there: no reading in the classics, no history prior to the sixteenth century, no natural sciences or philosophy (Frederick William called it "wind-making"), no Latin. He was, however, steeped in Calvinist theology. His father instructed his pastors not to teach the boy to believe in predestination, since he was convinced it would lead to desertions by fatalist soldiers, but they taught it to Frederick anyway. In fact, years later, even when he seemed not to believe anything at all, Frederick still spoke well of predestination.

Other than religion and economics, there was only one lesson that Frederick William insisted Frederick's tutors teach: They were charged to "infuse into my son a true love for the [life of a] Soldier . . . and impress on him that, as there is nothing in the world which can bring a Prince renown and honour like the sword, so he would be a despised creature before all men, if he did not love it, and seek his sole glory therein." The same year he was submitted to the Instruction—that is to say, at the age of six—the crown prince was given his own corps of human toy soldiers, the "Crown Prince Royal Battalion of Cadets," 131 luckless little boys whom he was to drill to Prussian standards. Two years later he was also given his own little arsenal, complete with miniature versions of the weapons in the Prussian armory, and a working cannon.

For a few years, Frederick appeared to be all his father could have hoped. Not long after he began working with his cadets, he wrote the king a letter in which he praised his troops for their precision in maneuvers and reported that he had shot his first partridge (Frederick William was an avid huntsman). The following year, at the age of seven, he sent his father an essay he had written, "How the Prince of a Great House Should Live" ("he must love his father and mother . . . he must love God with all his heart . . . he must never think evil," etc.). At the same time his teacher was reading to him from *Telemachus*, a novel by Fénelon, pen name of the Archbishop of Cambrai, who wrote his novel about the son of Odysseus as a manual on monarchy for the education of Louis XIV's grandson. Frederick William's mother had read the book to him, and it was filled with the sort of advice to a monarch-in-waiting of which the king very much approved. "The Gods did not make him king for his own sake," Mentor advises Telemachus. "He was intended to be the man of his people: he owes all his time to his people, all his care and all his affection, and he is worthy of royalty only in as much as he forgets his own self and sacrifices himself to the common weal." In the age of Louis XIV, that sentiment could not have been popular at the

French court, but both Frederick's later characterization of himself as "first servant of the state" and Frederick William's rebellion from the splendiferous court and self-image of his father have a root here.

As time went on, Frederick's curiosity ranged further and further from the cramped curriculum his father had prescribed for him. Fortunately for his education, his tutor Jacques Duhan was a wise and intrepid teacher, who followed his student's interests and even, over time, helped him to amass a secret library, hidden in the locked closets of a house he rented near the castle. The library eventually grew to almost four thousand volumes, ranging from pre-Socratic philosophers to the writers of the early Enlightenment. When his father ended Frederick's formal education at the age of fifteen and pensioned off the tutor, Frederick wrote Duhan: "I promise that when I have my own money I will give you 2400 crown a year and I will always love you, even a little more than now if that is possible."

§

FREDERICK WILLIAM'S PROGRAM for his son was subtly but relentlessly subverted by Frederick's mother. For much of his childhood he lived at her palace, called Monbijou, with his sister Wilhelmina, his elder by three years. Queen Sophia Dorothea was a Hanover, the daughter of England's King George I and sister of George II. (She was also the first cousin of her husband, whose mother was a Hanover.) In a replay of his parents' relationship, Frederick William loved his wife (he called her his *Fiechen*, a diminutive of Sophia), and Sophia Dorothea felt greatly diminished by her marriage. She painted Potsdam as rough and provincial in comparison to Hanover, and she let her children know of her distaste for her egregiously fat husband, who dressed every day in his faded military uniform, got drunk every night with his silly smoking party, and was forever talking about *ein Plus machen*. She was more than free with her opinions with her children: She consciously deployed them as part of a strategy to win them over to her vision of a *real* court (Hanover), the majesty of a *real* royal life (certainly not this one), the beauty of elaborate balls at which the latest in courtly music was played by the finest musicians. In this way and more direct ones, she made it clear to the children that they had a choice to make between her and their father. At one point, Wilhelmina wrote, her mother fiercely upbraided her for going to her father about some minor matter. She "reminded me that she had ordered me to attach myself to her exclusively; and that if I ever applied to the King again, she would be fiercely angry. . . ."

Their father placed no less claim on their affection, of course, so Frederick and Wilhelmina, caught between antagonistic parents and their separate, dueling courts, found shelter in each other. They giggled conspiratorially at both parents' dinner tables, made faces at each other when forced by their father to listen to his pastor's sermons, and delighted in their common passion for music, which was perhaps the only unalloyed delight of their young lives.

Both clearly came to favor their mother. In her memoir, Wilhelmina paints a distinctly (and justly) unfavorable portrait of both parents but reserves her faintest praise for the king. "His table was served with frugality," she wrote. "It never exceeded necessities. His principal occupation was to drill a regiment." As for Frederick, Wilhelmina (at least as a child) had only deep affection and loyalty. "He was the most amiable prince that could be seen," she wrote of her younger brother, "handsome, well made, of an understanding superior to his years, and possessed of every quality that forms a perfect prince."

What the queen wanted more than anything was that her children would marry Hanovers, who were now England's royal family. Wilhelmina was to marry the prince of Wales and Frederick his sister, Princess Amalia. Sophia Dorothea, then, would someday be mother not only to the king of Prussia but also to the queen of England, a prospect which suited her. The spies, of course, had to make sure that never happened, since it would put Prussia in England's camp rather than the empire's. Until the "double-marriage" plan could be completely unraveled, therefore, the spies worked "Fatty" hard, and so did the queen. Both sides used the same carrot: the aggrandizement of Prussia. The empire dangled two provinces on the Rhine, Jülich and Berg, that both the Great Elector and Frederick William's father felt, with justice, the empire had taken from them wrongly. (The empire had no intention of actually supporting the claim, and it was characteristic of their view of Prussia that they offered as a prize something they had blatantly appropriated.) England, in its alliance with France against the empire, held out a future for Prussia as a coequal, independent, sovereign state rather than the role of imperial lackey and also support for his claim to Jülich-Berg. In trying to gain advantage for that position, the queen played a very treacherous game. Among other things, she recruited the French ambassador to Berlin, Konrad Alexander von Rothenburg, to be the conduit for secret messages to the English court, essentially plotting with them against her husband and king.

Not surprisingly, Frederick William frequently had the feeling something was going on behind his back. Who would not have been confused and suspicious, caught between the pleading of an ambitious and deceitful wife whom he loved and the advice of spies whom he considered his best advisers and closest friends?

§

AS HE GREW older, Frederick seemed to be less and less his father's son and more and more his mother's. He had never really liked hunting, and now when they went to the hunting lodge at Wusterhausen, he hid. Once when he should have been stalking game, his father found him in a clump of bushes reading. He fell off his horse. He curled his hair. He slept late. He called his uniform "the shroud." He and his sister were ever more faithfully part of their mother's cabal, to the point that she was able to draw Frederick into her conspiracy with the French minister, at which point her little prince began to demonstrate a distinct taste for intrigue.

His mother's ability to bring Frederick into her perilous orbit owed a great deal to the fact that he was being physically abused and humiliated by his father. The beatings began when Frederick was twelve, and on a fixed date. Father and son were at a dinner party given by one of the spies, Field Marshal von Grumbkow. (Grumbkow was Frederick William's war minister, of all things. The other spy was the former imperial ordnance master Count von Seckendorff.) In his cups, the king wrapped his arm around the crown prince and began loudly to give him advice, the rest of the party his audience. According to a dispatch from the Saxon minister to Dresden after the party, as he spoke the king began patting his son's cheek for emphasis. "Fritz, listen to what I am going to say to you. Keep always a good large army [light tap], you cannot have a better friend and without this friend you will not be able to sustain yourself [harder tap]. Our neighbors desire nothing better than to make us turn a somersault. I know their intentions; you will learn [very hard tap] to know them. Believe me, do not trust in vanity—attach thyself to the real [harder]. Have a good army and money [harder]. In these consist the glory [harder] of the king [harder]." Word of the incident made its way to the capitals of all nations represented at the Prussian court.

From that point on, the beatings became increasingly frequent, humiliating, and severe. He beat Frederick for wearing gloves on a cold day at the hunt. He beat him for eating with a silver fork instead of a steel one. He beat him in front of servants, officers, and diplomats. He threw the prince to the floor and kicked him, berating him at the top of his lungs and beating him with his cane.

Frederick was not his only victim; his fury seemed omnidirectional. For a while it was thought that the king was going completely mad. So violently hostile was he even to his beloved giants that forty of them plotted to roast him alive by burning down Potsdam (a plot that gives us some sense of their collective intelligence). The penalty for desertion was to have one's skin pinched off with red-hot tongs and then have all of one's bones broken on the wheel, but there were hundreds of desertions anyway, and suicides at the garrison ran two a month. "The people are greatly discontented," Rothenburg wrote to Paris. "They hope and believe that this distress cannot endure always. There are all the appearances of a revolution. Everything is preparing for it."

§

AT ONE POINT, in one of his most profound depressions, the king began talking of abdication. Grumbkow and Seckendorff (and more so of course their imperial paymasters) were horrified: Should Frederick William abdicate and the crown prince succeed him now, the English alliance would be assured. So the Hapsburg emperor called upon his good friend Augustus the Strong, elector of Saxony, king of Poland, and grandmaster of the revels at one of the most sumptuous pleasure domes of Europe. The king of Prussia needed a rest, the emperor told Augustus, who was more than happy to oblige by sending Frederick William an invitation to Dresden.

Augustus the Strong was no doubt the most debauched ruler in Europe, which for the early eighteenth century is no small claim. His mistresses were legion, his illegitimate children numbered exactly 354, and some of his many daughters had become his mistresses as well. Obviously Frederick William disapproved such goings-on and knew what awaited. He took Frederick with him only because Wilhelmina plotted with the Saxon ambassador to pry an urgent invitation out of Augustus for the crown prince to join him. Frederick, of course, was thrilled with Dresden. He saw his first opera, he held his own in interesting conversation with smart dinner companions, he went to concerts, he even played his flute with the king's Kapelle. In a letter to Wilhelmina describing the scene (the first letter he signed in the French manner, "Fédéric"), he wrote grandly, "I have been heard as a musician." In that way and others Frederick greatly upstaged his father, whose most notable accomplishment in Dresden was to split his pants at a ball.

Perhaps Augustus's greatest gift to the young crown prince came as a result of a joke played on his father. Knowing Frederick William to be something of a prude, Augustus led him to a human diorama, covered at first by a red velvet curtain. When drawn, it disclosed, surrounded by hundreds of candles, the reclining naked figure of a startlingly attractive woman. Accounts differ as to Frederick William's reaction—he said she was beautiful and blushed, he slapped his hat over Frederick's face and pushed him out of the room, he huffed out and said he was going back to Potsdam immediately—but we have no trouble imagining Frederick's reaction. He had already been flirting with a certain very sexy countess who was among Augustus's illegitimate daughters and favorite mistresses. She was cheating on Augustus with one of her half brothers, but apparently she had time for a crown prince, because Augustus caught her looking. He took Frederick aside and told him the countess was unavailable but asked if he would like to get to know the lady behind the curtain. Frederick said he would. Credible speculation has it that he eventually got to know them both.

If Frederick left Dresden with a smile on his face, it was knocked off in short order. After Dresden, father and son made immediately for the king's hunting lodge at Wusterhausen. It was a banner hunt that year—the party brought in a grand total of 3,600 wild boar, 450 in one day—and Frederick was miserable. Apparently the king had not changed his attitude toward his son, because during their time at Wusterhausen Frederick wrote a letter to his father, who was in the next room:

> For a long time I have not ventured to present myself before my dear papa, partly because I was advised not to do so, but mainly because I . . . was afraid to disturb my dear papa further by the favor I shall now ask. So I prefer to put it in writing.
>
> I beg my dear papa to be kindly disposed toward me. I assure him that, after a long examination of my conscience, I find not the smallest thing with which I should reproach myself. But if, contrary to my wishes, I have disturbed my dear papa, I herewith beg him humbly for forgiveness, and I hope that my dear papa will forget the fearful hate which appears so clearly in his whole behavior and to which I find it hard to accustom myself. Until now I have always thought that I had a kind father, but I now see quite the opposite. Nevertheless, I shall take courage and hope that my dear papa will think this over and restore me once again to his favor. In the meantime, I assure him that I will never in my life willingly fail him, and in spite of his disfavor, I shall remain with most dutiful and filial respect, my dear papa's
>
> Most obedient and faithful servant and son,
> *Friedrich*

His father replied:

> You know very well that I cannot abide an effeminate fellow who has no manly tastes, who cannot ride or shoot (let

it be said—to his shame!), is untidy in his personal habits and wears his hair curled like a fool instead of cutting it. . . . For the rest, you are haughty, as indifferent as a country lout; you converse with no one outside of a few favorites, instead of being friendly and sociable; you grimace like a fool; you never follow my wishes out of love for me but only when you are forced to do so. You care nothing but having your own way, and you think nothing else is of any importance. That is my answer.

*Friedrich Wilhelm*

There was a terrible amount of animus, posturing, and truth in both letters, and the exchange had the predictable effect, which was none. Frederick did not modify his behavior, and his father kept beating and humiliating him for it. The prince seemed to have brought some illness back from Dresden, speculatively identified as venereal disease. Whatever it was, it laid him low, and was no doubt made worse by the constant battles with his father.

He had revived by the time Augustus paid a visit to Potsdam a few months later, and along with his many mistresses (including Frederick's favorite), he brought his Kapelle, for which he had recruited the best musicians in Europe. One of them was Johann Joachim Quantz, a flautist of formidable reputation with whom Frederick had played in Dresden. On this trip he agreed to become Frederick's teacher on the instrument, which was no small commitment, since the lessons and expenses were to be paid by the queen and kept secret from the king.

This little plot had the predictable outcome as well. The king came unexpectedly to Frederick's apartment in the middle of one of his musical evenings, where Frederick was decked out in the red-and-gold robe he wore when he played duets with Wilhelmina. His hair was curled and puffed, and everything was just so, very French. There was a mad scramble when the lookout spotted the king coming. Frederick tore off the robe and stuffed it in a corner, the others, including Quantz, grabbed their instruments and found a firewood closet to hide in, but Frederick's hair gave the game away. Very quickly the king sized up what was happening and began casting around the room for proof and co-conspirators. Where are they? he wanted to know. Hardened in his rebellion and protecting what was closest to him, Frederick said nothing. The king grew angrier, too angry, apparently, to think of looking in the closet. Finally he found and confiscated a few French books. Otherwise all he found was the red-and-gold robe. He stuffed it into the fire.

Sometime after that the king took Frederick with him again (for reasons unknown and unfathomable) to see King Augustus, who was holding military maneuvers in Mühlberg as the excuse for a great raucous party. On the last day, Augustus gave a dinner for all thirty thousand of his soldiers at two long—apparently very long—lines of tables, at each end of which was the head of an ox, with the skin of oxen covering the roasted quarters on the tables. Between the two lines of tables rode the kings of Poland and Prussia and their two crown princes, receiving the hosannas of the crowd. Frederick, however, could not have been regarded with unmixed awe. A day or two before he had been forced to stand at parade with his hair and clothes badly askew. For one reason or another, the king had beat him hard that day, throwing him to the ground, kicking him, and dragging him around by the hair, in full view of the crowd. When he had finished with his son, Frederick William spat at him: "Had I been so treated by my father I would have blown my brains out, but this man has no honor."

Not long after Frederick returned to Berlin, Rothenburg informed Paris: "I have reason to believe that he is thinking of making his escape."

## VI.

*THE  SHARP  EDGES  OF  GENIUS*

FREDERICK HAD NOT YET BEEN BORN AND HIS FATHER
was still just the fourteen-year-old maniac crown prince of Prussia, promising to hang his tutors the minute he took the throne,
when, at the age of seventeen, Sebastian finished his studies at St.
Michael's School in Lüneburg. By that time he was a skilled composer, his improvisations were dazzlingly original, and his virtuosity was outrageous. After what was probably his first audition
for a real job, the council of Sangerhausen, a large town with a serious musical tradition, voted unanimously to make him their
principal organist. For all the hard work his early mastery had required of him, however, and despite the obvious fact of his genius, all he could have taken from that remarkable early triumph
was confirmation of just how far the support of a town council
would get him: After they had voted unanimously in his favor
and made him a firm offer, the job went to a favorite of the local
duke. As a result, Sebastian's first job was as a "lackey" at the
court of Weimar, where he filled in for the aging organist and sat
in with the ducal Kapelle as needed. He later elevated himself to
"house musician" on his résumé, but in fact he worked at the level
of a valet, in livery full-time. Never one to underestimate his gifts
or his due, Sebastian quickly found his way out of Weimar, out of
uniform, and out of any vestigial naïveté of youth. The next time
he went into an audition, he had the job wired, possibly even
rigged.

The Thuringian town of Arnstadt needed an organist, and the
Bach family had deep roots there. During the Thirty Years War
Sebastian's great-grandfather had lived in the castle's clock
tower, responsible for winding the clock, caroling the hours, and
sounding the alarm for fires and approaching armies. Since then
no fewer than six of Sebastian's forebears had held musical positions in Arnstadt, including his father, so his connections could
hardly have been better. Beyond family pull, his main sponsor appears to have been Arnstadt's sometime mayor Martin Feldhaus,
who happened also to be Uncle Christoph's brother-in-law. Feldhaus had been charged with supervising the construction of an
organ for the town's so-called New Church, which by this time
was far from new. It replaced a church that had burned down
more than a hundred years before, but it had never had an organ.
Thanks to a wealthy citizen's bequest of a thousand thalers, a
third of the organ's total cost (three thousand thalers was the
equivalent of more than two hundred thousand dollars), it was finally completed while Bach was at Weimar.

Feldhaus nominated Bach* to do the final examination of the
organ. A coach was sent to Weimar for him, and he was paid a per
diem, a handsome fee, and all expenses. Why he was chosen for
the job is something of a mystery. He had as yet no history as an
organ expert, and although he certainly was one, there were quite
a few others around (including several Bachs) who were not still
in their teens. Having done the examination, he also played the
official concert to inaugurate the organ, for which he was given
another fee, recorded by Feldhaus as having been paid to the
"Court Organist to the Prince of Saxe-Weimar," a very impres-

---

* At this point it is time we begin to call him by the name of Bach. He was no longer a
child, and he was already very close to earning the right granted him by posterity to
have the name to himself.

sive and entirely fictitious promotion. Almost immediately there-
after Bach was offered the organist's job. There is no record of
anyone else even auditioning for it.

Not only did he get the job, he also got a very light workload
and an unusually generous salary: for only four services a week,
he was paid fifty florins (his father's salary for running all of the
town music in Eisenach), as well as an additional thirty-four for
board and lodging. By way of comparison, an Arnstadt organist
senior to Bach was paid twenty florins for ten services, and an in-
kind payment for board that was exactly one and a half bushels of
wheat. Bach's pay no doubt recognized his genius, but there is
more than a hint of self-dealing on Feldhaus's part as well. The
salary was drawn from various sources—twenty-five florins from
the church treasury, another twenty-five from the tax on beer
(among the biggest pots in many town treasuries), and, oddly, a
bonus of thirty-four florins from St. George's Hospital. Not coin-
cidentally, the inspector of hospitals was none other than Martin
Feldhaus, the amount of the hospital bonus was exactly what
Bach needed for room and board, and Feldhaus was the owner of
the house where he ended up living. (Also staying there was Feldhaus's niece, who would become Bach's first wife.)

A few years later, Feldhaus was the object of a nasty set of
charges, including "much incorrectness and embezzlement,"
and removed from his positions of responsibility. Still, his en-
trepreneurial flourish of 1703 launched one of world's great
composers—and made Bach's hagiographic memory a little
more human. Even at eighteen, fresh out of livery, he was working the system. "You have just come into the affairs and dealings
of the world," Luther wrote (in a passage of Bible commentary
that Bach marked for emphasis), "and you have just begun to understand . . . the world. You have swallowed some water, and you
have learned to swim."

§

AS A CHURCH organist, Bach had to confront at the very outset
of his career the need to incorporate Lutheran theology into his
musical ideas. The greatest part of his job at the New Church
was to introduce congregational singing with "chorale preludes," sometimes improvised but always artfully contrived introductions to the hymns that had become the soul music of
Protestant Germany. Seeded by thirty-six hymns handed down
from Luther himself, the chorale repertoire by this time had ma-
tured under a century and a half of care and propagation by a
thousand pastors, schoolmasters, and cantors, to the point that it
became the very melody of daily life. Like a later (much later)
generation's "golden oldies," Germany's beloved chorales carried widely shared meanings and memories with them, a world
of associations conjured in a phrase. During the Thirty Years
War, they were expressions of hope uttered in the face of violence and chaos. Soldiers sang them as they marched to war;
peasants and townsfolk sang them as they awaited the approach
of foreign armies, bracing themselves with memories of a better
time and the hope of better times to come. Not surprisingly, having been composed during years of plague, famine, and war,
many of the chorales dwelled longingly on the sweetness of
death.

Luther had encouraged making chorales out of popular
songs—"Why should the devil have all the best tunes?"—but he
insisted that each melody be yoked securely to its proper spiritual
message, the music chosen and arranged precisely to promote the
text. Luther's chief musical assistant, Johann Walter, harmonized
the first chorales during a marathon work session with Luther in
Wittenberg. "He kept me [there] for three weeks," Walter wrote
later.

It is clear, I think, that the Holy Spirit was at work. . . .
Luther set the notes to the text, with the correct accentua-
tion and prosody throughout—a masterful accomplishment. I was curious, and asked him where he had learned
how to do it. He laughed at my simplicity, and said: "The
poet Virgil taught me. He was able to fit his meter and dic-
tion to the story he was telling. Just so should music fit its
notes and melodies to the text."

Luther's idea of music as the faithful servant of theology inspired every Baroque composer's defining challenge: to devise
melodies and harmonies that could carry and dramatize meaning, or, to put it a bit oversimply, to make music speak in words.

Luther's mandate for music to deliver "sermons in sound" had
several important results over time. It gave new life to an ancient
connection between musical composition and classical rhetoric,
which after all shared music's new purpose of moving an audience
in a particular direction. It reinforced the Baroque composer's notion of himself as an artisan: not as an artist "expressing" a personal
idea or feeling—a conception the Baroque composer would have
found entirely strange—but as a professional with an assigned task
and learnable, teachable methods of doing it. Combined with the
Baroque infatuation with encoded allegory (viz. how much 3 plus 4
could really add up to, see page 50), this concept of music as an oratorical craft inspired a vast compositional vocabulary of passages,
rhythms, key changes, and other devices that could telegraph in
music the meaning of a text, the language of what came to be
known as "musical-rhetorical" figures. For example:

In the *Musical Lexicon* of J. G. Walther (namesake but no relation to Luther's musical assistant, actually Bach's cousin, of
whom more soon), the term *anabasis* or *ascensus* is defined as a
passage of rising notes

through which something ascending into the heights is expressed. For example on the words: "He is risen," "God has ascended," and similar texts.

Its opposite is a *catabasis* or *descensus*, which Walther defines as a passage of descending notes

through which lowly, insignificant and disdainful things are represented, for example: "He has descended," "I am greatly humbled," and similar texts. For that reason a phrase or a theme which descends in semitones by step and without any leaps is called a *subjectum catabatum*.

Another negative figure is a *saltus duriusculus*, a dissonant leap downward, literally "hard leap," used to point out, often didactically, something harshly negative. A *saltus duriusculus* of a falling diminished seventh, for example, signifies "false." A *passus duriusculus* is a chromatically descending *catabasis* "meant to express sorrowful emotions." All of these are examples of *pathopoeia*, a general term for figures that aim to elicit a specific positive or negative message, what Baroque composers called an "affection." There are hundreds of such terms, each of them representing an emotional or spiritual arrow in the Baroque composer's quiver.

Walther is to be cherished for having written all this down, because we might otherwise never suspect Bach's music contained such figures. For the Baroque composer, though, our ignorance of that would be neither here nor there, because consciously hearing and comprehending such effects did not, in theory, matter; the composer's evocation of an affection was thought to rely not on conscious perception but on a quasi-mechanical reaction to vibrations of the sound itself. Being able to move people without their having any idea how they were being moved made the Baroque composer into something of a wizard, and to understand the mysteries over which Baroque composers claimed command requires taking a moment to peek behind the curtain.

Descartes made one of the first attempts to explain the concept of the affections in his last book, *The Passions of the Soul* of 1649, which boiled our feelings down to six—wonder, love, hatred, desire, joy, and sadness. They were caused, he wrote, "by the spirits which are contained in the cavities of the brain, in so far as these operate by way of the nerves which serve to enlarge or contract the orifices of the heart." (This, remember, was from a patron saint of rationalism, albeit at a time when rationalism could still have saints.) Descartes's book was followed a year later by the *Musurgia universalis* of the "last Renaissance man," Athanasius Kircher. A Jesuit-trained mathematician and scholar of sometimes dubious credibility, Kircher was fluent in Hebrew and Greek and translated everything from Coptic script to Egyptian hieroglyphics, where he discovered "secrets" of the universe that no one ever found again. He actually was a creditable inventor, notably of the "magic lantern" that is the ancestor of the film projector; his tinkering also profited thermometers, microscopes, air pumps, and telescopes. On the other hand, his *Musurgia* spoke of echoes that could return in translation, bells that rang themselves, a keyboard that made melody by variously pinching the tails of cats, and other funhouse fictions. Still, it was the most widely read treatise on musical philosophy of the seventeenth and early eighteenth centuries. Kircher was very much a believer in music not only as a mirror but as a fundamental element of Creation itself: In the last chapter of the *Musurgia* he gives a chart of nine tones which he identifies not just as nice basic notes but as the framework of all that exists. How he gets there is a trip we need not take, but at his destination we discover that music was not so much a reflection or approximation of God's perfect design but an emanation of the divine Itself. Kircher's motto was: "Music is nothing other than the knowledge of the order of all things." He certainly seemed to think that he, at least, knew just about everything.

To explain how the Pythagorean numbers actually work to elicit the affections in music, Kircher invoked the four humors. (This will be over soon.) For those who may be a little rusty on their ancient Greek medical theory, the four humors were temperaments that were thought to correspond to the secretions of four organs and also to the four elements of matter (as well as certain animals, gems, trees, fish, and archangels). The four humors—sanguine (heart/air), choleric (liver/fire), melancholic (spleen/earth), and phlegmatic (brain/water)—correspond to specific affections: respectively, love and joy; anger and fury; sorrow and pain; and middling degrees of both sadness and joy. As Kircher explained it, affections result from anything that changes the balance of the humors and so releases a certain gaseous "animal spirit" that rises through the blood. This animal-spirit-gas flows into the nerves, which are narrow tubes that take it all around the body and in particular to the soul, which is located in the pineal gland, the place where affections are produced.

For the Baroque composer, the point was that this animal-spirit-gas can be launched into the tube nerves by evoking numerical proportions through musical intervals. Yes, that is what they thought: The animal-spirit-gas can be launched into the tube nerves by evoking numerical proportions through musical intervals. Unfortunately, Kircher's explanation of how this was supposed to work is, perhaps not surprisingly, unhelpful: "When the *harmonic numerus* (i.e., the musical proportions and the vibrations emanating therefrom) first stirs up the spiritual breath, and when these *vapores* [vapors] are mixed with the inner breath or mind, then they move a human being in the direction they are going; and in this way harmony moves passions and affections." Just like that.

Against the suspicion that this whole project of the affections was just one last neuronal series firing off in the medieval mind, here is Handel's friend Johann Mattheson, a music critic for the Enlightenment, in 1739:

> With nothing more than gigue [a quick French dance] I can express four important affects: anger or eagerness, pride, simple-minded desire, and flightiness. On the other hand, if I had to set *open-hearted* and *frank* words to music, I should choose no species of melody other than the Polish one, the *polonaise* [ceremonial, processional music].

Far from being anachronistic, the doctrine of affections had an almost Newtonian character: Specific musical figures had been demonstrated empirically—by Baroque audiences said in contemporary reports to swoon, wail, weep, and shout for joy at just the right moments—to evoke specific emotional results, with a force as reliable as the one that attracts an apple to the ground. But of course they worked: Our reaction to the numerical proportions (thus musical intervals) was divinely ordained, after all, given that they are the fundament of our universe and ourselves. "It cannot be otherwise that an individual's temperament is moved and controlled through well-written music," Werckmeister wrote. "For an individual is both inwardly and outwardly, spiritually and physically, a divinely created harmonic being."

There will not be a quiz on the foregoing. It will be enough to remember that Baroque composers, very much including Bach, practiced a craft of somewhat mysterious and arcane causes and effects, that they used rhetorical figures consciously to invoke specific emotional and moral messages, and that these messages, whether or not they are felt or heard, can be found on the pages of the score.

Making beautiful music and articulating literal messages at the same time seems to have been as difficult as it sounds. Some were better at it than others, and even the best composers' attempts were not always successful. Among the little of Bach's earliest work that has survived is a keyboard suite called *Capriccio on the Departure of the Beloved Brother* (BWV 992). Most of Bach's biographers believe it was written as a send-off to his brother Johann Jakob,* who had signed on as oboist with the expeditionary army of Sweden's Charles XII—a good job for a musician in service to a cause that must have seemed glamorous to a boy in his late teens. The *Capriccio* is about the most literal work of music that can be imagined. The first movement, in keeping with certain other such storytelling compositions, is titled "Friends Gather and Try to Dissuade Him from Departing," and sure enough there they are, audibly mingling, softly dissuading. In later movements, just as obviously, we find out that "The Friends' Lament" and then, "Since He Cannot Be Dissuaded, They Say Farewell." The finale is a fugue that imitates the horn of a postillion, or lead horseman, presumably trumpeting Jakob off to glory.

In the current context, however, another part of the work bears notice, of a sort that it first received by the musicologist Michael Marissen. In the movement entitled "Various Misfortunes That Could Befall Him Abroad," Marissen heard Bach do something very unusual: To get across the idea of misfortune, he modulated the piece radically downward, deep into the flat keys, well outside the range that would then have been considered appropriate. As Marissen noted, he did this later in choral works to underline a textual point. Such a "distant tonal movement in the

---

* Christoph Wolff has made a strong case that it may have been written for Bach's school chum Georg Erdmann or for a graduation party at Lüneburg (*NBR* no. 18n), but the departure for war of his closest brother remains a plausible and attractive occasion for it as well. Finally, the question is unanswerable.

flat direction outside the ambitus," in the language of a tweny-
first-century musicologist (Marissen), could be used as a *pathopoeia*,
in the language of Baroque musical rhetoric, meant to signify
suffering, sadness, grief, and death. After the *Capriccio* Bach
rarely employed this device in his instrumental works, but for one
important instance when Marissen heard him doing it again, we
will have cause to remember this one.

§

BACH'S LIFE WAS hardly a swamp of esoteric music theory, but
he had plenty of time to think up rhetorical solutions to musical
problems in Arnstadt because he had very little else to do. He was
therefore on somewhat shaky ground when the consistory called
him on the carpet for refusing to train the Gymnaseum's choral
students for anything beyond simple hymns, even though he was
correct in pointing out that he was not required to do so by the
terms of his contract. To be fair, his refusal is understandable.
The council records contain a complaint about the Gymnaseum
students with whom he was saddled:

> They have no respect for their masters, fight in their pres-
> ence, behave in a scandalous manner, come to school
> wearing swords, play at ball games in their classrooms,
> even in the House of God, and resort to places of ill re-
> pute. Out of school they play games of hazard, drink, and
> do other things we shrink from naming.

These were not choirboys. To complicate matters, some of them
were older than their twenty-year-old director.

One twenty-three-year-old instrumentalist actually started a
fight with Bach one night when he was coming home from an
event at the castle. As Bach made his way home, according to the
consistory records, a student bassoonist named Johann Heinrich

Geyserbach braced him in the market square, accused him of comparing his playing to the bleating of a goat, called him a cowardly dog, and swung a stick at him. Bach swore later that he would never have drawn his dagger (a not uncommon dress-up accessory in those feistier days) if Geyserbach had not swung at him first. According to the consistory's account of the matter, "the two of them tumbled about until the rest of the students who had been sitting with [Geyserbach] . . . separated them."

Bach's denial that he had said Geyserbach played like a goat was never taken seriously. Where music was concerned, he was famously unforgiving. He is credibly reported to have thrown his wig at an organist once, with the forceful suggestion that the man think about becoming a cobbler. While censuring Geyserbach, the consistory drily observed that Bach "might very well have refrained" from calling Geyserbach a bleating bassoonist and once again censured him for not taking the students' musical advancement more in hand. Bach replied that he would be happy to help out if there were a director of music to impose some structure and discipline on the effort, to which the consistory remarked, in just so many words, that life is not perfect. The consistory concluded with an admonishment to its young organist: "[Bach] must get along with the students and they must not make one another's lives miserable."

Bach never did get along with the students. Some weeks after the Geyserbach incident, about six weeks before Christmas, he requested and was given a leave of four weeks. He returned four months later.

§

WHAT INTERVENED WAS another of Bach's very long walks in search of his future, this one a two-hundred-fifty-mile journey to Lübeck, where Dietrich Buxtehude presided at the great organ of

St. Mary's Church. Given Buxtehude's advancing age (he died the next year) and what had just happened in Arnstadt, Bach may well have been investigating the possibility of becoming Buxtehude's successor. Handel, who was Bach's exact contemporary and in some ways his exact opposite, had come to Lübeck on the same errand two years before, invited to audition for Buxtehude's job by the president of the town council. In this oddly rare juncture in the lives of Bach and Handel as young men, Philipp Spitta shrewdly took the measure of both.

> Handel arrives from Hamburg in the bright midsummer days, in the gay society of Mattheson, and in obedience to an invitation from the president of the council; he enjoys an affable welcome, and festivities in his honour. Bach comes on foot in the dull autumn weather from remote Thuringia, following his own instinct, and perhaps not knowing one single soul that might look for his coming.

In the end, the same problem that had put others off the idea of becoming Buxtehude's successor would have put off Bach as well. Like many such important posts, this one came with the stipulation that the candidate marry his predecessor's daughter, who in this case was ten years older and a great deal larger than both Bach and Handel. It may not be entirely cynical to imagine that Bach wanted to consider the alternative before settling down with Martin Feldhaus's niece in Arnstadt; marriage could be a very practical matter in those days.

He may have left Lübeck without a new job or a wife, but he left anything but empty-handed, having witnessed that Advent season's *Abendmusiken*, Buxtehude's occasional concerts for choir and orchestra, which this year were especially grand: back-to-back oratorio evenings to commemorate the death of Emperor

Leopold and the accession of Joseph I. Extra security was required to hold back the crowds, the church was decorated and lit for the occasion, and the oratorios were productions on a scale that Bach had never before witnessed. There were several orchestras and choirs arrayed around the church, including two bands of timpani and trumpets and two horn-and-oboe ensembles, and at one point no fewer than twenty-five violins played in unison. Fittingly for the occasion and venue, the music was a mixture of secular and sacred, and to judge by the libretto and by Buxtehude's *oeuvre* (the score did not survive), both oratorios were works of bold, sweeping strokes. Buxtehude's music is like the thunder of Jove. He took on huge harmonic and compositional challenges with both hands (and feet), and his life was like his music: He was fiercely independent, as a musician could only be in one of the free (meaning prince-free) imperial cities. He had managed to create for himself several thriving musical lives, as composer, teacher, performer, and entrepreneur. The *Abendmusiken,* for example, were entirely his show: He courted sponsors and raised the money, printed the music, chose the musicians, conducted the performance, and of course wrote the music. A serious theorist as well (though, like Bach, one who wrote nothing on the subject but his works), he was thoroughly intrepid. At a time when collections of music from England, France, Italy, and the Netherlands could seem to be from different continents and when composers tended to aim for epitomes of their own national styles rather than to reach across boundaries for something new, Buxtehude drew everything from everywhere. All German composers fell under the influence of the Netherlands, but Buxtehude also wrote arias in the Italian manner, and his harpsichord suites sound French. He wrote for the viola da gamba like an Englishman and choral movements in the style of Lully. He actually borrowed one of Lully's airs for a set of variations, and was so taken by the works of Lebègue that two of the French composer's works were long attributed to him. Bach, who may or may not have taken formal lessons with Buxtehude, was his most attentive student.

§

RETURNING TO HIS cramped professional life in Arnstadt must have been either profoundly depressing or profoundly motivating; possibly it was both. The consistory, predictably, inquired what he could have been thinking as he unilaterally and so greatly extended his leave, missing the entire Christmas season. In his defense, Bach lamely replied that he was sure his cousin had filled in well in his absence and said that he had needed the time "to learn one thing and another. . . ." Perhaps emboldened by his inexcusable absence, the consistory went on to scold him for making "strange variations in the chorale, mixing many outlandish tones in it so that the congregation has become confused thereby." They actually went further than that, prescribing how he *should* compose: "In the future, if he wishes to introduce a *tonus peregrinus,* he must prolong it and not shift too swiftly to something else, or, as he has hitherto been accustomed, even play a *tonus contrarius.*" Being told his improvisations were ranging too far harmonically—being told by a consistory how to make music—cannot have been a welcome experience. In any case, Bach was finished with Arnstadt, in spirit if not immediately in fact.

Well known by now as the best organist in Thuringia (which was saying something), he did not have to look far for his next job. He found it only a few miles away in Mühlhausen, a free imperial city like Lübeck where he was now to preside at a big organ in the main church, St. Blaise's. As he took over his new responsibilities, he married his rooming-house sweetheart, Martin Feldhaus's niece, and providentially inherited more than half a year's salary when his mother's brother died.

∫

IT MAY WELL have been for that uncle, Tobias Lämmerhirt, that Bach composed the funeral cantata *Actus tragicus* (BWV 106), his first major work. Had any of his contemporary composers heard it or been able to see it in print, they would have known they were sunk. At the age of twenty-two, Bach delivered himself of a funeral cantata in which messages of deep spiritual wisdom were married to music of heartbreaking and impossibly apposite lyricism. Let us take them in that order, wisdom first—though in truth, amazingly, the theological message and artistic merit of the work are really inseparable.

A work of twelve movements (some very short; the entire work is less than twenty minutes long), its subject is time, on several levels: the great span of spiritual history on earth, from Creation to the Second Coming; the analogous arc of every human lifetime, facing up to Old Testament judgment on the way to New Testament redemption; and most of all God's time, in which, says Psalm 90, "a thousand years are a single day, a yesterday now over, an hour of the night."

The *Actus tragicus* begins in human time. The opening lament for recorders and strings, set to a steady heartbeat rhythm in the bass, starts in the innocent key of E-flat major and refuses to leave it, as if to say we may mourn but we may not despair, because death is the door to eternal life. Just in case we missed the point, the first chorus is a sweet, happy work of Renaissance-pure polyphony: "God's time is the very best time" (*Gottes Zeit ist die allerbeste Zeit*). Having given us an encouraging glimpse of the joy to come at the final destination—of today's funeral, of our lives and of all eternity—Bach begins a long and steep descent, through the keys and through the stages of life and history. After staying in E-flat major for the phrase "in Him we live," the chorus takes a sudden, stomach-turning drop to C minor for "in Him we die" and then for a quote from Psalm 90: "Oh Lord, teach us to remember how few days we have so that our hearts may grow in wisdom." Sinking ever deeper, into F minor now, a rigorous, muscular fugue sets forth the fearsome law of the Old Testament ("It is the ancient covenant: Man, thou must perish"), followed by a plaintive aria for soprano, "Come, Jesus, come." The fugal death sentence returns as if to deny relief, but this time, after the third statement of the subject (theme), the soprano returns to join the fugal dirge, literally topping and finally outlasting it with the prayer, "Come, Jesus, come."

Only then, after a rest fraught with silence, do we come to the nadir, B-flat minor, in which an alto sings a tender, painfully tentative aria to the last words Christ uttered from the Cross, "Into Thy hands I commend My spirit," a declaration of hopeful surrender at the very moment in life when hope and surrender are most dangerous. In all the choral works of Bach, this is the only movement in the key of B-flat minor, the *extremum enharmonium*, in the phrase of one of his contemporary theorists, the deepest-but-one of the deep-flat keys, a key to which Bach would later descend only for moments of the most profound grief and despair, as in the *St. Matthew Passion*, when the crucified Christ is at His weakest and most human: "My God, My God, why hast Thou forsaken Me?" (In a very different context Bach will be going through this key again, about forty years from now.)

Then begins the ascent, the triumph over death in Christ's resurrection and humankind's salvation through grace, which here as elsewhere evokes from Bach his most inspired displays of musical and theological wisdom. A bass solo, rising to F minor and even slipping in and out of A-flat major, sings Jesus' promise to the thief on the cross next to him, "Today thou shalt be with Me in paradise," and after a virtuoso flourish, the aria is joined by sopranos singing in long, held notes (otherwise known as *cantus firmus*) one of the most beloved of Lutheran chorales, "Mit Fried und Freud" ("In Peace and Joy I Now Depart"). The bass drops out just before the sopranos emerge again into the sunlight of E-flat major for the line *wie Gott mir verheissen hat* ("as God has promised me"), which after a chorale of thanks becomes the subject for a four-voiced fugue. Here Bach gives us music in its divine aspect, where time disappears into simultaneity. Only in music—and nowhere better than in counterpoint—can two complementary or contrasting thoughts combine in the same moment, in this case "as God has promised me" (in the fugue subject) and "through Jesus Christ" (in the words sung to the fugue). Earlier, at the very center of the cantata, history itself is conflated, when the Law ("Thou must die") and Gospel's promise of mercy ("Come, Jesus") are sung together, as they exist otherwise only in God's time.

Enough about rhetoric and theology: Considered simply—or not so simply—as a work of art, the *Actus tragicus* is almost unspeakably beautiful. In fact its beauty is unspeakable, though we can talk about it. We can marvel at how Bach lulls us in the deceptively simple first movement into a world of delectable pain and exquisitely broken hearts, or how the chorale "Mit Fried und Freud" emerges from Jesus' promise of paradise like a tissue being offered to someone who is crying. We can talk about his brilliantly melodic part writing, the richness of his counterpoint, the way his music follows text the way roses follow a trellis, in perfect fidelity and submission but at not the slightest sacrifice of beauty. Finally, though, one comes up against the fact that the greatness of great music is in its ability to express the unutterable. Having reached that point exactly, and not for the last time, we would be best served to put down this book, get out the score, put on the music, read the words and the music together; and after playing it through several times, consider the power of inspired (as well as rigorously educated and deployed) genius. The *St. Matthew Passion*, the B-minor Mass, the *Brandenburg Concertos*, the cello suites: All of Bach begins here.

§

ONLY A FEW people ever heard the *Actus tragicus* in Bach's lifetime. Like almost all of his work, it was never published and never performed outside Leipzig until he was long dead. His biggest public moment in Mühlhausen, the same year as the *Actus tragicus*, was the performance of a cantata marking the annual rotation of the town council, not nearly so great a work as the *Actus tragicus* but a larger one in terms of its audience and its demands on his musical resources, which would have been stretched to the point of breaking. The title was *God Is My King* (*Gott ist mein König*, BWV 71), which seems a bit provocative for an event meant to glorify civic bigwigs, and it takes until the last movement to get around to mentioning them, but either they missed the point or were flattered by the comparison because they paid for the work to be elaborately printed. This and another cantata he wrote for the town council were the only cantatas ever published in Bach's lifetime. The publications were meant to mark the occasions, of course, not to acknowledge the composer's genius, but no matter: *God Is My King* is a work of Buxtehudian ambition and scale, complete with a spectacular fugue that, for the first time, promoted instruments from accompanists to center stage, with coequal voices in the fugue's development. Bach even let the last statement of the fugue subject ring out triumphantly from the trumpets. With *God Is My King*, the student surpassed the master. Mühlhausen had surely never heard the like of it.

On the other hand, even a slight miscalibration could turn rhetorical figures into compositional dynamite, and a bit of it goes off in Bach's hands in the penultimate movement, where a

relatively innocuous line in the libretto ("O, never to adversaries
deliver the soul of Thine own best beloved") is delivered by a
chorus of deeply sorrowful, chromatic sighing that goes right
over the top, culminating in what Spitta aptly describes as

> a terrible expression of suppressed pain [that is] the height
> to which the character of the whole piece naturally leads
> us. . . . The composer has here overshot the mark. . . .
> That he allowed himself . . . to be carried away too far by
> his subjective bias must have become plain to him later,
> when he wrote a chorus with . . . many similar details (as
> particularly the wailing minor sixths) to the words
> *Weinen, Klagen, Sorgen, Zagen,* etc.

*Weinen, Klagen, Sorgen, Zagen* means "Weeping, Wailing, Sor-
rowing, Fearing," surely better occasions for a deeply scarifying
motif than a town council event, and he would have an even better use for it later.

In the end, Bach's ambitions were too great for Mühlhausen
and especially for its church, which had not only a temperamental
strain of musical conservatism but also was a stronghold of
Pietism, with which Bach sympathized in just about every way
but one: They disapproved of the use of "concerted" music in
church, meaning elaborate music with instruments, reserving
their favor only for hymns. Like Ohrdruf, Mühlhausen was riven
by the strain between orthodoxy and Pietism, a city so long and
passionately involved in its spiritual disputations that it had
hosted the execution of the Anabaptists' leading light, Thomas
Münzer. Now a couple of centuries later, reviving the old dispute,
a war broke out between the Pietist pastor at St. Blaise's, who was
also the Mühlhausen superintendent, and the pastor at another
church, who like Bach was orthodox Lutheran. Despite enough
Pietist sympathy to straddle the issue in good conscience, Bach of

course placed himself squarely in the middle of it, siding against his own superior.

More important to Bach than Pietist conservatism, though, was a siren's call from the opera, which was serving up tantalizing new forms capable of bringing music for the church, especially the cantata, to a higher level of eloquence and beauty: free recitatives, which lifted virtually all structural constraints; and a robust, compelling form of aria that supported and inspired not only biblical quotations but boldly interpretive poetry as well. These innovations could never have been embraced by the clergy or parishioners of a town like Mühlhausen, and just a year after he had moved there, he wrote a (somewhat petulant) letter of resignation to the town fathers:

> Although it was my intention to advance music in the divine service toward its very end and purpose, a regulated church music in honor of God; although it was also my intention here to improve the church music, which in nearly all villages is on the increase and is often better treated than here . . . I have not been allowed to do my work without vexation and opposition. . . . So God willed to bring about an opportunity that will make it possible for me [to pursue] the creation of an organized repertory of church music.

Thus did Bach inform the town fathers of Mühlhausen of a delicious vindication, the offer to return, as a member of the ducal Kapelle and principal organist, to the very court where he had been a "lackey." His new salary of 150 florins, eighteen bushels of wheat, twelve bushels of barley, four cords of firewood, and thirty pails of tax-free beer represented a significant raise, and Weimar was a large court town—a third of its five thousand residents worked for the court—known to be a venue of serious new music, as forward-looking as Mühlhausen was stultifying. The court secretary and keeper of the ducal coin collection was an accomplished poet, Salomo Franck, whose cantata texts required just the sort of freedom Bach was seeking for his choral music. There was a link to the latest musical theory there as well in the person of J. G. Walther, who was just then finishing his latest book on the subject, having been aided in the project by Andreas Werckmeister himself. Bach was about to learn all he needed in order to choose the final course of his career, and that choice would decisively influence his response, in the last years of his life, to a more than musical challenge from the king of Prussia.

VII.

WITNESS TO AN EXECUTION

As FREDERICK RODE BEHIND HIS FATHER AND THE
Saxon elector Augustus the Strong in the grand procession at
Mühlberg, after the fiercest beating of his life, he had cause to feel
more like the butchered oxen on the banquet tables than like the
crown prince of Prussia. By then he had concluded that his relationship with his father was both desperate and hopeless: He
was at the malevolent whim of a gout-ridden drunk whose best
friends and wife (not to mention the emperor) handled their
"Fatty" like a dolt. By such a man was the crown prince beaten
and humiliated in front of servants and officers, a man who split
his pants at parties and replaced a Leibniz with a Gundling. He
belonged with the boars of Wusterhausen. Frederick did not. On
his first visit to King Augustus's lavish court in Dresden, Frederick had become Fédéric, someone who was not just inclined but
destined to curl his hair and play the flute—and *not* necessarily
someone meant to sit straight on a horse or eat with a steel spoon.
On this his second and last visit to Saxony as crown prince (he
would be back some years later as a king, to the next Saxon elector's deep regret), Fédéric decided he would not let himself be
bullied anymore. He was not yet sure how, but the humiliation
was going to stop.

The fury of the king's assaults seemed to increase with the
pressure of diplomacy over the "double marriage," the queen's
longed-for scenario in which Frederick and Wilhelmina both

married into Britain's royal family, securing not only a Prussian-English alliance but a glamorous (meaning: Hanoverian) court for herself. The attack at Mühlberg, for example, coincided with the visit of a special envoy from London whose mission was to break the long deadlock: Frederick William was ready to let Wilhelmina marry the prince of Wales but would not commit himself to Frederick's marriage as well. The British king, obviously more interested in having a Prussian king as a son-in-law than a Prussian princess as Britain's next queen, insisted on both marriages or neither. In the interest of foiling Frederick William, Frederick and his mother had taken up a back-channel correspondence with London, and in Potsdam they plotted behind the king's back with the ambassadors of both England and France. Frederick went so far as to put in writing a secret promise to his grandfather, the English king, that if he (George I) would consent to Wilhelmina's marriage to the future prince of Wales, he (Frederick) would pledge to marry no one but the English Princess Amalia while Frederick William lived. Such a commitment to a foreign power in contravention of the king amounted, of course, to treason.

Frederick William, even when he suspected her of conniving, treated his wife with deference, out of affection and respect for her position as a Hanover, but he could not be expected to make any such allowances for his son. Even Wilhelmina, Frederick's co-conspirator in all things and especially the double-marriage plot, which she no less than her mother dreamed of, warned him that he was placing himself in danger by acting as he did.

Only his youth and the severity of his father's abuse can explain Frederick's recklessness. Beyond plotting with England, he began shaking down foreign governments to support his various forbidden hobbies, such as his library, which included two thousand thalers' worth of musical scores alone by the time he was fifteen. At first he raised five hundred ducats from Austria, but then, his appetite aroused, he started asking for more and more until he was collecting huge sums regularly from Austria, England, and Russia. Each of the loans was secured by his promise of friendship and repayment on taking the throne, which even then he was plotting intermittently to do.

"The Crown Prince is loading me with favors," the French ambassador Rothenburg wrote to Paris, and later: "I pretend never to speak to the prince, but I have several sure, faithful ways of making known to him what I desire and of receiving his messages." In Rothenburg's diplomatic dispatches there were dark hints that Frederick William could be declared insane or in some other way dethroned by the crown prince. "[Frederick William] is absolutely hated by every class in his kingdom," Rothenburg wrote, citing the king's harsh treatment of Frederick. "In order to disarm the father, it will be necessary to form a party for the crown prince, and to attach to his side a number of officers. I believe that this scheme would succeed." King Louis himself replied to that message: "Profit by the relations you have with those who surround [Frederick and] present to him my acquiescence in his sentiments and the assurances of my interest in his welfare."

Frederick William was not so naive or confused that he failed to sense something was afoot, even if he could not say exactly what it was. He got his son drunk one night to try to discover the truth but got nothing from him. When he found out about the foreign "gifts" to his son, he made it a capital crime to loan money to royal minors, but the money kept coming in. He had already put a stop to Frederick's education by pensioning off his beloved teacher Jacques Duhan and assigning Prussian officers to be his minders, but then he became convinced that one of the officers assigned to the task was only encouraging his son's disloyalty. The British ambassador to Potsdam wrote to London: "The other day the King asked the Prince, 'Kalkstein [his minder] makes you English, does he not?' to which the Prince answered, 'I respect the

English, because I know their people love me'; upon which the King seized him by the collar and struck him fiercely with his cane, in fact rained showers of blows upon him; and it was only by superior strength that the poor prince escaped worse. There is a general apprehension of something tragickal taking place before long."

Frederick William's inchoate frustration with his crown prince, if not the violence that attended it, inspires a certain empathy. For all that he ranted and raved, he had no words for the plainest and worst fact of his life: He had lost his son, just as Frederick had lost his father.

After the beating reported by the British ambassador, Frederick wrote to his mother:

> I am in the utmost despair. What I had always apprehended has at length come on me. The King has entirely forgotten that I am his Son. . . . I am driven to extremes; I have too much honor to submit to such treatment; and I am determined to put an end to it one way or other.

§

FREDERICK MADE HIS first attempt at escape while still at Mühlberg, telling the British emissary that he was planning to run away first to Alsace (where the French ambassador Rothenburg had an estate), then, after a few months in France, to England.

He was abetted in this and later such plans by a new friend, Lieutenant Hans Hermann von Katte. The son and grandson of high Prussian officers, Katte was also a flautist and a painter who loved to talk. One of the king's Tobacco College chums said Frederick and Katte acted like lovers with each other, and Wilhelmina also suspected that her brother's relationship with Katte was of a scandalous, "unnatural" sort, an opinion that clearly informed her physical description of him in her memoirs: "His eyes

were almost hid under two large black eyebrows; his counte-
nance carried in it a certain ominous trait that seemed to mark his
destiny. . . . He affected to be a free-thinker, and led a most dissolute life: with these vices he combined great ambition and
much levity."

The escape attempt in Mühlberg was entirely lame. Frederick
sent Katte to the post office for a map and asked the Saxon minister to arrange horses for two officers who wished to go incognito
to Leipzig. The minister, who like everyone else knew about
Frederick's humiliation at the hands of his father, saw through the
ruse immediately, and Frederick's chief minder, Colonel Wilhelm Friedrich von Rochow, closely questioned Katte, who denied all. Von Rochow was not stupid, however, and now he was
on notice.

That plan foiled, Frederick next told the British emissary that
he planned to escape during a tour of their western provinces
with his father the next month. According to the diplomat's notes,
Frederick said, "I prefer to go to France first [because if] I should
go immediately to London the king would think that my mother
knew of my plan and treat her cruelly." Appalled at the possible
consequences of such a course of action, Uncle George (who had
succeeded Frederick's grandfather to become England's King
George II) sent back word that he should sit tight, and he offered
Frederick another large "loan" if he would. Frederick took it, and
continued with Katte to plot his escape.

Befitting the defection of a reckless and romantic crown
prince, his plans were richly dramatic, involving aliases, secret
meetings, safe houses, and highly incriminating correspondence,
most of it carefully preserved in a chest that Frederick left with
Katte. The prince—in a smashing new red cape he bought for
the occasion—was to slip away from the king during their tour,
and Katte was to meet him at The Hague, where Frederick
would be staying under the name of "Count Alberville." The ex-

ecution of the plot was pitiful; in fact, it never reached a point that could be called execution because Frederick's intention to flee was so plain and his circle of conspirators so large and flimsy. The plan had been easily frustrated more than once during the trip when finally the king was informed of it by a frightened page who had been caught bringing Frederick a horse in the middle of the night.

Frederick William was beyond angry. In his view, Frederick had plotted desertion, probably in a treasonous conspiracy involving the French and British governments, which was a harsh but not wholly unreasonable construction of the facts. At first he did not let Frederick know he knew. "I thought you would be in Paris by now," he baited his son at the next halt. Frederick answered boldly, "If I had wished it I could certainly have been in France," but now he knew his father knew, and he wrote to one of his pages, "the plot has taken an unfavorable turn. Arrange for our leaving." Colonel von Rochow, however, was already on orders to see that Frederick be kept in hand, and Frederick overheard officers saying that he was to be taken to a nearby town for detention and interrogation, "dead or alive."

The king himself was his first interrogator.

"Why did you attempt to desert?"

"Because you have not treated me as your son, but as a worthless slave."

"Then you are nothing but a deserter, without honor."

"I have as much honor as you. I have only attempted what you said a hundred times you would do, if you were in my place."

At that the king drew his sword, and one of Frederick William's generals had the courage and presence of mind to step between them, sensibly suggesting that if the king really wanted to get at the truth, Frederick should be questioned not this way, by his father, but by a formal board of inquiry.

Presumably chastened by his father's rage and the sentries

who were now stationed outside his door with bayonets fixed, Frederick next day gave at least a version of the plot, but apparently he was not yet sufficiently frightened to tell the truth. "He said he wished to go incognito to Landau, Strasburg and Paris, to take service, enter Italy, distinguish himself by brilliant action and obtain in this way His Majesty's pardon." The king knew that The Hague had been Frederick's rendezvous point and so had caught him in a lie. This convinced him that there had been a conspiracy, and one that might even have included his own assassination. At this point the crown prince was formally placed under arrest.

When the true gravity of the situation began to dawn on him, Frederick wrote his father a letter.

> I take the liberty of writing to my dear father to ask him to recall my arrest, giving assurance that all that I have said or have told to my dear father is true. As to the suspicions held against me, time will show that they are groundless, and I affirm that I have not had the bad intention that they accuse me of having. I implore my dear father's pardon, and I remain, for life, his most respectful, most submissive and very devoted son.

The king responded by having Frederick sent to the fortress prison of Küstrin and ordering the arrest of all of his co-conspirators, including Katte. He sent off two letters by pouch to Potsdam, one to the queen, another to her lady-in-waiting. Only the second letter survives, a pitiable testament to his compassion for his wife: "Fritz has attempted to desert. I have been under the necessity to have him arrested. I request you to tell my wife of it in some good way, that the news may not terrify her. And pity an unhappy father."

Frederick was kept in isolation, without pen or ink, without his flute, without visitors or books to keep him company. Frederick William composed another of his compulsive "Instructions": "The door [to his cell] must be well closed day and night, with two heavy locks across it; the keys must be in the keeping of General Lepell. Every morning at eight o'clock it must be opened, and two officers shall enter to see if everything is right; a stocker of the post shall bring to the arrested a glass and a basin of water to make himself clean, and . . . the whole must not take more than a few minutes," and so forth.

A second interrogation was undertaken by one General Mylius, who put to him almost two hundred questions, and finally, under protest, five from the king that were clearly meant to elicit an admission of guilt but each of which Frederick answered with a perhaps all-too-clever grace.

Q. What does he deserve and what punishment does he expect?

A. I submit myself to the mercy and will of the king.

Q. What does a man deserve when he has broken his faith and plotted desertion?

A. I do not think I have failed in honor.

Q. Does he deserve to become a king?

A. I cannot be my own judge.

Q. Does he wish his life to be spared or not?

A. I submit myself to the mercy and will of the king.

Q. As he has rendered himself unfit to succeed to the throne by breaking his faith, will he, to preserve his life, abdicate his succession and renounce it in such manner that it will be confirmed throughout the whole Roman Empire?

A. I do not cling much to life, but His Royal Majesty will not use such rigorous means against me.

They were rigorous enough. As soon as the king returned to Berlin, he fired Frederick's servants, sold his carriages and horses, found and disposed of his secret library (as well as the librarian, who was exiled, as was Frederick's old tutor Jacques Duhan). On the discovery that Frederick had played harpsichord-and-flute duets with the daughter of a cantor in Potsdam, the king ordered that she be placed under arrest, whipped in front of her father's house and all around the city, then sent to work in the hemp factory at Spandau prison, for life. (A midwife and surgeon certified that she was still a virgin or it might have been worse.) Stirred up by the spies, who were at this point afraid of the vengeance Frederick might wreak on them were he ever to become king, Frederick William became convinced of ever more monstrous and far-ranging conspiracies suggested by his son's attempts at escape—involving, for example, poison and France. His fury toward Frederick became steadily more ferocious, sufficiently so to keep at least one diplomat awake at night, thinking about the foam at the king's mouth as he spoke of his son. "If the King of Prussia persists in these sentiments," the Dutch ambassador wrote, "we will see the most dreadful, bloody scenes that have ever happened since the creation of the world."

It was not at all certain that Frederick would emerge from this crisis with his life, much less the throne. The king was deaf to the pleas of his wife and Wilhelmina and resented those of various heads of state, including the Russian czar, the emperor, and the kings of Sweden and England, who felt it necessary to plead for Frederick's life. Frederick William might actually have had Frederick killed had it not been so difficult to bring off without hurting himself as well. Beyond that, there was precious little hard evidence of a conspiracy; Queen Sophia had destroyed all the correspondence with England, and the French ambassador Rothenburg had covered his tracks as well. For his part, Frederick would not admit to desertion, only to attempting to escape his father's brutality. To the king, this seemed the ultimate trickery. "This little knave," he muttered at one point, "has invincible cleverness and hard-headedness in defending himself."

He decided therefore to call a court-martial, charging a panel of his officers—three major generals, three colonels, three lieutenant colonels, three majors and three captains—to pass on the fate of Frederick and his co-conspirators. They heard evidence for two days, and on the third rendered their verdicts. For a lieutenant who had been Frederick's intermediary with Katte, imprisonment for two to six months. For another who had ordered a carriage for Frederick, two to six years. As for Katte, who had clearly aided Frederick's ambition to escape and had admitted that he would have gone with the prince had the attempt succeeded, the panel was divided: Some favored his execution, some favored the death penalty conditioned on its being commuted by the king, and others voted for life imprisonment. Finally the head of the panel exercised his prerogative to break the impasse and voted for life in prison. These verdicts were sent to the king, along with the panel's unanimous finding that, as the king's subjects, they were not empowered to pass sentence upon a member of the royal family.

Frederick William was incensed. He accepted their reluctance to judge the crown prince, and he found their verdicts against the other two lieutenants just, but he could not abide their mercy toward Katte. "They must judge according to the law. . . . The court-martial will have to convene again and . . . judge otherwise." They convened again, but the head of the panel, an old and upright general, refused to reverse the finding: "To change it would be against my conscience, and is not in my power."

General Hans Heinrich Graf von Katte, the lieutenant's grandfather, addressed a moving petition to the king, appealing to the distinguished service of the Katte family, the foolishness of youth, the magnificence of mercy, and "the prayers and tears of a very old man." The response was swift and beyond firm. "This man much deserved being torn with red-hot tongs," Frederick William wrote. "However, in consideration of the General Field Marshal and Lieutenant-General Katte, I have mitigated the penalty. . . . He must have his head cut off. I am your most affectionate king."

Frederick had no idea of the court-martial's verdicts or the king's order for Katte's execution, though both were accomplished facts, when he wrote his sister Wilhelmina a letter signed *"Le Prisonnier"*: "They are going to make me out a heretic, after the court-martial is finished [but] the anathemas pronounced against me will disturb me very little, provided that I know my gentle sister inscribes herself my champion. . . . From the bottom of my heart, I wish . . . that we could recover those happy days when your *Principe* [her lute] and my *Principessa* [his flute] kissed each other. . . ." In fact, however, after what Frederick was about to endure, nothing would be the same for him, including even his relationship with Wilhelmina, the only woman he ever loved.

§

MANY YEARS LATER, when Frederick told the story to his aide, Henri de Catt, he said he did not learn about Katte's fate until five o'clock in the morning on the day of the execution, when a captain and a colonel came to his cell in tears.

> "Oh my prince my poor dear prince!" blurted out the officer amid his sobs, "my good prince!" I was sure they were going to cut off my head.
>
> "Just tell me, am I about to die? I am quite ready for these barbarians to finish me off, and quickly."
>
> "No, my dear prince, you are not going to die, but al-

low these grenadiers to lead you to the window and hold
you there."

He was confused by the odd request, and even more so when
he saw Katte in the courtyard, surrounded by officers. "What is he
doing here?" he said. Then the scene took shape before him: the
scaffold, the pile of sand, the two pastors flanking Katte, whose
shirt was loose at the neck. When Frederick fully realized his best
friend was about to be executed, he began to plead frantically with
his guards to do something to stop it: He offered to renounce the
throne, to accept life imprisonment, to give his own life, to do
whatever the king required, anything to spare Katte's life, but the
guards were impassive; obviously it was too late for any reprieve.
Katte had been brought to Küstrin for his execution precisely so
that Frederick could be forced to watch it. In his fashion, Frederick William had prescribed in minutest detail how the execution
scene would play out, from how long the headless corpse should
remain where it fell (seven hours) to the sort of men who should
carry it away ("burghers of a respectable standing").

According to the king's script, Katte was walked in procession
to the place of his beheading, a place chosen for its central point
in the narrow compass of Frederick's cell window. The prince
struggled with his guard, who could not now have pried him
away from the window in any case. "My dear Katte!" he screamed.
"Forgive me!"

Katte sent Frederick a kiss with his hand and, with a gallant
bow, said there was nothing to forgive. He seemed to witnesses
incalculably calm, carrying his hat under his arm, listening to the
formal sentence of death, saying good-bye to his bodyguard and
the others assembled around him, taking off his coat, opening his
shirt, and kneeling on the sand that had been put there to accept
his blood. He refused a blindfold, and a last prayerful cry—
"Lord Jesus Christ!"—was interrupted by the fall of the execu-

tioner's two-handed sword. Frederick did not see the fatal stroke because just before it came he fainted.

He returned to consciousness in a delirium. He spent the day weeping and in shock, much of the time at the tiny window of his cell, staring at the body below, on which someone (defying the king's instructions) had thrown a black cloth, now caked with Katte's blood. Unable to eat or sleep, Frederick spent the night, in a high fever, talking to himself. "The king thinks he has taken Katte away from me," someone heard him say, "but I see him all the time."

## VIII.

*SONG   OF   THE   ENDLESSLY*

*ORBITING   SPHERES*

WHEN THEY ARRIVED IN WEIMAR, SEBASTIAN BACH was twenty-three, and his wife Maria Barbara was twenty-four and pregnant with their first child. Since her husband had now left two jobs in a little more than a year, it may have occurred to her if not to him that it was time to settle down for a while.

Not much is known about Maria Barbara Bach, but it is suggestive that she was a Bach even before their marriage; through her he secured a new hold on the family that had abandoned him as a boy. She was Sebastian's second cousin, daughter of the Erfurt musician Johann Michael Bach, who was the brother of Uncle Christoph and a composer whose work Sebastian always admired. Maria Barbara was herself musical and clearly helped her husband with some of his professional chores; a good deal of the music in his library was copied in her hand. Otherwise we know only that she provided a home of which he never gave recorded complaint and a number of children that suggests they were on very good terms. In Weimar that December of 1708, fifteen months after their marriage, Maria Barbara gave birth to their first child, a daughter, Catherina Dorothea, and they had five more children during the next seven years. Maria Barbara was lucky to have help with the housekeeping and childrearing from her elder sister, who had lived with them since their marriage, because in no time the small house on the market square in Weimar that they shared with the master of pages (who was also a dance instructor and falsetto singer at court) teemed not only with children but also with the students Bach had begun picking up in Mühlhausen, to be joined in time by two of his nephews.

Bach was obviously the sort of person who thrives on chaos because his output of work during their nine years in Weimar was enormous, including the lion's share of his organ works, a great deal of instrumental music (he could now call on full-time court musicians), and, assuming the same percentage of his works was lost from the Weimar period as from the others, a hundred or so multimovement cantatas (finally, he had professional singers). He was almost frantically productive in these years, hungrily assimilating all the latest music of every nation and just as avidly subsuming it in works that were completely his own. By the time he left Weimar, in his absorption of such extremes of form and style as strict canon and the concertos of Vivaldi, he had learned everything he needed to turn music on its head.

§

LUCKY FOR HIM, Bach had a compatriot in his studies now in a distant cousin, Johann Gottfried Walther, who had been in Weimar for a year when Bach arrived. The two men, nearly the same age (Walther was older by six months), were hardly equals, but Walther was no slouch. He knew far more about the history of music theory than Bach did, having just finished his first book on the subject, and as a composer he was described years later by no less than Johann Mattheson, referring specifically to some of the chorale settings that he wrote while he and Bach were working together, as a second Pachelbel, "if not in art the first." At the same time, Walther had lost out to Bach when he made a run at the job in Mühlhausen, and this job as town organist in Weimar had been his consolation. Now Bach was coming to Weimar as chamber musician and principal organist at court, in effect bettering him again. However Walther may have felt about that, the two men clearly benefited from working together in what seems to have been a rivalry of friends.

For example: Bach was given to boasting that he could play any music at sight, no matter how technically difficult or how densely scored. Whether because he was tired of hearing about it or just for a little slightly malicious fun, Walther invited him to breakfast one day for a trick challenge. Knowing Bach's habit of going to the keyboard and playing through whatever music was there as soon as he arrived, Walther put an inordinately difficult keyboard piece among the others on his music desk. Sure enough, Bach went straight to the keyboard, and while Walther started making breakfast Bach began to read and play what was there. Carl told the story in a letter to his father's biographer Forkel.

> In a few minutes Bach got to the piece which was destined for his conversion and began to play it. But he had not proceeded far when he came to a passage at which he stopped. He looked at it, began again, and stopped at the same passage.
> "No," he called out to his friend, who was laughing to himself in the next room. "One cannot play everything at first sight. It is not possible."

Not "I cannot do it," understand, but "it is not possible." One thing Bach did not lack was a proper estimation of his powers.

The most common genre for Walther's and Bach's dueling compositions was the chorale prelude for organ; both of them, after all, had been hired as organists, and in Bach's case that

meant primarily playing chorale preludes at Sunday and week-
day services in the palace. It was in these organ works from
Weimar, which Bach later collected into his *Orgelbüchlein*, that
his biographer and fellow organist Albert Schweitzer noticed
for the first time certain figures embedded in the score that had
no apparent relation to the music but seemed to have been taken
from spoken language—"an independently conceived motive,"
as Schweitzer put it, "not derived from any of the lines of the
melody, but from the text of the chorale, and embodying the
poetic idea that Bach regarded as characteristic of the music and
expressible in musical terms." What he was seeing in the scores
more than hearing in the music was Bach's deployment of the
musical-rhetorical figures to carry the "affection" of the
chorale message, and though Schweitzer has been accused since
then of discovering somewhat more than what was there, his
discovery was a great achievement. As in other works, the
rhetorical figures in the *Orgelbüchlein* can be difficult to hear as
such without reference to the text and score. For example, rip-
pling scales in the prelude to "From Heaven Came the Host of
Angels" are not meant to be merely ornamental: They give
sound to the flight of angels. An odd dissonance in the course of
"Jesu, My Joy" is an evocation of the disquiet in the heart of a
sinner. In the prelude to "With Peace and Joy I Now Depart,"
rising bass figures depict the soul's ascent to heaven. Schweitzer
had discovered in the organ chorales written during the years in
Weimar nothing less than what he called "the lexicon of Bach's
musical speech."

§

ONE OF BACH'S favorite forms—in the *Orgelbüchlein* and later
elsewhere as well—was canon, which he often used to connote
law, the meaning of the word's Greek root, and sometimes specifically the Ten Commandments. The most compressed, rigorous,

and esoteric form of counterpoint, canon is to fugue as haiku is to blank verse, and although Bach must have come across them in his studies, there is no evidence of a practical interest in them until Weimar. Walther had long since undertaken to learn everything about speculative music theory, from Pythagoras and Plato to his own time, including the most arcane forms of counterpoint; he was also then making a comprehensive list of the musical-rhetorical figures, classified by their related affections. His study of theory represented a devout and lifelong project that would result years later in his *Musical Lexicon*, the first music dictionary, but even now Walther's library of musical esoterica was large, and Bach's curiosity was as rapacious as it would ever be. If he had not already immersed himself in the theoretical thinking of Werckmeister, Kircher, Boethius, and their ancient Greek ancestors, he surely did so now.

In the book Walther finished before Bach arrived, he defined music as "a heavenly-philosophical and specifically mathematical science." This quasi-scientific and quasi-cosmic view of the composer's art was of course mainstream, certified as such by none other than Leibniz, who started in on most great metaphysical problems with his motto, "Let us calculate." For Leibniz and in the Baroque worldview, harmony was both an ideal and a fact. Leibniz believed that everything in the universe was composed of "monads," the smallest, indivisible units of matter, whose forms and flow in the physical world were regulated by God in accordance with the "pre-established harmony" with which He created and imbued the universe. While Bach was in Weimar, Leibniz received a letter from his foremost disciple, Christian Wolff, requesting his definition of perfection. He answered this way: "Perfection is the harmony of things . . . the state of agreement or identity in variety; you can even say that it is the degree of contemplatibility. Indeed, order, regularity and harmony come to the same thing. . . . Hence, it also follows quite nicely that God, that is, the supreme mind, is endowed with perfection, indeed to the greatest degree; otherwise he would not care about the harmonies."

Leibniz did not concern himself with the practical business of composing music, but his dancing monads presented a wonderfully evocative metaphor for canon, especially perpetual canon, in which a single phrase, played against itself at different points in time and space, becomes an infinitely unfolding harmony similar to (and thought by some to be the same as) the continuous playing out of Creation, the ultimate "identity in variety."

Leibniz memorably defined music as "the hidden arithmetical exercise of a mind unconscious that it is calculating," but when he did so he was clearly not thinking about canons, whose composition is conscious to the point of brain frying. Take, for example, the piece of music for which Bach was probably most famous in his lifetime, known (for its dedicatee) as the Houdemann canon (BWV 1074). It became famous because it was a widely published "puzzle" canon, so called for its enigmatic notation.

The nine notes between the vertical bars present the subject of the canon, and the subject specifies the work's entire content. Unlike fugues, whose subjects can be elaborated with secondary melodies and other harmonic devices, the only figures allowed in a strict canon are statements or variations of the subject itself. It may be transformed in different ways—played backward, upside down, in different keys—but otherwise a strict canon must be composed of its subject and only its subject. Likewise, in a "canon a 4" such as this one, every "solution," or "realization," of the canon subject must involve four voices—no more, no less. What must be "solved" is at what intervals the voices should come in—three notes higher, or five, or eight, or none—and when or how soon the subjects must follow one another, by one beat, two or three or twelve. In the simple canon "Frère Jacques," for example, the theme always comes in on the same note, eight beats later, but in more complex canons the subjects follow one another much more closely than that and begin on a different note each time. The markings to the left and right of the subject in puzzle canons like the one above give clues to what solutions there might be.

In the Houdemann canon, it turns out, the subjects follow one another immediately and on four different keys, the tightest possible canon to write, and despite that it has several very different solutions. In somewhat more readable if no less enigmatic form than Bach's and with a guide to what all those strange markings are about, the Houdemann canon looks like this:

Successive clefs suggest that each voice, like the canon for Walther, should enter on the pitches G, C, A, and D respectively.

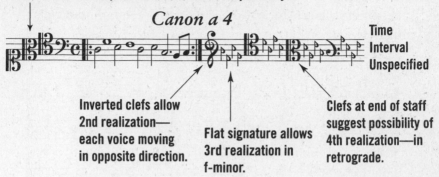

*Canon a 4*

Time
Interval
Unspecified

Inverted clefs allow 2nd realization— each voice moving in opposite direction.

Flat signature allows 3rd realization in f-minor.

Clefs at end of staff suggest possibility of 4th realization—in retrograde.

Bach gave the "prime" solution—the one that uses the subject as written and in the order of keys that he specified with the four clefs at the beginning—to J. G. Walther:

But he clearly foresaw other solutions, and every theorist of
Bach's time took a shot finding them. Johann Mattheson inverted the subject (turned it upside down) and used the four-
flat solution:

Friedrich Wilhelm Marpurg, author of the first book on the theory
of fugue, inverted it too, but left it in a major key, without the flats:

Bach also suggested a minor-key "retrograde" solution, in which the subject is played backward—

and a major retrograde-inversion solution, which puts the melody both backward and upside down:

All the solutions result in "perpetual" canons, since by the nature of the subject there is no place for it to end, and all of them make sense musically, though some are less gainly (the realizations in retrograde and inversion) than others (the retrograde inversion and the prime).

Solving such canons, not to mention making them up, was clearly not work for the easily frustrated, and Bach wrote at least fifty of them during his career, of which eight are in the *Orgel-büchlein*. Walther wrote canons too, though he did not exploit the

form as thoroughly and elegantly as Bach did. Bach commemo-
rated their mutual passion in a perpetual canon for four voices
(BWV 1073), which he wrote on the birth of his godchild,
Walther's eldest son. Critics will say, and said very loudly in
Bach's time, that canons are not always tuneful or pleasing to the
ear, and they have a point, but nowhere better than in a perpetual
canon like this can you hear so clearly the connection between
music and celestial harmony, the canonic voices weaving in and
around one another like so many orbiting planets, eternally in
motion and eternally the same. In that sense even when they are
not pretty they can be beautiful.

IT WAS JUST Bach's luck that when he had finally mastered the
highest art of contrapuntal writing, not only breaking into but
making himself right at home in the sanctum sanctorum, hea-
thens came banging at the door, decrying the elitist and esoteric
nature of counterpoint (though some of them were at the same
time demanding to be let in on it). Friedrich Erhard Niedt, a well-
known organist of Copenhagen, for example, wrote, "Many an
honest bore has spent many an hour of his life trying to excel at

canons." He thought counterpoint had been ridiculously mystified by its practitioners.

> There are doubled, inverted, salted, larded, roasted coun-
> terpoints, and those basted with hare drippings that occur
> when voices are inverted and bass, alto, tenor and discant
> are interchanged. . . . I do not think it worth the trouble
> and expense to waste paper and ink on [them].

The Kapellmeister in Dresden, Johann David Heinichen, said
that as a student, he "could hardly eat, drink or sleep until I found
the solutions to all canons." Now he wanted someone to put together a book containing all the rules of counterpoint. "Such [an
undertaking] would greatly lessen the general wonderment at
these kinds of paper witches." The most unrelenting and painstak-
ingly reasoned attack on canons and other forms of learned
counterpoint came from Mattheson, who began his argument
with their practical worthlessness. "Do not expect that after all
that quill-chewing and toiling to be rewarded for your pains," he
advised students. "There will probably be not a single one among
2000 listeners who will notice your finesse, unless he be alerted to
it beforehand."

More broadly, the critics of counterpoint were renouncing
music's allegorical and cosmic nature, its claim to be a manifestation of the divine. To this generation, music was not to be written
according to any higher theory or objective than that of sensual,
aural pleasure. "Rules are valid as long as I consider it well and
sensible to abide by them," Mattheson wrote. "They are valid no
longer than that. . . . The rule of nature, in music, is nothing but
the ear."

Mattheson vented his most provocative polemics against counterpoint in his journal *Critica Musica*. One particularly incendiary

article prompted a friend of Bach and Walther, the prominent contrapuntist Heinrich Bokemeyer, to leap rather unwisely to counterpoint's defense, overstating his case, which allowed Mattheson to continue the attack by publishing the defense along with his own devastating commentary on it. Bokemeyer was eventually so undone by the war of words that he actually capitulated in a letter he allowed Mattheson to print. "When I look at my old ideas," he wrote Mattheson later, "I am filled with the greatest disgust."

Obviously, given the heat of the debate, this was an intense moment in the history of music. Theorists were full of ideas, newly able presses were there to deliver them up to a ready audience, and there really was something important to talk about. Music was now at the intersection of what could be thought of as a horizontal-vertical crossroads: the point at which the idea of music as a spiritual weave of independent voices moving roughly equally and together through time (polyphony) was giving way to the ideal of a sensuously beautiful and all-important melody hoisted aloft and borne forward by an undergirding of chords (homophony). The arrival of thoroughbass accompaniment— the part played by the harpsichord and perhaps a bass viol or a similar "continuo" group—put a roof and floor on this divided house, as it were, by giving priority to the highest and lowest voices, but it was still a house without walls, and it was on the brink of collapse.

We will be coming back to this subject (if not the mixed and overextended metaphor) because this is the point at which Bach parted company with his sons and their generation, including Carl and his royal employer, and where they parted company with him. And we will be returning to the subject of canon—the pride of counterpoint's defenders and the bane of its detractors— because inside the exploding bouquet that was Bach's *Musical Offering* to Frederick the Great there were exactly ten of them.

§

AS A COMPOSER in Weimar Bach was everywhere all the time. For the cantatas he wrote there he continued to plant allegorical meanings in his key changes, as he had done in the *Actus tragicus*, but now he began also to sharpen his theological and musical ideas with new interpretive poetry being written for the liturgy and new forms from the opera, especially recitatives (a free, formless passage of music, usually for a solo voice, that follows the natural accents and rhythm of a piece of text) and da capo arias (*da capo*, literally "from the head," indicating a work of two parts and a repeat of the first, resulting in the A-B-A form familiar from every popular song).

In his study of every structural and stylistic device of his time, Bach was a musical omnivore (and given his taste for food and drink, which were now beginning to show, not an exclusively musical one). At the same time that he was mastering the intellectual rigors of canon, he was trying to understand the passionate intensity of the latest music from Italy, especially that of Antonio Vivaldi, whose *L'Estro armonico* was published while he was in Weimar. The young duke Johann Ernst brought it back with him from Amsterdam, along with so many trunks full of the latest music that new shelves had to be built in the palace to hold it all.

Once they had music in hand, old or new, Walther and Bach—like every other conscientious composer of their day— went about studying it as they had been taught in school to study oratory, through the threefold discipline of *praeceptum*, *exemplum*, and *imitatio* (learning principles, studying examples, and imitating good execution). In just this way, Bach and Walther studied the Italians: first by copying out their works note for note, then by arranging them for various instruments, finally by transfiguring them in works of their own. Both men did transcriptions of Italian violin concerti for harpsichord and organ. From this period date Bach's fugues on themes of Albinoni, Corelli, and Legrenzi, as well as his F-major concerto "after Vivaldi" for harpsichord.

Bach did more than study and replicate his models, though, and he was more than "influenced" by them. Unlike his contemporaries Handel and Telemann, whose ambition was directed toward creating the epitome of a particular style, Bach deconstructed styles and put them back together again combined with his strengths in invention, orchestration, and counterpoint. The result especially of his encounter with the structural and melodic strength of Vivaldi was not only a sum greater than its parts but something utterly new: a burlier, grander, ever more confident Bach, who was now fully armed and ready for glory. First, however, there would be a fall.

§

AFTER FIVE YEARS in Weimar, he had already become sufficiently well known and respected that, at the age of twenty-eight, he was asked to succeed no less than Friedrich Wilhelm Zachow, the teacher of Handel, who had presided at the Market Church in Halle since the year Bach was born. During his courtship by the Halle consistory, he was put up for two weeks at the best hotel in town, where he appears to have had a very good time; his room charges included more than thirty quarts of beer, as well as respectable quantities of brandy. Given the likely result on his mood, it is perhaps not surprising that he was very receptive to his hosts' offer, but several weeks later he reversed himself. In Halle, this change of heart was taken as evidence that his romance with them was only a ploy to better his position in Weimar. Bach objected in the strongest possible terms to the inference but gratefully accepted a large raise and promotion from the duke.

The promotion was to concertmaster, a position inferior only to that of Kapellmeister Samuel Drese and his son the Vice Kapellmeister. More important, it required him to compose new works for the duke's Kapelle at least once a month. For the next three years he poured forth an extraordinary amount of work in every form and style—music for choir, chamber music, music for orchestra and keyboard. When Kapellmeister Drese died at the end of 1716, Bach no doubt considered himself the best possible replacement, and if any proof were needed, his work of this period should have been more than sufficient. Ultimately, however, the job went to Drese's son, and it later became apparent that Bach had never been seriously considered for it.

He did not have to look for long for another job. The young prince Leopold of Anhalt-Cöthen quickly signed Bach to be his Kapellmeister, the position with the duties and authority he had always wanted. Bach accepted even before his release by the duke because he was so certain of it. If all else failed, he could count on the fact that, in this world, a prince outranked a duke. Of course all else did fail, and dukes, it turned out, had their devices, prince or no prince.

While the duke was still considering his options for the next Kapellmeister, Bach was invited to Dresden for what was clearly set up to be a battle of titans: the organ virtuoso Louis Marchand versus the master of Weimar in a keyboard duel. The match was probably instigated by Count von Flemming, the Saxon elector's prime minister and an admirer of Bach, at whose castle the contest was to take place. Bach certainly knew Marchand by reputation and through his music, but he apparently had not heard him play, because before he wrote the letter setting forth the challenge he surreptitiously attended a performance to take the measure of his opponent. Obviously undaunted, Bach wrote the letter, received Marchand's agreement, and turned up at the appointed time. Bach, his hosts, and the expectant audience waited . . . and waited, until finally someone went to Marchand's hotel to fetch him, only to find that he had left that very morning by the fast coach out of Dresden.

It says something about the common perception of Bach's mastery that the great Marchand's absence was taken immediately for capitulation. Bach had been dodged before. He twice attempted to meet Handel, only to be eluded with somewhat flimsy excuses. After one of Handel's visits to Dresden, Count von Flemming wrote to Bach:

> I tried to get a word with Mr. Handel and to pay him some civility for your sake but I could accomplish nothing. I used your name on my invitation to him to come and see me, but he was always out or else ill. *Il est un peu fou, ce qu'il me semble* [It seems to me he's a little crazy].

Possibly inflated from his triumph over Marchand and the fuss made over him in the court of the Saxon elector, Bach returned to Weimar and pressed the duke for his immediate release with all of his usual political delicacy. A note in the ducal records tells the rest:

> On November 6, [1717] the quondam concertmaster and organist Bach was confined to the County Judge's place of detention for too stubbornly forcing the issue of his dismissal.

No doubt struggling at his bars round the clock, he was nevertheless kept in prison for four long weeks before finally being sent away from Weimar with a dishonorable discharge.

No mention is made of Bach's imprisonment in any contemporary account of his life except for a passing reference by one

Ernst Ludwig Gerber, who wrote that Bach had written the first book of his *Well-Tempered Clavier* "in a place where ennui, boredom and the absence of any kind of musical instrument forced him to resort to this pastime." Once again, in being passed over for a lesser musician and then imprisoned for his trouble, Bach's career had been brought up short by the peremptory power of aristocracy.

§

THE TWENTY-THREE-YEAR-OLD Prince Leopold of Anhalt-Cöthen loved music, was a musician himself, and was interested in the relationship between music and social structures. He had hired the right man. In works he began in Weimar and finished in Cöthen, Bach was exploring just such issues, though perhaps without thinking of it that way. In the *Brandenburg Concertos,* for example, the musicologists Michael Marissen and Laurence Dreyfus both found any number of places where Bach seems intentionally to confront and subvert both musical and social conventions. In the first Brandenburg, for the first time in any concerto, he uses flashy, aristocratic hunting horns, only to devalue them by making them an equal contrapuntal partner with the lowly oboe, which was associated with downscale, town-piper music. In the fourth Brandenburg he promotes over the violin the even lowlier recorder, an instrument too common even to be claimed as one of a town musician's proficiencies in applying for a job. Bach put canons into his most elaborately ornamental developments; he blurred the distinction between full-orchestra and solo episodes; he put French and Italian forms together to comment on each other; and far from simply absorbing the styles he studied, he seemed to go out of his way to break them, writing in the French or Italian manner, as Dreyfus memorably puts it, "like a surly foreigner."

To ask if Bach was doing this intentionally or not would be to imply an insult. Bach was nothing if not thorough, intentional about everything he did.

§

ONE OF THE most persistent and provocative dialogues in the history of Western culture takes place between those who claim for art a universal, metaphysical basis and those who see it as culturally determined, the articulation of the artist's response to a particular time and place. On one level it is clear that both positions must be correct. It seems quite obvious that a composer writes from and about a particular time and place and equally obvious that a composer's power of expression and a listener's empathy have a more complex system of roots.

In Bach's time and as far back as Plato's, the question was framed in terms of *ratio* and *sensus*, or intellect vs. emotion/intuition, as alternate faculties by which one could most properly create or appreciate a piece of music. The proponents of *ratio* cited Pythagoras' galactic harmony and numeric proportions, the intellectual, quasi-scientific aspect of music that linked it to astronomy, geometry, and arithmetic in the classical *quadrivium*. Although even Plato reluctantly had to admit that aesthetic pleasure rather than intellectual purity was the ultimate judge of music, the proponents of *sensus* had to wait many centuries for less grudging advocates—for example, Mattheson. But the *sensus* position did not really come into its own until the once-unquestioned imperative of social conformity was challenged by the assertion of the individual and personal feelings, a very gradual process that heated up considerably during the eighteenth century and culminated in the Romantic hero of the nineteenth. One of Bach's most dramatic contributions to this mind-vs.-feeling and order-vs.-freedom debate was the fifth Brandenburg concerto, in which, very oddly for his time, he seems to come down strongly on the side of the passionate, self-asserting, singular human being.

The development of the modern concerto heralded the advance of the individual and in a way enacted it: There was the orchestra, representing the collective society, who would articulate the subject (theme) of the evening, and in front of it stood the soloist. The interaction between them was a kind of discourse between the individual and society, one that could at times take on the character of argument. The knowledge that in the end we would always return to the place, or key, where we began offered a kind of reassurance that the tension in this play of the one and the many would be resolved, that all would be well in the end. (When music could no longer be relied upon to end up where it started, two world wars and the atomic bomb had taken away the assurance of such happy endings.)

Into the dialectic of the concerto entered, for one example, Vivaldi, house composer to an orphanage and the Republic of Venice, a far from traditional aristocracy. Doges were generally installed toward the end of their lives, had no real power, and were told on their installation to remember that life is short. At least one doge's life was shortened for him when he forgot he had no power. In other words, Vivaldi composed in a relatively free aesthetic environment, and in part for this reason his solo parts could be dazzling, virtuosic statements that unapologetically upstaged the orchestra. In some parts of the world, such a role for the individual would have been regarded as downright subversive.

One such place was the absolutist court of Louis XIV, whose resistance to Italian passion we have confronted before (page 57). To say individualism was not tolerated at Versailles is to understate the matter considerably. Once all the Italian composers and musicians in his court were fired, no Italian opera was heard at the court of France for sixty-seven years. Lully's luxuriant propaganda and ceremonial ornamentation took its place. From this

eventually came the *galant* style that figured in the schism between Bach and his sons' generation, which finally was an argument about what music was to be—serious work by serious people
about serious things or light amusement for connoisseurs. We
know where Bach stood in this debate, but if we did not we would
have only to listen to the first movement of the fifth Brandenburg
concerto (so named for their dedicatee, the Hohenzollern Margrave Christian Ludwig of Brandenburg, youngest son of the
Great Elector, who knew Bach from before his years at Cöthen).

The work opens as a concerto for flute and violin. It would
have been a masterpiece if that is how it ended as well, but three-
quarters of the way through this movement Bach does something
that had no precedent in the history of music: He gives the cadenza not to the flute or violin but to the harpsichord, an instrument that had never had a solo in front of an orchestra. It had
always functioned in the thankless role of accompanist (and a not
terribly audible one at that), a peppy but harmless orchestral
gofer. What's more, he seems to be announcing that he is doing
something revolutionary with a kind of malicious glee, as the musicologist Susan McClary wrote in a remarkable essay entitled
"The Blasphemy of Talking Politics During Bach Year." The
piece is not so much interrupted as "hijacked". . . .

Bach composes the parts of the ensemble, flute, and violin
to make it appear that *their* piece has been violently de-
railed. They drop out inconclusively, one after another,
exactly in the way an orchestra would if one of its members started making up a new piece in the middle of a performance. Their parts no longer make sense. They fall
silent in the face of this affront from the ensemble's lackey,
and all expectations for orderly reconciliation and harmonic closure are suspended. . . . On the surface, closure
is attained; but the subversive elements of the piece seem

far too powerful to be contained in so conventional a manner. Certainly social order and individual freedom are possible, but apparently only as long as the individuals in question—like the sweet-tempered flute and violin—abide by the rules and permit themselves to be appropriated. What happens when a genuine deviant (and one from the ensemble's service staff yet!) takes over?

To put this in terms of the debate about music's ultimate source and meaning: Was Bach expressing his frustration with the aristocratic hierarchy, writing from his place and time? Or was he intuiting the way to new modes of expression, opening up musical vocabulary, simply as a result of his genius? One good answer is yes and yes. Bach was a man of his time, and so, as Luther did, he respected the hierarchy for what it was—certainly to be observed in most things, even when it hurt—but he also saw it for what, on the theological plane, it more truly was, just another flawed necessity of a fallen world, a side effect of human weakness. He would of course obey, but he would not be bowed. In music, where hierarchy was simply a matter of conventional expectation, Bach delighted in defiance. The current taste was a matter of indifference to him if not contempt, whether the taste was that of a commoner or a king.

In any case, he managed to turn over a lot of furniture with all his hierarchical inversions and stylistic improprieties. Every piano concerto in the history of Western music has its antecedent in the fifth Brandenburg concerto, when the lowliest member of the orchestra was turned loose to become Liszt.

§

BACH'S RELATIONSHIP with Prince Leopold seems to have gone at least somewhat beyond patronage. Three years after he had left Cöthen, Bach marked the birth of Leopold's first son by sending the infant an early copy of his six keyboard partitas, complete with a dedicatory poem by himself, who was no poet.

> *[This] is the first fruit of my strings in music sounding;*
>   *Thou the first son round whom thy Princess's arms*
>     *have curled.*
> *It shall for thee and for thy honor be resounding,*
>   *Since thou art, like this page, a firstling in this world. . . .*
> *So may I, Prince of all our hopes, e'er entertain thee,*
>   *Though thy delights be multiplied a thousand fold,*
> *But let, I pray, the feeling evermore sustain me*
>   *Of being, Serene Prince, Thy humblest servant*
>
> BACH*

With a sympathetic and generous patron behind him, Bach had one of the most comfortable professional situations of his life in Cöthen. He had no regular responsibilities in the churches, since the official religion was Calvinist (which tolerated only the least adventurous music); and the Lutheran church, where Bach and Maria Barbara rented pews, had an organist and cantor of its own. Since there were no singers on the prince's regular payroll when he arrived (they were apparently hired ad hoc for the occasional secular cantatas Bach composed for New Year's Day and Leopold's birthday), he could and did turn his attention to instrumental work. The partitas—a mix of styles and genres the like of which had never been seen before—as well as Bach's magnificent works for solo cello and violin date from the years in Cöthen, and it was there too that he completed the first book of the *Well-Tempered Clavier*, the French and English suites, the two- and three-part inventions, and of course the six Brandenburg concertos.

* This poem obviously doesn't gain anything in translation but the author is assured it doesn't lose anything either.

Leopold and Bach had more than music in common. They had both lost their fathers when very young, and they both lost children. Leopold's first wife died after they had been married for less than two years, and the son by his second wife to whom Bach dedicated his poem died in infancy. Sebastian and Maria Barbara had lost twins at birth, the baby they named for Leopold died before his first birthday, and perhaps the greatest tragedy of Bach's life occurred while he worked in the court at Cöthen.

Frail since boyhood, Leopold took the waters at a Bohemian spa each summer on the advice of his doctors. On at least two occasions he took his Kapellmeister and members of his Kapelle to Karlsbad with him. No doubt he did so in order to enhance his prestige among the other wealthy and noble patrons of the spa, which had become "the earliest regular summer festival of the performing arts," and Bach must have made important connections for himself there as well.

When he came home from their second trip to Karlsbad, Bach learned that Maria Barbara, who had been perfectly healthy when he left a few weeks before, was dead. The cause of her death is unknown to us and perhaps was unknown then as well. Aside from the fact of her burial, the deaths register of Cöthen records only that the full choir of the Latin school sang at her funeral.

§

BY CHANGING HOW the world is perceived, every great movement of ideas changes everything. To understand Bach's reaction to his wife's death, therefore—to make sense of his music at all—requires turning back the calendar to a point in time before there had ever been the faintest glimmer of an Enlightenment; because among the Enlightenment's least explicit legacies to us is a common understanding that there is a gulf, a space that defines a substantial difference, between spiritual and secular life. For Bach there was no such place, no realm of neutrality or middle ground for action that was not a commitment to one side or the other in the great battle between God and Satan. This did not preclude his being very much a man of this world. In his "Peasant Cantata" of 1742, a bass aria exclaims, "How good a bit of smooching tastes!," to a melody that clearly invokes a popular folk song of the time:

*With you and me in the feather bed,*
*With you and me in the hay,*
*No feather would poke us,*
*No flea would bite us.*

Bach the religious man was simply Bach the man, who like Luther was a lover of strong drink and the conjugal bed. Bach had an untroubled sense of the central Lutheran paradox that to be human is to be *simul justus et peccator,* sinful and righteous at the same time, and just as his physical life in no sense tainted his spiritual one, his religion was no less vigorous for its roots in the world. As he wrote in one of his very few prose works for students, the purpose of music "can be nothing else but the glory of God and the restoration of the heart [by which was meant the reform of the whole person]. Where this is not the case there is no real music but only a demonic noise." Martin Luther wrote very much the same thing in the preface to the first evangelical hymnal of 1524.

As with Luther, God and Satan were vividly alive for Bach, and his own life was their battleground. It is difficult to listen to his music—by turns gruesome and angelic, tormented and enraptured, mournful and exuberant—without hearing the warfare raging inside him, just as it had raged in Martin Luther; and in that respect his sacred and secular music were the same. Bach did not separate them even in his filing system, and both alike bore the epigram S.D.G. (*Soli Deo Gloria,* "All Glory to God"). At the moment of the direst atonement in a cantata Bach not infre-quently breaks into a dance, since in his worldview (Luther's worldview) the knowledge of weakness was precisely the way to grace and the ultimate joy.

There are some who say he did that now, in the gravely beau-tiful *Chaconne* from the solo violin sonata in D minor, a work at first of almost unbearable sadness, music from a cold and distant darkness which, as it slowly comes closer, begins to sing a quiet song that speaks of a hope that is filled with pain. The belief in joy is there, but the joy itself is not. It does not stay for long in a major key, but the end is not quite dark; finally a single note dies away into silence. There are serious people who say this was his *tombeau* or epitaph for Maria Barbara (though it must be said the claim is controversial). It was written very close to the time of her death, on paper he had bought at a mill near Karlsbad, and his copy of the whole set of suites for solo violin is dated the year of her death, 1720. Musicologists who believe Bach used *gematria*, or the number alphabet (A = 1, B = 2, etc.) to encode his music with hidden messages say that there is numerological evidence in all six of the violin suites that identify them with the liturgical seasons of Christmas, Easter, and Pentecost, that they contain in code the words of the Latin creed and Magnificat, and that Maria Barbara's name is hidden in a cryptograph at the opening of the work. What is clearer is that Bach has quoted several chorales in the work, which he frames with parts of the melody from the Easter hymn "Christ lag in Todesbanden."

> *Christ lay in death's bondage;*
> *For all our sin was given;*
> *He is once more arisen*
> *And hath us brought true life now;*
> *For this shall we joyful be,*

*To God giving praise and gratitude,*
*And singing Hallelujah*
*Hallelujah!*

§

SIX MONTHS AFTER Maria Barbara's death Bach's oldest
brother Christoph died in Ohrdruf. Christoph had of course
been the closest he had to a father since the death of his parents
when he was nine years old. A year after Christoph, Bach's youngest brother Jakob, who had gone with him to Ohrdruf when
their parents died and whom he had later piped off to glory with
his *Capriccio,* died as well. Bach's eldest son Wilhelm Friedemann
was ten years old now, the three others were younger, and Bach
knew he had a decision to make. The children would soon
outgrow the school in Cöthen, which was only mediocre, and
Leopold was being pressed so hard for funds to settle family disputes and to underwrite the Prussian military of King Frederick
William, which was responsible for the defense of Cöthen, that
he had been forced to reduce his support of music. Perhaps the
death of Maria Barbara, compounded by that of his brothers, reminded him of the mission that began forming itself when he and
Jakob had moved in with Christoph as boys, with their freshly in-
flicted pain. Whether for that mission or for the comfort he knew
it could bring him, or perhaps for both, Bach decided to take the
same path now that he had taken as a nine-year-old orphan. Once
again, this time once and for all, he gave himself to the church.

IX.

*A  CHANGELING*

*AMONG  THE  SWANS*

THE CLERGYMAN WHO HAD WALKED KATTE INTO THE
prison courtyard to his beheading, Pastor Friedrich von Müller,
had instructions from the king to go immediately afterward to
Frederick's cell—when the event was "right fresh," as Frederick
William put it in his letter—in an attempt to sharpen his sense of
guilt and remorse. Having just witnessed his friend's gruesome
death, delirious with grief and running a high fever, Frederick
took the pastor's appearance at his cell to mean that he was about
to be led to his own execution, and he could not be convinced otherwise. He was sure the medicine Müller brought for his fever was
poison, and the pastor was finally forced to swallow some before
Frederick would take it. Müller's instructions were to "wring"
and "break" Frederick's heart, but it was plain to him that that
was already done.

Frederick was too weak to talk or listen much that day, and
Müller had only limited success the day after. He brought a letter
Katte had given him for Frederick two nights before, on the eve
of his execution, and both men cried as they read what he had
written: Frederick was absolved of any guilt in his fate, he still
loved Frederick, and he hoped that somehow Frederick could
make amends with his father.

After that, Müller began the king's prescribed lessons in repentance and salvation that he would repeat, over and over, for the next two weeks, during all of which time Frederick remained under the implicit threat of execution. Müller reported the prince's predictably receptive reactions to spiritual guidance in detailed letters to the king, whose replies were predictably skeptical. "I know his wicked heart. . . ."

Finally, Frederick William's blood lust having been appeased by Katte's death or possibly just discouraged by pleas for the crown prince's life, the king sent word to Küstrin that his son would not be killed but would be kept in prison indefinitely under the strictest guard and regimen. The spy Grumbkow delivered this message in person, in order also to deliver the message that it was his paymaster the emperor (aided by his own not inconsiderable persuasive powers) whose appeal had saved the crown prince's life. Frederick was so relieved to hear of the reprieve—and and so disoriented by what he had just gone through, which apparently made him temporarily forget the spy's many treacheries—that he tearfully made Grumbkow the gift of Katte's last letter to him.

Metaphorically, psychologically, and perhaps even strategically, this very strange gift seems to have been a gesture of surrender: Far from clinging to his friend's memory, he wanted to deliver himself of Katte and join with the forces that killed him. In no time, his keepers said that Frederick seemed to be "happy as a lark." He told someone that Katte's fatal flaw was ineptitude.

It was far from the last time that Frederick would do and say things that seemed completely inimical to his affections and ideals. In the crucible of this ordeal, the graceful dissembling he had always employed to further his interests hardened into a reflexive survival instinct for deceit, and his character was fractured. After that, he never felt more secure than he did when he was successfully deceiving others about his own thoughts and intentions.

In international diplomacy, he once said, "the great art is to conceal one's designs." The split in his character made for a very lonely man and for a very great practitioner of power politics.

§

THE REGIMEN PRESCRIBED for him at Küstrin was loosened a little after his reprieve, but only a little; he was out of his cell, not yet out of the woods. In a new "Instruction," the king sentenced him to work in the Chamber of War and Domains responsible for governing Küstrin—a sentence to months of boring government meetings, the study of dry administrative details and provincial economics. He was to learn about taxes and rents and various methods of addressing the ultimate imperative, *ein Plus machen*. Much of what he learned he would later put to good use, but he could not have what he most desperately wanted, his freedom and his privacy. He was never to be left alone, but was to be accompanied at all times by one or more of his keepers. His chief minder was the director of the Chamber, Christoph Werner Hille, who was also to instruct him in the history of Brandenburg-Prussia. "Frederick knows perfectly Aristotle's poetry," Hille complained early on, "but he is ignorant as to whether his ancestors gained Magdeburg at cards or some other way."

Frederick proved a quick study, though, and as the old deference and perquisites due a crown prince slowly but surely settled on him once more, he began to regain a little of his swagger. He was still confined to quarters, but his keepers began to loosen the chains a bit, recognizing the increasing probability that they would soon be his subjects. In coming weeks he got his flute back, and he began to write poetry feverishly if not well. (Since his mother tongue was German but he was educated in French, he was never comfortable writing in any language, and it showed. Asked for his opinion of the work, Hille told Frederick diplomatically that it was not bad for a prince.) He even felt secure enough to renew, in a letter to his father, their old argument about predestination, a tenet he quickly renounced, however, when his father made that a condition of his increasing liberties.

Frederick began around this time to think like the ambitious monarch he would soon be, and to imagine for himself a place on the world stage. Two months after Hille gave him a lesson on the indefensibility of Prussia's many and disconnected borders, Frederick wrote a letter in which he concluded that to knit his country together he would be required to increase its territory by force. He would do so from "political necessity" but also "to cut a striking figure among the great men of the world and play one of the great roles, neither giving nor maintaining the peace by any other reason than love of justice, and not by fear, or, if the honor of the House [of Hohenzollern] demanded war, being able to pursue it with vigor." In the same letter he said he saw himself advancing "from country to country, from conquest to conquest, like Alexander proposing new worlds to conquer." In this sense, Frederick the Great was born in captivity.

§

ODDLY, OR PERHAPS because he was bent on a reconciliation, Frederick William paid his first visit to the crown prince on his own birthday, August 15, 1731, about ten months after Katte's execution. He found in his son a changed man—or, what is perhaps more accurate, a changeling. Frederick utterly abased himself, washing his father's feet with tears of remorse, pledging undying love and fealty, pleading for forgiveness. In front of a crowd, the father forgave his son and embraced him.

The prize for Frederick was a little more freedom. The king prescribed a list of domain lands he could now visit outside of Küstrin, in each of which he was to learn economy by observation. He was to visit farms and mills and foundries, and he was to ask careful questions, see how they worked, and consider how they could be improved. Frederick did his father's bidding and more. Soon his letters were full of practical suggestions. Some marshes around the Domain of Wollup should be drained because doing so would create a good field for wheat. The old sheepfold at Carzig was in good condition, and its fields would soon be yielding 10 percent more barley and rye. The brewery at Himmelstadt was in bad shape, but there was an old church nearby that could be restored to replace it. In Lebus, Frederick wrote, his heart leaped at the sight of a new giant for the Potsdam Grenadiers. He only wished he had more time for hunting, and he wanted nothing more than to be restored to his uniform (formerly known as the "shroud") and his place in the army. His father began to address his replies to "My dear son."

How much of Frederick's change was cynically calculating and to what extent he was seriously interested in the husbandry of flax is difficult to estimate, but it is clear that his identification with his father was neither wholeheartedly sincere nor wholly an act. He was caustic about his father in private, but he also increasingly expressed admiration for him that was not meant only for an audience. Given his more distant relations with his own feelings and sentiments, which he had reason to consider of no help to him in the past, perhaps even he was not sure of the degree of his sincerity.

§

A FEW MONTHS after the reunion scene, a courier awakened Frederick at midnight with a letter from the king.

My dear son Fritz,
. . . I pardoned you with all my heart, and since that time I have thought of nothing but your welfare and to establish you well, not only in the army but with a suitable

daughter-in-law. . . . The Princess of Bevern . . . has been found good and modestly reared, such as all women should be. You must tell me your sentiment immediately. . . . [If you agree] I will give you enough to carry on the expenses of your household and, in the month of April, I will send you to the army. The princess is not beautiful, but she is not ugly. . . . Be obedient and faithful, then all will go well for thee in time and eternity. And the one who desires this with all his heart says: Amen. Thy faithful father unto death.

*F. W.*

Frederick wrote to his father, "Nothing is better than to be able to show my most gracious father my blind obedience, and I await in most humble submission further orders. . . ." On the same day he wrote Grumbkow, his new best friend: "I have always wanted to distinguish myself by the sword. . . . Now I will have only the duty to fuck. I pity this poor person [the princess of Bevern], for she will be one more unhappy princess in the world." In a letter to Grumbkow a week later, compassion for his intended had given way to a somewhat histrionic despair.

I have suffered sufficiently for an exaggerated crime. . . . I have still resources, and a pistol-shot can deliver me from my sorrows and my life. . . . If there are honest people in the world, they must think how to save me from one of the most perilous passages I have ever been in. I waste myself in gloomy ideas. . . .

In later correspondence, with Grumbkow and others, he would call his intended "a goose . . . my mute . . . the abominable object . . . the *corpus delecti*," or simply "the person." He wrote to Wilhelmina, "She is neither pretty nor ugly; not stupid but ill-educated, timid and awkward in society; there is a true portrait of this Princess, and you can judge if I am pleased or not." He told Grumbkow he would rather marry the most infamous whore in Berlin than she, and if forced to marry her he would abandon her to her own home and court. He promised Wilhelmina that she would be treated as his queen when he got the throne, and told her the best part about his engagement was that it "procures for me the liberty to write to you, my only consolation in your absence. You cannot imagine, my adorable sister, how often I form wishes for your happiness. . . . Believe me, no brother ever loved so tenderly a sister as charming as mine."

Not long after he wrote that letter, though, he seemed to change in his attitude toward Wilhelmina. When she was married off to the Hohenzollern margrave of Bayreuth, Frederick was allowed to attend the wedding. There she saw someone she no longer recognized, literally and figuratively. He had gained a great deal of weight, and he did not smile. "I . . . tendered him a thousand endearments, using the most affectionate language," she wrote, "but he remained cold as ice, and answered only by monosyllables." He seemed contemptuous of everyone, she said, and when she reproached him later for his attitude and the apparent change in his affection for her, "he answered that he was still the same; and that he had reasons for acting as he did."

There were reasons, that much is true. After his engagement and his reinstatement in the army, he wrote to his old tutor Jacques Duhan, who was still in exile, "You know that my situation has greatly improved, but what you possibly don't realize is that they have cut deeply into the marble, and that stays forever." We know that the man of stone had not ceased to feel anything, however, because several people noted that at the ceremony of his betrothal to the princess of Bevern there were tears in his eyes.

§

HIS PROMISE OF marriage had the promised effect: He was given his own household, his own regiment, and, for the most part, his freedom. He was still not free to leave the country, and some of his activities (having a company of twenty musicians, for example) required keeping his father carefully uninformed and placated by gifts of food and newly kidnapped giants, but that given, he could do as he pleased. His father pledged a large portion of Elizabeth's dowry to a château for Frederick at Rheinsberg, which needed a lot of work, but to Frederick that was of little consequence: It had a lovely view over a broad lake, it was surrounded by woods and fields, and it was not in Potsdam or Berlin.

In any case the more important part of his wife's dowry to him was the composer who was to come with her from the Bevern establishment in Wolfenbüttel, Carl Heinrich Graun, who became Kapellmeister to Frederick's growing band of musicians. Graun's brother Johann Gottlieb would eventually be Frederick's concertmaster, and Frederick also managed to recruit the brothers Franz and Johann Benda, great virtuosi from the chamber group of Augustus the Strong in Dresden (who had conveniently died in 1733, after a drunken binge with Grumbkow from which neither of them completely recovered). Even before moving into Rheinsberg, Frederick had several instrumentalists and singers on his payroll, and he sent an emissary to look around the hospitals of Venice for a castrato. Later his old flute instructor Quantz would join him in Rheinsberg, as would a young but already formidable keyboardist, Carl Philipp Emanuel Bach.

Frederick lived with his regiment in Neuruppin while the Rheinsberg château was being renovated (his princess bride-to-be was put up and away in Berlin), and it was there, with his officers and soldiers in camp and a group of intellectual friends and musicians at his nascent court, that Frederick for the first time could begin to live both of his lives in one place. He reveled in his life at Neuruppin, whose only shadow was his imminent marriage. "I live here in peace with my regiment," he wrote Wilhelmina, "and I should be perfectly happy if I could see you every day and if I never married. . . . The King tries to force me to love my beauty, but I fear he will not succeed. My heart cannot be dragooned. If it loves, it loves sincerely."

He seemed at times almost happy, occasionally even exuberant. As if to declare his own new day, he ordered a new insignia and new uniforms for his regiment, and with his men before a bonfire one night early in his command, he stripped to his underwear and threw the uniform of the old Goltz Regiment into the blaze: It would now be the *Crown Prince* Regiment. All his men of course followed their leader's example and threw their uniforms into the fire as well. We do not know exactly how they felt about this as they made their way home in their underwear, but in coming years they performed for him remarkably in the rigorous spring reviews, exemplary in close-order drills and maneuvers even by the king's notoriously exacting standards. Frederick, to a degree which perhaps surprised even him, proved to be a natural leader of military men.

For the first time in his life, there are stories in Neuruppin of pranks: He was said to have mistresses in town; he was said to be "debauched"; and when a local minister made a disparaging remark about him in his Sunday sermon, he and a few of his officers bombed the pastor's home with "missiles" (presumably nonballistic). He would from that time forward always enjoy the camaraderie that came with being among his soldiers (and there are occasional suggestions of something beyond camaraderie). The duality of his life, then and later, may have given him some comfort as well: His officers and soldiers could not participate in his intellectual and artistic interests, and his literary and musical friends knew nothing of the military.

For the first year or two in Neuruppin, perhaps because it had only recently been restored to him (he had been drilling a regiment since the age of six, after all, and was educated by Prussian officers), the military side of his life was predominant. Having already convinced himself of the necessity of military aggression on Prussia's behalf—for the "aggrandizement" of his country and himself—he began to elaborate his geopolitical thinking in what would become a book-length essay, *Reflections on the Present State of European Politics*. In at least one respect the present state of European politics was then much as it had been for a century or two, which is to say in a state of continuous readiness for war, a volatile mix of fragile alliances in a continent that seemed bent on breaking and remaking itself willy-nilly. Every monarch's death set every other monarch thinking, and what ensued each time was like nothing so much as a geopolitical scurry of musical chairs in which the one left standing was a defeated army and a smaller nation, diminished in influence if not in territory. No nation was left standing quite so prominently and often as Prussia, and notably so during the reign of Frederick William.

Just as Frederick was getting settled in Neuruppin, for example, his father was dealing badly with the latest pan-European tangle, the War of the Polish Succession, which had been set off by the death of Augustus the Strong. France took the occasion to bribe the Polish Diet into electing Louis's father-in-law the king of Poland, upon which both Austria and Russia marched on Warsaw. Having pocketed the bribe, the Diet then amiably elected Augustus's son, choice of the czar and the emperor. France, taking advantage of Austria's distraction, then made a secret pact with Spain and invaded not only Austria's duchy of Lorraine but also, with Spanish help, its territories in Italy. The emperor, of course, turned to his German princes for help, and while most of them dithered, Frederick William—no doubt encouraged by the spies—offered to put a forty-thousand-man army on the march immediately. Apparently the spies had done their work all too well, because the emperor was horrified: His own army was not ready yet; a large deployment of Frederick William's well-trained forces now would reach the field of battle before his own and so would be independent of him, capable of working its own will—for example, on the provinces of Jülich and Berg, his claims to which Frederick William had been pushing the empire to support (without success) throughout his reign. The answer to Frederick William's offer was that the emperor wanted only ten thousand men from him, and they were to wait for his order to march. Frederick William was furious at what he perceived to be a slight, yet another slight, from someone who was supposed to be his ally.

The crown prince watched his father's dealings with the empire now with a jaded sense of having seen it all before—how they ill-used their hapless "Fatty," always keeping Prussia on its heels, talking friendship but giving nothing. In Frederick's view, his father, blinded by his treacherous drinking buddies, was just being played for the fool again.

On the other hand, Frederick's work with his regiment and his dreams of "new worlds to conquer" had awakened in him an ambition to lead men into battle. He really had no brief against the French position, but he urged his father to let him be a part of the deployment against them so that he could learn the arts of war from the emperor's famous general Prince Eugene.

Thus did Frederick first lead men to war, though in truth it was not much of a war. Frederick and his father's good friend and general, the "Old Dessauer," were actually invited to dine in the French camp, where they enjoyed vintage wine and lively conversation. Frederick returned the favor in the large dining room in his tent, recruiting a few French officers to the Prussian army in the

process. In the course of things, there were a few obligatory ex-
changes of fire, during which Frederick displayed courage and
coolheadedness. The Austrian commanders were impressed.

Frederick was not. He concluded that Prince Eugene alone
was responsible for the awe in which the emperor's army was held
by its enemies and that the army itself was ill-trained, ill-
equipped, and unprepared, and so took away from this first experience of war something a great deal more valuable than Prince
Eugene's advice on tactics and strategy: He had seen the weakness of the empire.

A couple of years later, when another round of diplomatic and
military gamesmanship among the great powers left Prussia
standing alone once again and finally persuaded Frederick
William that his real enemy was in Vienna and nowhere else,
Frederick wrote to Grumbkow:

> Heaven appears to have destined the king to make all the
> preparations . . . we should make before beginning a war.
> Who knows whether providence may not be reserving me
> to turn these preparations to glorious account and use
> them for the accomplishing of those designs for which the
> king's forethought intended them?

Grumbkow replied that Frederick William's ambiguous
diplomatic position was artful rather than inept, that the king of
Prussia "must be a fox rather than a lion." Frederick's reply was
straightforward: "I am not enough of a subtle politician to be able
to make threats while giving way at the same time. I am young. I
would perhaps follow the impetuosity of my temperament; under
no circumstances would I take only half an action." Frederick, of
course, knew exactly to whom he was speaking. After that, no
one could say the empire had not been warned.

§

DURING THE "WAR" with the French, the king, never healthy, was suffering acutely from all the diseases that would eventually kill him. He had had a massive apoplectic seizure, his lungs were full of fluid, his gout and dropsy flared mercilessly, and at one point he was given only two weeks to live. "Pray with me," Frederick wrote to Wilhelmina when he heard the news, "that we shall soon be free of him." Later, however, it dawned on him that the king's death would mean he would gain the throne at the expense of the liberty he had been seeking for so long, and when the king recovered, Frederick was, among other things, relieved. "To recover entirely from three mortal illnesses at the same time is superhuman," he wrote to Wilhelmina then. "One must believe that the good Lord has very good reasons to restore his life. Once again I must stand aside."

The king's recovery saved two lives: his own as king and that of the crown prince in Rheinsberg, where Frederick had created for himself the life he had always dreamed of (funded by more large loans from Austria, England, and Russia—which, it must be said, he did repay as king, probably to his sponsors' shock). He drew around him an ever larger court of musicians, wits, and intellectuals, reassembled the library that had been taken from him, and determined to give himself the education of which he had been deprived. He read the classics of France and Greece— Racine, Corneille, Plato, Aristotle, histories of Caesar and Alexander; he read poetry and history and politics; and in the evenings he played the flute, accompanied by some of the best musicians of his time. After the concert, he read some more. Sometimes he read all night.

His days at Rheinsberg were filled with books, conversation, and correspondence. Frederick was an almost compulsive letter writer, and never more so than now, when his time was his own. His correspondence is the greatest part of the thirty-volume edition of his complete works, titled simply *Oeuvres*. Published in the nineteenth century by the government of Prussia in huge red leather volumes, the edges of its cardboard-thick pages lovingly gilded, the work has a stateliness that sorts oddly with Frederick's many outpourings of prosaic verses and verbose effusions, but it is clear from the letters of these years before his accession to the throne that he was never happier than at Rheinsberg, where, as he put it in a letter to his friend the count of Schaumburg-Lippe, "I am sequestered from the world, in a solitude where the great men of antiquity and the wisest thinkers of today keep me company."

Actually he had a great deal more company than that. The court at Rheinsberg was lively and in every sense gay. The record is somewhat unclear on just who was sleeping with whom, but with the exception of his first few months there, when he was notably failing to create an heir with his bride (paying his "tribute to Hymen," as he put it), there were no women at all. Some biographers state flatly, from the circumstantial evidence, that Frederick was homosexual; others demur for lack of what in another context might be called the smoking gun. (Carlyle only says that Frederick was inclined toward "ways not pleasant to his Father and not conformable to the Laws of the Universe.") He wrote homoerotic poetry, his letters refer often to Socratic love, and he called one of his favorites who was openly gay his "Swan of Padua." It is of course possible that he was asexual or pseudo-homosexual and misogynistic, or any number of other things, but it seems most likely on weighing all the evidence (which includes his fun at Dresden with Augustus's daughter-mistress) that he was bisexual. At a certain point not late in his life, there ceases to be evidence of any libido at all.

Not all of his friends were gay, but several were. One was the Count Francesco (Swan of Padua) Algarotti, author of the recent

*Newton for Ladies*. Frederick fell in love with him, according to his biographer Nancy Mitford. If so, he was in good company, with lords and ladies alike. There was another "Swan" in Frederick's court, this one his "Swan of Mitau," who was Count Dietrich von Keyserling, also known as "Caesarion," an "extremely debauched" linguist and poet, in Wilhelmina's opinion, "who thought himself a wit and was nothing more than a walking encyclopedia." (Keyserling, who was fourteen years older than Frederick, had been one of the officers assigned to him as a teenager, with strict instructions from his father never to leave him alone, even in his sleep, with the result that Keyserling had often shared the crown prince's boyhood bedroom.)

One of Frederick's strongest influences and most prolific correspondents was the Saxon diplomat Ulrich Friedrich von Suhm, nicknamed "Diaphanes." Besides bearing news of having successfully secured large "loans" for Frederick from the Russian court where he served as envoy, the letters from Diaphanes bore a gift that Frederick considered beyond price: translations of the works of Leibniz's disciple Christian Wolff, one of Germany's few early champions of the Enlightenment. Accused of atheism by the Pietist faculty at the University of Halle, Wolff had been banished from his chair in philosophy by Frederick's father, a characteristically rash and wrongheaded act that even Frederick William came to regret, but one which can be seen as a symbolic birth of the Enlightenment in Germany, or that strange sibling of the Enlightenment that came to be known by the German word for "clarification," the *Aufklärung*.

§

THE ENLIGHTENMENT WAS difficult enough to define. Even the term itself was not in use at the time, and it would be decades before Immanuel Kant would think to pose the question in his famous essay "What Is Enlightenment?" But never mind: Even early in the century they knew it when they saw it. It was the wish and the freedom to question everything, to submit everything to the rigor of reason and experiment, to take nothing on faith, and to resist the long-standing practice of using abstract principles to generate other abstract principles. In the mid-eighteenth century they knew also what they were against; the cry was to *écraser l'infame!*, and while the infamy to be smashed was mainly Christianity, it was more broadly the great muddle of philosophical and theological speculation. There were no immutable, divine laws, only those which arose from human experience. Truth was observable and calculable, and what was not could not be true. In Peter Gay's magisterial study of the Enlightenment, he cites a dream of the great encyclopedist Denis Diderot:

> The dreamer sees himself transported to an enormous building suspended in space, inhabited by feeble, aged and deformed men. Then a small healthy child enters, grows into a colossus, and destroys the building. That building (as Diderot interprets the dream) is the land of hypotheses, the cripples are the makers of systems, the colossus is Experiment.

These were heady times. Given enough time and the courage to follow empirical fact where it led, all was knowable and would be known; all diseases would be cured; all secrets of the universe would be disclosed.

What the *Aufklärung* had that the Enlightenment did not was a Lutheran upbringing. German thinkers did not have the liberty claimed elsewhere of writing off Christianity as a weedy blight of superstition choking off the flower of right reason. In Germany, the spirit of Martin Luther insisted that faith and reason be reconciled. This was, of course, quite the job. The most elaborate attempt before Wolff's prodigious gloss was made by Leibniz, who (to put his elegant reasoning very bluntly indeed) deduced from the fact that God made the world that it must be the best world possible, whatever its appearance. His ideas were systematized, popularized, and in the process somewhat flattened by Wolff, who was at least clear about his ambition: The title of the book Suhm was translating for Frederick was *On God, the World, the Human Soul and All Things in General*. Wolff delved deep into sophistry to explain miracles in rationalist terms: Moses parted the waters because he had a deep understanding of liquid dynamics, and it was Jesus' transcendent knowledge of chemistry that enabled him to turn water into wine.

Just as Frederick never had a language in which he was entirely at home, he was lost in religion as well, having given up on Christianity but without a footing in any other faith or philosophy. What he found so admirable in Wolff was the squaring of absolute confidence in human reason with a nondoctrinal notion of soul. This gave Frederick, who read his work extremely carefully—religiously, you might say—a measure of comfort.

$\int$

ONE CAN ONLY imagine Voltaire's reaction when, one summer day in 1736, the post brought a letter from Rheinsberg with the seal of Prussia's crown prince. Although they had never met, Frederick wrote, he felt he knew Voltaire sufficiently through his works to know he would appreciate the enclosed French translations of the works of Christian Wolff, whom he recommended to Voltaire as "the greatest philosopher of our time." This phrase might have carried a bit of a sting, since Voltaire no doubt thought that title might have been his, but Frederick had plenty of compliments left over. "Your works," he wrote, "are treasures of the mind. . . . You alone are able to combine the wisdom of a philosopher, the talents of an historian and the brilliant imagination of a poet in the same person." It goes on like that.

He signed it, in the French manner, Frédéric PR (prince royal) of Prussia.

At this point in his career, at the age of forty-two, Voltaire had already had numerous theatrical triumphs with now very dated neoclassical works for the theater. *Candide*, whose Le roi Bulgare would owe so much to Frederick, was decades away, but Voltaire was already both famous and infamous, having been imprisoned and exiled for what were taken as (and were) slights on religion and the court of Versailles. He had been forgiven and was allowed to return to Paris in 1729, but after his rigorously freethinking *Lettres philosophiques* was published in 1734, he felt the need to flee to his country house in Cirey. There he stayed. Chronically under threat of arrest, he nevertheless wrote in his *Discours sur l'homme*, for example:

> This world is a great dance in which fools, disguised under the laughable names of Eminence and Highness, think to inflate their being and elevate their baseness. All mortals are equal. . . . All are born from the same mud; they drag out their childhood in the same weakness; and the rich and the poor, and the weak and the strong, all go on equally from sorrow to death.

As a result, Frederick's letter found him in the midst of troubles: He was being spied on, betrayed by friends, persecuted in various ways for his writings, and always in danger of being exiled or sent to prison again.

The gesture of affection and prospect of protection by a crown prince, even at so provincial a court as Potsdam, was no doubt responsible at least in part for Voltaire's drippingly obsequious reply, which hailed "a prince who thinks like a man, a royal philosopher who will make men happy. . . . [Your] divine character . . . will be adored by your people and cherished by the entire world." The scholar Adrienne Hytier found that in the letters that followed, Voltaire managed to call Frederick "a Caesar, an Augustus, a Marcus Aurelius, a Trajan, an Anthony, a Titus, a Julian, a Virgil, a Pliny, a Horace, a Mécène, a Cicero, a Catullus, a Homer, a Rochefoucault, a Bruyère, a Boileau, a Solomon, a Prometheus, an Apollo, a Patroclus, a Socrates, an Alcibiades, an Alexander, a Henry IV and a Francis I." Of course the Voltaire–Frederick correspondence went on for more than forty years, filling three volumes of Frederick's *Oeuvres,* but the great majority of such references were in the early days, when their correspondence sounded more like love letters than a meeting of minds.

Not long after their correspondence began, Frederick told Voltaire he was reading Machiavelli's *The Prince.* He was horrified, he said, by its assertion that every ruler's most important occupation was war. Machiavelli's power politics, Frederick argued, was "opposed to virtue and the true interests of princes," and he was at work on a book-length refutation of it. The idea that he wished to promote was that the ruler was in fact the servant of the state and not the other way around, that war was justifiable only in certain circumstances, such as self-defense, and that the true interest of the ruler lay in the best interests of his subjects. "I venture to undertake the defense of humanity against this monster [Machiavelli]," he wrote, "to oppose reason and justice to [his] sophistry and crime. I have always regarded *The Prince* as one of the most dangerous books in the world."

Voltaire took the bait, not knowing—or preferring to ignore the suspicion—that Frederick already saw himself at war for Prussian territory to which ambition was his only claim. The book that would come to be titled *Anti-Machiavel* was, as Frederick's biographer Friedrich Meinicke observed, "a secret dialogue with himself and with the passionate impulses inside him." Actually it was not even secret. He had already confessed himself to Grumbkow, and the new French envoy to the court in Berlin told Paris almost as soon as he arrived that it seemed to him Frederick's "true desire is for fame, indeed for martial fame; he is burning to follow in the footsteps of the Great Elector." A year before, the former imperial ordnance master Count von Seckendorff had warned Vienna that Frederick liked the military "even more than his father [did]. . . . His principle is to begin with a thunderbolt."

As Voltaire and others would soon learn, Frederick was not much bothered even by the ideas he embraced most passionately. To be charitable, perhaps he was gifted with what Keats called the poet's "negative capability," the capacity to entertain contradictory feelings and ideas without attempting to resolve them. Less charitably, he would be called two-faced. Perhaps both are true. On the one hand he wrote Wilhelmina he could not wait for "the fat one" to die, and on the other he told his wife, "I do not want my father to die, and I believe that I shall be more grieved by his death than many others who pretend to idolize him during his life; natural feeling is an instinct too powerful in me and I am not sufficiently strong to smother it." This was the last we would hear of Frederick's "natural feeling" for his father. Two played this double game, of course. Frederick's father still throttled his son at one moment and embraced him at another. On his deathbed, Frederick William said he would laugh at Frederick from his grave at the terrible king Frederick would be; and he thanked God for such a wonderful son and heir.

§

A DAY OR two before Frederick William drew his last breath, in the spring of 1740, he called to his bedside the "Old Dessauer," his best and favorite general, his most devoted drinking companion of the Tobacco College, one of the few there whose loyalty was never in question, his friend in the best and blackest times. The king had his horses brought into the courtyard outside his window and asked the general to choose one. "Not good enough," he said to Dessauer's choice, and pointed out another he said was better. Knowing he would not see his friend and king again, the old warrior retired in tears.

Of course Frederick William prescribed every detail of his postmortem, dictating another of his long "Instructions." "As soon as I am dead my body is to be washed, dressed in a clean shirt and placed upon a wooden table. . . . The lid of the coffin is to be fastened with screws. . . ." and so on, page after tiresome page, through the procedure for the autopsy ("no organ [is] to be taken out") to how the body would be displayed to the arrangement of the horses drawing the caisson.

That done, he was ready to die. He called for his pastors and their absolution. At least at first they did not tell him what he wanted to hear. Frederick William pointed out that he never coveted what did not belong to him, that he was faithful to his wife, that he honored the Bible and always went to church. A pastor inquired: What about that man you hanged in Königsberg without so much as a trial? And what about the forgiveness of enemies? You have to forgive everyone else if you are to be forgiven yourself. The king told an orderly to write to one of his enemies when he was dead. The pastor said that would not do, but the king would not budge. In particular he refused to forgive his hateful cousin George II for a string of slights that went back to their childhood days. Eventually one of the pastors must have got to him, though, because among his final words were, "Death, I fear thee not!"

Frederick was awash throughout the deathwatch, clawing at his father's sheets, pledging his love and devotion: There would never be a greater king, he would do his best to be the equal of him, etc. He was not in the room when his father died. When the news came to him, he collapsed in tears once again, but he was not so overcome that he forgot to order the gates of Berlin to be closed so word of the king's death would not get out before he could be assured of his grip on power.

A while later the old Dessauer came to console Frederick on their mutual loss. Almost as an afterthought, he said he assumed Frederick would wish him to continue in command of the army, and suddenly the new king's eyes were dry.

"I know of [no authority] but that of the king," said the newly minted, twenty-eight-year-old monarch. The general withdrew with what Carlyle called "a painful miscellany of feelings, astonishment . . . among them."

Another old veteran came to give Frederick his condolences, this one the general who had run Frederick's court-martial, who had stood between him and the king at the worst of the crisis and had refused the king's demand that Katte be sentenced to death. Frederick scolded him for leaving his post without permission.

That night at the palace in Rheinsberg, the sound of horsemen arriving at two o'clock in the morning was followed by exciting news of Frederick's accession. There were shouts in the halls: "Get up, get up, the king is dead! Frederick is king!" Someone in the card room was so excited that he upset the table, scattering bets all over the floor. As someone bent down to scoop them up, another said, "What, grovel for groschen now, when it is going to rain ducats?"

Frederick's friends came to call what followed "the day of the dupes." There were to be jobs for only two of them, no wonderful new positions at court, no replication of the Rheinsberg idyll. They were out, though they could come to dinner when summoned. As Frederick bluntly put it to Keyserling, his close friend since boyhood: "My dear Caesarion, you're a dear fellow, you are well-read, you have a pleasing wit and a nice singing voice, but your advice is that of an imbecile." They were shocked by his brutal treatment of them. He sounded almost like his father.

## X

# THE ARTIST IN A PAINT-

# BY-NUMBERS WORLD

FREDERICK'S HALCYON YEARS-IN-WAITING AT RHEINS-berg were the worst years of Bach's life. By now more than a decade had passed since he had left Cöthen to become cantor at the school of St. Thomas's Church in Leipzig, and the honeymoon was long over. At this point, despite his surpassing work and genius, his superiors were scorning and undermining him on a regular basis. A few weeks after the premiere of his *St. Matthew Passion* he was actually docked in pay, proof of their shortsightedness, surely, but also of his ferocious stubbornness, which lost nothing with age. He had discouraging family problems as well. Bach's two oldest sons had long since left home, well launched on careers of their own—no small thanks to himself—but Bernhard, the third, was running up huge bills and bad loans again at his organist's post in Sangerhausen, the same problem that had forced him to leave Mühlhausen (and Bach had had to pull strings to get him both jobs). Finally in his *annus horribilis* of 1737, the journal *Critischer Musikus* published an attack on him by a certain Johann Adolph Scheibe, one of his former students and the son of a longtime colleague, who called him a composer of turgid, outdated, academic music and—this really hurt—an undereducated social climber.

These troubles hit him at a tender psychological moment. Two years before the Scheibe attack, he had turned fifty, the age at which his father, his mother, and his older brother Christoph had died. As others have been known to do when reminded of mortality much less forcefully than this, he started that year to work on a genealogy, reclaiming the family he had lost by digging up all known traces of the Bach line of musicians. He compiled a collection of their music as well, as if to make sure there would be a record of his own distinction, if only as part of a distinguished clan. At this point in his life, he had reason to doubt he would be remembered at all, except perhaps as an exemplary anachronism.

If he was hurt by such ignominy, he could not have been entirely surprised by it. It was of a piece with his whole life.

§

WHEN MARIA BARBARA died in 1721, Bach was thirty-six and at the top of his form, well known for his virtuosity as a performer and as a composer of great mastery. Still, when he reached out for a good church job, that did not seem to be enough. For a senior position that came open in Hamburg, he gave a concert on the great organ at St. Catherine's, where a long, bravura improvisation on the chorale "An Wasserflüssen Babylon" prompted from the near-centenarian Johann Adam Reinken a very rare compliment indeed: "I thought that this art was dead, but I see that it lives on in you." Virtually the entire musical establishment of Hamburg turned out to hear Bach play and to conduct one of his cantatas, apparently including Johann Mattheson, now director of music at the Hamburg cathedral, who always praised Bach as a keyboard virtuoso but took from the cantata only a case study in bad declamation. In his *Critica Musica,* he quoted the libretto word for word in order to make fun of it:

"I, I, I, I had much grief, I had much grief, in my heart, in my heart, I had much grief etc., in my heart etc. etc., I had much grief etc., in my heart, etc., I had much grief etc., in my heart etc., etc."

Possibly if he had known of Maria Barbara's very recent death, he would not so blithely have poked fun.

Mattheson aside, Bach's concert was a huge success, and still the job went to a nonentity, for the price of a large donation to the church, an outcome over which even Mattheson expressed indignation. Several months later, in the summer of 1722, when the job of cantor at the St. Thomas School and director of music in Leipzig presented itself, Bach was near the bottom of a list of twelve candidates. His friend Telemann, the favorite, took himself out of the running, as did two others; another could not win his release from court employment; and Bach, the only candidate without a university education, before a selection committee replete with doctorates, finally got the job almost by default. At the crucial meeting, one town councillor, Dr. Abraham Platz, concluded, "As the best are not available, I suppose we must take one of the second-rate men"—a statement for which he has been justly immortalized.

The appointment process was, it must be said, highly politicized, a proxy for the ongoing battle between the absolutist ambitions of the Saxon elector, Augustus the Strong, and the contrary assertion of power by Saxony's nobility and cities, known together as the Estates. The two sides had two very different ideas for the job, a fact that doomed anyone who took it to a world of political wrangling. The absolutist party (led by Augustus's de facto prime minister, Count von Flemming, Bach's host for the noncontest with Louis Marchand) wanted a Kapellmeister, someone who would bring musical distinction to the city of Leipzig as a whole. The Estates wanted a school cantor, someone clearly under local auspices. As a candidate of the absolutists (after all, he had spent the last fifteen years in court employment and had long known where the real power was), Bach represented for the council of Leipzig an intrusion by the elector into civic matters. Finally, however, all of their own candidates bowed out for one reason or another, and after passing the requisite examination in theology, Bach was, without recorded enthusiasm, hired.

The position, in Philipp Spitta's opinion, was "not a brilliant one," though it had a distinguished musical lineage going back for more than a century. Among other problems, discipline at the school had been deteriorating for years. In a report as early as 1717 the rector admitted to "a very sad state of things. . . . [P]articularly of the *chorus musicus* . . . there is more of evil to be guarded against than of good to be hoped for." Spitta reported that the singers spent all they made at weddings and funerals on "prohibited pleasures" and were "often enfeebled and miserable from disease." A new code set in place by the rector the year that Bach arrived was largely ignored, and even after Bach had been at St. Thomas's for seven years, the superintendent reported that the school was "fast going to ruin and had almost run wild." For all that, Bach's first years at St. Thomas's were among the most productive of his life.

§

HE HAD HIS SECOND wife to thank for that, at least in part. About a year after Maria Barbara died, while he was still in Cöthen, Bach had hired into the court Kapelle a gifted nineteen-year-old soprano named Anna Magdalena Wilcke, daughter of the court trumpeter at Weissenfels. He gave his new singer the unusually lofty title of "chamber musician" and a salary second only to his own. We do not know whether the musical relationship came before the romantic one or whether Bach was being the clever dog, but six months after she arrived, they were married, and a year later they had their first child. When Anna Magdalena Bach was sufficiently recovered to travel, the twenty-one-year-old bride set out with her thirty-six-year-old husband and his family—including his first wife's sister and four children, now ranging in age from eleven to five—for their new home in Leipzig, where they would spend their entire married life.

Compared to how little is known about Bach's relationship with Maria Barbara, what we know of his marriage to Anna Magdalena is abundant and evocative. We know that she loved songbirds and flowers, that she sang beautifully and often at home (though she gave up her career after she married). We can surmise that she wanted to learn to play keyboards because of a notebook Bach began making for her not long after the wedding, which he assembled in a green binding that was stamped with her initials and tied with a band of silk. Some of the pieces in it are copied out in her own elegant hand, some are songs Bach wrote for her to sing, and other songs were clearly addressed to her.

> Your servant, sweetest maiden bride:
> Joy be with you this morning!
> To see you in your flowery crown
> And wedding-day adorning
> Would fill with joy the sternest soul.
> What wonder, as I meet you,
> That my fond heart and loving lips
> O'erflow with song to greet you?

Every evidence suggests that theirs was a loving home.

Typically for Bach, it was a busy one as well, with more newcomers to the family virtually every year. Ten months after their first child came the second, fourteen months later the third, and so on, and so on: Anna Magdalena Bach presented her husband with thirteen children in nineteen years. He loved them all but always doted on his three sons from his marriage to Maria Barbara, and particularly on the eldest. During their first year in Leipzig, Bach gave Friedemann, who was twelve years old at the time, the notice of his future admission to the university wrapped as a Christmas present, and he used the music book he wrote for Friedemann to teach all of his children to play. He boasted in a letter to a friend that all of his children were "born musicians, and I can assure you that I can already form an ensemble both [choral] and [instrumental] within my family, particularly since my present wife sings a good, clear soprano, and my eldest daughter, too, joins in not badly." But Friedemann was clearly the favorite and Bach's intended musical heir, the son he took with him to Dresden to hear what he gently disparaged as the "pretty little ditties" of Johann Adolph Hasse, a friend of Bach's who wrote in the *galant* style favored by the Saxon elector's court. And yet the son who would create the greatest legacy as a musician and the one who wrote most about his father is the second son, Carl, or C. P. E., as the world has remembered him. It is from Carl, for example, that we hear his father could predict, at the first entrance of a fugue subject, every way in which it could be developed contrapuntally— and that when the performance proved him right he would proudly give Carl a nudge and a wink. Both sons spoke frankly of having to distinguish themselves from such an outsize character as their father, but Carl seems to have felt that need more keenly than Friedemann, perhaps because he was so clearly not the favorite.

Plainly, Bach enjoyed the role of *haus-pater* to all of his children, and a family life that was traditionally and devoutly Lutheran: Children were to show respect for the parents, and parents were to learn patience and diligence in dealings with their children and each other in that challenging nexus of family relationships which Luther called the "school for character."

Their apartment in the south wing of the St. Thomas building made for a very crowded school. Carl remembered his father's home as a "beehive, and just as full of life. . . . No master of music was apt to pass through [Leipzig] without meeting my father and being heard by him." His students and assistants lived with the family, and there were frequent house concerts, probably in the largest room, the heated living room on the second floor, which was all of 250 square feet. With more than a dozen people at a time living in the 800-square-foot apartment (which apparently had only one unheated bathroom), it is possible to understand why, when he shut himself off in the evening to work in his composing room, he sometimes took along a bottle of brandy.

There were instruments in the composing room, but he had long since stopped composing at the keyboard. He wrote music at his desk, where there were stacks of paper, the raven-quill pens he always used, and rastrals for drawing staves on the scores, single staves for instrumental parts, double for keyboard. There too was the powder to make the ink, the red and black ink pots in which he mixed it with water, and a box of sand for blotting the ink dry. On a sunny day he could find his thoughts while gazing out the window of this corner room, which overlooked the river Pleisse and, in the far distance, the castle and cathedral of Merseburg.

He must have spent a good deal of his time in that room, because his output was astonishing, especially in the early years. On the Sunday he took over his duties in Leipzig, in late May of 1723, he presented the first cantata in the project of "well-organized church music" that he had considered his great goal as a composer ever since he left Mühlhausen fifteen years before, citing in his letter of resignation the "opposition" and "vexations" he had experienced in pursuit of it. This was the first cantata in what would become five complete annual cycles, a cantata for every Sunday and feast day of the ecclesiastical year, some three hundred in all. There are few achievements in the history of art to compare—in ambition, scope, or artistry—with Bach's composition of cantatas during those first years in Leipzig, and to them he added his passions, the *St. John Passion* for his first Easter, the *St. Matthew* for his fourth. Only a deep sense of mission could sustain such an extraordinary outpouring of work. As the Bach scholar Friedrich Smend observed, the cantatas and passions were "not intended to be works of music or art on their own, but [were meant] to carry on, by their own means, the work of Luther, the preaching of the word and of nothing but the word."

From his first job in Arnstadt, Bach had worked with the words of Luther and the Bible virtually every day of his career, and as he grew older his pursuit of spiritual understanding became ever more gripping. The library of books on theology that he accumulated, much of it in Leipzig, would have been the pride of any pastor. He owned the best-known works of the Pietists and Christian mystics and numerous works of commentary on Luther's works and the German Bible. In 1733 he bought a three-volume version of the Lutheran Bible that had been published in 1681 with commentary by Dr. Abraham Calov, and later he spent a large fraction of a year's salary to buy the seven-volume edition of Luther's collected writings on which Calov had based his work. This joined an eight-volume set he already owned that had been published in the mid-sixteenth century. Most of Bach's theological library disappeared after his death, but the Calov Bible was found in the attic of a farmhouse in Michigan in 1934.

More telling than the extent of the library are all the heavy underlinings and the exclamations he wrote in the margins of his Calov. As anyone who has ever read a used book knows, nothing exposes readers to quite such a high degree of nakedness as the underlinings and marginalia they leave behind, and Bach was no exception. Many of the passages he marked clearly address issues related to texts of his music, but others clearly speak to very pressing issues in his life. Since he bought his Calov in 1733, we can be quite certain that as he scrawled and underscored his way through it, he was often thinking about the constant battles he was having with his superiors, which reached a high pitch in the mid-1730s but began not long after he arrived. Unfortunately for Bach, the close, nearly obsessive attention to matters of form that served him so well as a contrapuntist did not translate at all well to the world of office politics. But it is in these small, sometimes almost slapstick squabbles that we see the character of a man who could ignore everything about him but his own vision.

§

ANGER MUST EXIST, BUT TAKE CARE THAT IT OCCUR AS IS PROPER AND IN YOUR COMMAND, AND THAT YOU EXPRESS ANGER NOT FOR YOUR OWN SAKE BUT FOR THE SAKE OF YOUR OFFICE. . . . FOR YOURSELF YOU MUST SHOW NO ANGER, NO MATTER HOW SEVERE THE OFFENSE HAS BEEN. HOWEVER, WHERE IT CONCERNS YOUR OFFICE, *YOU MUST SHOW ANGER.**

A few months after he began his new job, Bach decided to raise the issue of who was in charge of music at the university church. Telemann and Christoph Graupner had been offered that job as part of their portfolio, but after they dropped out, and before Bach was hired, the organist who was filling in temporarily, Johann Gottlieb Görner, came forward and was given the position

---

* Emphasis original. This passage and all those that follow were annotated, checked in the margin, or underlined by Bach in his Calov commentary.

for an annual remittance of all of twelve florins, about enough money to buy four cases of good wine. For Bach, however, as so many things were with him, this was a matter of principle. He petitioned the council for the job, and the twelve florins that went with it, but the council said he had no standing to claim the job or the salary, which was their prerogative to give to anyone they chose. Bach argued back on precedent: Kuhnau had had authority over the university church, *and* the twelve florins. Since their new cantor was obviously not letting this go, the council decided to split the difference: Bach could have six florins for programming and conducting the music at four annual events at the church, Görner would keep Sundays and other services. For Bach that was not good enough. (Keep in mind that now we are talking about only two cases of wine.)

IF YOU CHOOSE TO PLACE YOURSELF IN VIOLENT
OPPOSITION YOU WILL BE POURING OIL ON THE
FIRE AND RUBBING AGAINST THE BARB.

Bach took it up with the king of Poland. This, of course, was also the elector of Saxony, his ultimate patron, Augustus the Strong (whose prime minister had helped to put him in the job). He wrote to Augustus once, then again, and finally delivered himself of a several-thousand-word essay that dissected the small matter into very tiny particles. At that Augustus ruled decisively against Bach—by now this issue had been going on for almost three years—declaring that the council's compromise had been a fair one. On the other hand, the records indicate that, somehow or other, Bach did finally wrangle the full twelve florins, and even a bit more, for the four annual performances he conducted at the university (of recycled cantatas), which he kept doing for the next twenty-five years. Wine, after all, is wine.

§

THOSE WHO DIG TRAPS EASILY ERR AND FALL
IN THEMSELVES. THUS DEALING WITH
GOVERNANCE AND SUCH MATTERS IN THE
WORLD IS NOTHING OTHER THAN DIGGING
PITFALLS, AND YOU MAY BE FOREWARNED TO
EXPECT ALL SORTS OF DANGERS.

A few months after the king sided with the council, Bach stepped on Görner. He accepted a commission to write a cantata for a service to honor the recently deceased wife of Augustus the Strong that was to be held at the university. Predictably, Görner blew up, but Bach got away with it, minus some fast-waning goodwill with the council.

The next year he got into another ridiculously petty feud with St. Thomas's subdeacon over his right to choose hymns for the service, which became the subject of another arch, nanoscopic argument in a letter to the council, which was beginning to get more than a little tired of its cantor.

One would think the performance of his first version of the *St. Matthew Passion* the following Easter might have quieted them down a bit. Besides being the greatest of all Bach's passions, besides being perhaps the greatest oratorio and one of the most ambitious and powerful works of music ever written, the *St. Matthew Passion* was also one that used to maximum effect the new forms of recitative and da capo aria with which Bach had been enriching the repertoire of Lutheran church music for several years. Clearly, however, his superiors and parishioners were not particularly grateful for this technical and aesthetic achievement, because the only recorded review of the *St. Matthew Passion* in Bach's lifetime was from an aged widow in the congregation: "God help us! It's an opera-comedy!" A few weeks after that, four choral scholars that Bach had deemed "useless" were admitted to St. Thomas's over his protest, and things were getting worse.

§

THOSE WHO WANT TO ASSIST THE PEOPLE AND
THEIR AFFAIRS AND WHO HELP FAITHFULLY ARE
THANKED AS THE WORLD IS ACCUSTOMED: IT
KICKS THEM AND WIPES ITS SHOES ON
THEM. . . . THEREFORE LEARN TO RECOGNIZE
THE WORLD; YOU WILL NOT MAKE IT DIFFERENT;
IT WILL NOT DIRECT ITSELF ACCORDING TO
YOU; ABOVE ALL OTHER THINGS LEARN AND
KNOW THAT THE WORLD IS UNGRATEFUL.

Plainly and understandably discouraged, Bach began to move away from the church in that fall of 1729. He filled an opening for organist at the New Church with his own man and took for himself the leadership of the secular collegium musicum that traditionally came with that post. Predictably, as he began to compose orchestral music and conduct the weekly concerts of the collegium musicum at Zimmerman's coffeehouse, his superiors at St. Thomas's became even more clearly focused on his inattention to them. His contribution to the bicentennial of the Augsburg Confession in June 1730, three new cantatas performed over three days, was followed in a few weeks with a town council meeting in which Bach's failure to teach his regular classes (trying to make musicians out of numbskulls, in his view) was discussed in near-apocalyptic terms. One councillor said he showed "little inclination to work," and another said he "did nothing. . . . A break would have to come sometime." A third called Bach "incorrigible" and wanted to see him fired. Instead, at least for the moment, they reduced his income, and at the same time doubled the salary of the New Church organist and gave him money for new instruments. Bach had every reason to feel that an attempt at his ouster was imminent, which it was. He clearly did feel that his efforts were not sufficiently appreciated, which they were not.

Into the teeth of this vexatious opposition, in his fashion, Bach hurled a memo entitled "Short but Most Necessary Draft for a Well-Appointed Church Music, Plus Some Modest Reflections Concerning Its Ruin." The council may never have got past the title. In any case there was no reply to the document, which began with a statement so dry as to leave no doubt of the author's contempt for the memo's recipients: "To perform concerted music . . . both singers and instrumentalists are required."

His complaints were many: that incidental fees for town musicians and other vocal and instrumental fill-ins had been reduced, that he needed at least eleven more paid instrumentalists, that more than a third of his student choristers were "not yet serviceable," and that many others—he listed seventeen by name—were "useless." Putting on works of the scope of the *St. Matthew Passion* would obviously have been challenging in such circumstances, but by this time the council had exactly no patience for their cantor or his complaints.

In the absence of a response, Bach wrote an old friend, now an ambassador in Danzig, asking whether he might know of an opening there and, interestingly, complaining about the many Leipzigers who were clinging so obstinately to life. "My masters are strange folk, with very little music in them," he wrote, with his customary dips into Latin and French.

Consequently, I am subjected to constant vexation, envy and persecution. . . . My present *station* is worth about 700 thalers a year, and if the death-rate is higher than *ordinairement* my *accidentia* increase in proportion; but Leipzig is a healthy place, and for the past year, as it happens, I have received about 100 kronen less than usual in funeral *accidentia*. The cost of living, too, is so *excessive* that I was better off in Thuringia on 400 thalers.

His sense of injustice and ingratitude would never leave him, and from this time forward his work for the church fell into the background. His *Passion According to St. Mark* for Easter 1731 featured music he had written years before.

§

A FOOL AND A HAPLESS MAN IS OF NO USE TO HIMSELF. . . . SUCH PEOPLE ARE FOUND IN ALL LEVELS OF SOCIETY; WE MUST LIVE AND WORK AMONG THEM, NO MATTER HOW UNBEARABLE AND INSUFFERABLE THEY MAY BE. . . . WHAT IS THIS WORLD BUT A LARGE THORN GROWTH THAT WE MUST TEAR OURSELVES THROUGH. . . . THIS EARTH IS THE DEVIL'S KINGDOM.

By the time he actually got his Calov, in 1733, he had a lot of pent-up underlining and marginal exclaiming to do. Given what was going on with him and against him at the time, it is easy to see him with his Calov open, a brandy at his elbow, jowls quivering, wig shaking, the quill in his thick fingers hacking at the page.

In truth, although he understandably could not see it that way, his rejection by the church was a liberation. In the years that followed, he became ever more inventive and self-confident about going his own way musically. His memo to the council seems in this respect a turning point for him. Here for the first and only time, Bach reflects on his sense that the public taste has changed, that "the old fashioned music sounds strangely in our ears," and that "the greatest care must be taken to obtain [musicians] capable of satisfying the modern taste in music." Of course, he was making a case for his request, appealing to the burghers' interest in appearing to keep up. Bach had no interest in following fashion. He was, however, clearly driven to engage the music of his time, just as he had swallowed Vivaldi whole and devoured Couperin (and Marchand) and bettered the best of his fellow contrapuntists. Having witnessed the silence that was his superiors' worst response to the *St. Matthew Passion,* he set about finding new avenues for his ambition—for example, with the collegium musicum and the composition of new keyboard music. The year after his memo to the council, he published the first volume of his *Clavierübung* ("keyboard practice," an understated title if ever there was one), containing the finished version of his six masterpieces for keyboard, the Partitas. Hugely diverse and yet entirely comfortable as a set, they are a veritable catalog of styles and devices from every time including his own: In strict and free counterpoint mixed with extraordinarily elegant *galant* writing, he embraces the traditions and fashions of half a dozen countries, and yet all of the suites and their parts are uniquely his own. *Clavierübung II,* published four years later, consists of his *Italian Concerto* and *French Overture,* works admired by the most avid advocates of both counterpoint and the *galant.* For all that he had already done in these works and in bringing new forms and life into his music for the church, including his "opera-comedy" the *St. Matthew Passion,* his most dramatic confrontation with the music of his own time had just begun. His freedom for that program of work would have been much curtailed had he depended for it on his superiors at St. Thomas's, especially since the worst of his problems with them were still ahead.

§

AFTER THE DEATH of Augustus the Strong, Bach sought a court title from his son Friedrich, the new elector (amazingly, Augustus's only legitimate child; all of his hundreds of other children were born to his various daughters and other, extra-familial mistresses). Bach clearly thought this would give him some protection from the authorities in Leipzig. To this end, on a trip to Dresden to visit Friedemann, he brought with him a suitably spectacular composition, the first two sections of what years later would become the B-minor Mass, in a dedication copy for the new elector. He gave it to an intermediary along with a letter to Friedrich which appealed to "Your Highness's World-Famous Clemency" to take him "under Your Most Mighty Protection." It was a little early for the new elector to be world-famous, but this was the sort of thing Baroque composers said to absolute rulers. What followed was not quite as common.

> For some years and up to the present moment, I have . . .
> innocently had to suffer one injury or another, and on oc-
> casion also a diminution of the fees accruing to me in this
> office; but these injuries would disappear altogether if
> Your Royal Highness would grant me the favor of confer-
> ring on me a title of Your Highness's Court Kapelle. . . .

His application was decidedly ill-timed, coming before the official mourning period for Augustus was over and as Friedrich's claim to the Polish throne was under attack, but Bach pursued it with almost undignified but oddly uncompromised zeal.

For the birthday of the new elector's young son that fall, he wrote one of his secular *drammi per musica*, this one called *Hercules at the Crossroads* (BWV 213), which used a classical myth to celebrate the boy's prestige and also gave Bach the opportunity for a sermon, an attempt to put this young man on the right path (not a bad idea, considering his grandfather). The story was well known despite somewhat esoteric origins. In Xenophon's *Memorabilia*, it is told by Socrates, who attributes it to his teacher. As the story goes, Hercules was just coming into his young manhood when two women came to him in a vision, one representing virtue, the other vice. Vice promises him "a short and easy road to happiness. You shall taste of all life's sweet and escape all bitters . . . your only speculation what meat or drink you shall find agreeable to your palate, what delight of ear or eye, what pleasure of smell or touch." Virtue admits that hers is the more difficult path but warns him of the easy road to ruin and promises that if he chooses her, "you shall be moved to accomplish many a [great] and noble deed."

Bach, of course, enjoined the new elector's crown prince to answer as Hercules does, and just to make sure his dedicatee got the message, Hercules' love duet with Virtue is followed by a recitative from Mercury singing:

> *Behold, you gods, here is a portrait*
> *Of the youth of Saxony's Crown Prince. . . .*

Three months after *Hercules* he wrote and staged another *dramma per musica* for the new elector's wife. In the fall of the following year, on very short notice—Friedrich decided suddenly to visit the Michaelmas Fair in Leipzig—he cobbled together still another one. We can infer the full measure of his desire to please from the fact that he pulled its nine movements together in only three days and that its lyrics approach Lullian heights of sycophancy over Friedrich's contest for the Polish throne. At that it was entirely in keeping with the rest of the festivities, for which the town and all its towers were illuminated by hundreds of torches, visible for miles around. Six hundred students carried candles in procession (past little verse messages posted in the windows of hopeful shopkeepers along the way, clearly meant for a merciful and philanthropic elector: "Debts oft bring me incarceration / But tonight I have illumination" and "I love my King with heart devout / I have a lot of pain from gout"). Four lucky counts presented the score of Bach's work to the elector and got to kiss his hand, after which came the music. According to the town chronicler, the visiting royalty "did not leave the windows until the music was over and listened most graciously and liked it well." It must have been long on brass, because Bach's sixty-seven-year-old lead trumpeter suffered a fatal stroke the next day, brought on, the chronicler said, by smoke from the torches combined with exertions required in Bach's music.

Bach's works for the elector, despite their practical purpose, were composed with no less dedication and conviction than any of his other music. If further proof were needed that Bach drew no distinction between his secular and sacred work, there is this: No fewer than six movements from *Hercules* turned up at the end of 1734 in his *Christmas Oratorio* (BWV 248). The love duet between Hercules and Virtue becomes an aria for baritone and soprano giving thanks for the nativity of Jesus. The chorus in praise of young Prince Friedrich becomes in the oratorio a hymn in thanks to God for His Son. Virtue's promise becomes a plea for faith. Hercules' rebuke to Vice becomes a challenge to recognize the Messiah upon His birth. And the aria in which Hercules ponders his decision becomes, with little more than a key change, the soliloquy of a devout Christian. Most of the rest of the *Christmas Oratorio* was taken from his other encomia to Friedrich over the past year.

Even after the last of these musical tributes to the elector and

his family, there was no answer to Bach's plea for a royal title until two years later, by which time Friedrich was securely installed
as the Polish monarch and Bach was finally given the estimable
but largely honorific title "Royal Composer to the Noble Court
of the King of Poland and Elector of Saxony."

§

WHEN THINGS ARE GOOD CONSIDER THAT THEY
CAN EASILY TURN BAD, AND IF THINGS ARE BAD
THAT THEY CAN TURN GOOD, AND DO NOT
PRESUME THAT THINGS WILL GO THE WAY YOU
WANT. . . . HE WHO TROUBLES HIMSELF WITH
HAVING THINGS TURN OUT THE WAY HE
WANTS . . . WILL HAVE NOTHING BUT SADNESS,
UNREST, AND PAIN OF HEART.

Bach's new title did not insulate him as he had hoped. In fact, his
situation deteriorated badly that very year, when he and the new
rector of the St. Thomas School got into a catfight over who had
the right to choose which students could act as Bach's assistants,
or "prefects," an embarrassment for both men that was actually
just one ridiculous scene in a serious drama. The rector, Johann
August Ernesti, a distinguished but cold, acerbic academic, was
bent on submitting the St. Thomas curriculum to the new light of
reason. Twenty-nine when he was made rector, Ernesti was
twenty-two years Bach's junior, which cannot have helped their
relationship, especially since the war of ideas under way at that
time between Bach's world and that of the Enlightenment was
distinctly generational.

The battle with Ernesti began when one of Bach's prefects in-
flicted too harsh a punishment on a boisterous chorister. According to Ernesti, the prefect's method of discipline (he beat the

singer with a stick) warranted a public flogging. Rather than submit to that, the boy left school. Ernesti then determined that his replacement was to be a boy named Krause, who Bach felt was musically unfit and, he said, "a dissolute dog." Nevertheless, Ernesti got the backing of the burgomaster to deliver Bach an ultimatum: Make the appointment or Ernesti would do so himself. Bach's response was the predictable one.

Ernesti talked to Krause very early on the second Sunday of August 1736, early enough that Bach had time before the main service to appeal the decision to the head of the council, who hedged. By the time Bach got to church the service was begun, and Krause was in the choir loft conducting. Furious, Bach collected another prefect and with him in tow stormed up to the gallery, where he relieved Krause brusquely and apparently with a great deal of noise. Hearing the commotion, Ernesti left the service to find out if Bach was acting with the council's support. Finding he was not, Ernesti told Krause after the service to take over conducting at vespers that afternoon, and in the meantime he forbade the choir to sing under anyone else on pain of expulsion. Once again at Vespers, of course, Bach drove Krause from the gallery. The second prefect, who sensibly refused Bach's request to take Krause's place, was punished that evening when Bach, who had to eat dinner with the students because it was his week to act as school inspector, drove the traitor from his table. As Bach put the students to bed with their evening prayers, those who were not still stinging from the absurd set-to of the day would surely have been snickering about it.

Bach's first long, detailed letter to the council about the matter was dated that very day. A longer and even fussier one was dated the next day. There was another two days later, and they kept coming. The next Sunday Bach and Ernesti played out the same awful scene, bringing forth yet another piteous tome from Bach.

The "affair of the prefects" dragged on for more than a year before finally Bach once again—this time over the earth-shattering issue of a teaching assistant—went right to the top, to the elector of Saxony and king of Poland, for satisfaction. Bach's king and elector ruled forcefully that he could not care less:

> Whereas Our Court Composer, Johann Sebastian Bach, has complained to Us . . . that [Ernesti] has had the effrontery to fill the post of Prefect without his concurrence . . . We therefore desire herewith that you [the town council] shall take such measures, in response to this complaint, as you shall see fit.

The council minutes do not disclose exactly what happened after that, but both sides seem to have been accommodated to some extent, and the practical issue had been resolved when Krause left school at the end of the previous academic year. (Bach must have appointed his replacement, because there was no quarrel over the matter.)

The silliness of this bizarre wrangle does no credit to the real issue between the rector and his cantor, which was important and which never did go away. Ernesti was a prototypical rationalist of the early Enlightenment, a grammarian, translator, and professor of philology who sensibly posited that the Scriptures should be submitted to the same objective, scholarly approach as the classics. He was determined to bend the curriculum of St. Thomas toward the humanities and liberate it in particular from the notion of music as handmaiden of theology, his idea of a school being light-years from Luther's educational ideal of "the training of men toward God as a consequence of the practice of music to the glory of God." An ardent follower of the *Aufklärung*'s Christian Wolff, Ernesti believed strongly in the need to rationalize the spiritual, the same bootless project that led Wolff to such contorted solutions as Moses' expertise in fluid mechanics. It is some measure of his firmness of purpose that he could write this: "Greater weight in exegesis should be attributed to grammatical considerations than to doctrinal ones." To be fair, he is still felt to have had a salutary impact on biblical scholarship if not on faith.

Ernesti was far from alone in seeking technical clarity about the mysteries of faith. Typical was one contemporary theologian, Hermann-Samuel Reimarus, who achieved posthumous fame for his massive *Apologia for the Rational Worshipers of God*. Among other conclusions, his reading of Matthew led him to believe that Jesus not only did not foresee his crucifixion but was completely undone by the prospect: "He began to quiver and quake when he saw that this adventure might cost him his life." Reimarus reads the climactic crucifixion scene, in which Christ calls out from the cross, "My God, My God, why has Thou forsaken me?" not as the moment which proves that even the Son of God was subject to human weakness, doubt, and pain, without which of course the crucifixion would be meaningless, but as a simple, horrified realization that

> God had not helped him to carry out his intention and attain his object as he had hoped he would have done. *It was then clearly not the intention or the object of Jesus to suffer and to die*, but to build up a worldly kingdom, and to deliver the Israelites from bondage [emphasis original].

A practical interpretation certainly, but not the basis for much of a religion.

In such a cold-lighted world there would be no more cosmological-theological privilege for music, no more number mysticism or claims about divine harmonies and proportions, no more pseudocosmic nonsense. One of the school's founding principles—"to guide the students through the euphony of music to the contemplation of the divine"—was to be discarded. If

Ernesti could have had his way, the curriculum of St. Thomas
School would have dispensed with music entirely. He was known
to stop music students at their practice to say derisively, "What,
you want to be a beer fiddler too?"

One of Ernesti's guiding lights and kindred spirits, a professor of aesthetics at the university named Johann Christoph
Gottsched, followed Christian Wolff down somewhat different
blind alleys. The task he set for himself was to rationalize the creative process, which produced results about as edifying as
Reimarus's reading of the Gospel. Gottsched's *Kritische Dichtkunst*
of 1730 was a dry, pedantic compendium of rules and formal hi-
erarchies by which German poets were to write poetry and German dramatists were to write drama, presupposing that every
proper aesthetic device and effect could be classified and that such
a classification, if rigorously adhered to, would produce a true
German literature. In his *Kritische Dichtkunst,* Gottsched ridiculed
the use of da capo arias, recitatives, and operatic forms in general.
"By an extravagantly wasteful musical art the work of poetry becomes invisible, or so hidden that it is not discernible." He
praised Graun and Hasse, devotees of the *galant* style, mentioning his Leipzig neighbor Bach not once. As Peter Gay pointed out
in his study of the Enlightenment, Gottsched at least had the
problem right: German literature and drama had no public, and
the language itself, a crude vernacular with no stylish written
form, was a large part of the reason.

Bach showed Gottsched what he thought of his prescription
for change—and served notice of his opinion on certain aspects
of the Enlightenment in general—when Gottsched worked with
him as librettist on a cantata to mark the death of Augustus's wife,
the Electress Christiane Eberhardine (the cantata Görner wanted
to write). Gottsched, of course, wished his libretto to be a model
of his theories in practice. Knowing Bach's use of librettists who

were pliant about letting him shove their words around and even writing to order, he adopted a formal structure that he felt would force Bach to follow his script. The beauty of his ode, he wrote, lay in "the equality of its divisions, in the euphony of its syllables and in the order of its rhymes." Not for Bach, who bent the text entirely to his purposes, setting Gottsched's dated, over-the-top libretto ("Your Saxony and dismayed Meissen / are struck dumb at your royal tomb; / the eye weeps, the tongue cries; / my woe can be deemed indescribable. . . .") to a work of great range and beauty. There is this to be said for Gottsched: His belief was genuine and well intentioned. Beyond that, he was a very large target (literally as well as metaphorically; he only narrowly avoided being drafted into Frederick William's regiment of giants) and so presented for the next generation a clear guide to what he himself had missed: that there is more to making great literature than observing unities or strophic regularity, that neither an artist's nor an audience's reactions are invariable and fixed, that sentiment, emotion, and imagination are involved both in creating and in responding to art, that one cannot paint by numbers.

In his remarkable book *Bach and the Patterns of Invention*, Laurence Dreyfus raises the interesting question of whether a university education might actually have got in Bach's way: His willful mixing and matching, destroying and rebuilding to his own specifications the forms and styles of his time was distinctly at odds with contemporary aesthetic theory. The Enlightenment's way of knowing a thing was to identify, separate, and classify it, the encyclopedic impulse. Bach's way of understanding something was to get his hands on it, turn it upside down and backward, and wrestle with it until he found a way to make something new. The fact that he kept himself well away from the theoretical mainstream—of Germany, not to mention Europe—may indeed have helped him follow where his own drive and genius took him, which is to say well beyond notions of music as merely a craft or a depiction of theological texts or a graceful appeal to good taste. Rather, Bach presented the model of a composer grappling creatively with himself and the world. This relation of the artist to his art would be truly adopted only a century after Bach and Gottsched, by the Romantics of the nineteenth century. Before the next few generations could figure this out, however, there were casualties among theorists in all the arts, music very much included.

§

ONE OF GOTTSCHED'S students, who was at the performance of his funeral ode with Bach, was none other than Johann Adam Scheibe, whom Bach had passed over for the organist's job at St. Thomas's. The son of an organ builder who was a longtime friend of Bach, Scheibe had since then become a highly respected commentator on music, and he now became Bach's most outspoken and hurtful critic. His campaign began with the March 1737 issue of his *Critischer Musikus*, in which he said that Bach

> would be the admiration of whole nations if he had more amenity, if he did not take away the natural element in his pieces by giving them a turgid and confused style, and if he did not darken their beauty by an excess of art. . . . Every ornament, every little grace . . . he expresses completely in notes: and this not only takes away from his pieces the beauty of harmony but completely covers the melody throughout. All the voices must work with each other and be of equal difficulty, and none of them can be recognized as the principal voice. . . . Turgidity has led [him] from the natural to the artificial, and from the lofty to the somber. . . . [O]ne admires the onerous labor and

uncommon effort—which, however, are vainly employed, since they conflict with Nature.

Scheibe spoke as a member of his musical generation in claiming the primacy of what was called the "natural" in music (accompanied melody) over "artificial" harmony (counterpoint), and had he stopped there, his critique would have taken its place with others simply as evidence of the aesthetic theory of the moment. But Scheibe did not stop there. He proceeded into an ad hominem attack, suggesting that the royal court composer was overly impressed by his new title, employing the derogatory term *musikant* for Bach, the word for a journeyman performer rather than a serious musician; and he referred sharply and painfully to Bach's lack of a university education.

How can a man be faultless as a writer of music who has not sufficiently studied natural philosophy, so as to have investigated and become familiar with the forces of nature and of reason? How can he have all the advantages which are indispensable to the cultivation of good taste who has hardly troubled himself at all with the critical study . . . as necessary to music as [it is] to oratory and poetry.

Bach made no immediate reply to Scheibe, perhaps in part because just now the criticism was put into perspective by a far more serious problem at home.

§

JUST AS NO MAN CAN BE CERTAIN AT WHAT
HOUR A CHILD WILL BE BORN OR DIE; THUS
SHOULD WE SAY: LORD GOD, THE HIGHEST
GOVERNANCE IS WITH YOU, MY LIFE AND DEATH
ARE IN YOUR HANDS. . . .

Of the thirteen children Bach had with Anna Magdalena, only six, three sons and three daughters, lived longer than a few years. Some of the children were born dead or died shortly after birth, but their first child, a daughter, died at the age of three, as did their second son, and their second daughter died at the age of four. A third daughter died at seventeen months. Usually around the time one of his children died, a note would appear in the St. Thomas Church records indicating that Bach had taken Communion, which he did otherwise only twice or three times a year.

So many losses can only have focused his attention more sharply on his surviving children, and particularly on his three eldest sons. Three months after their four-year-old died, Friedemann, having finished his university studies, applied for the job of organist at St. Sophia's Church in Dresden. His father wrote a letter of recommendation for him, copied out the piece he was to play for his audition, and not only wrote his letter of application but even signed Friedemann's name to it himself.

After Friedemann moved to Dresden to take the job, Carl left the University of Leipzig to study in Frankfurt an der Oder, a strange and abrupt move. He had not yet finished his studies, and Frankfurt, a city once noted for its university and its patronage of the arts, had been downgraded by the elector of Brandenburg— Frederick's father Frederick William—to a garrison town, its former virtues subjected to his patented ridicule. The year after Carl arrived, the king sent to the university an essay he had written entitled "Sensible Thoughts on Fools and Folly," and ordered that there be a debate on the subject between professors and his court jester, which of course duly took place, no doubt to everyone's embarrassment, including the jester's. By that time the faculty had already declined markedly. The legal faculty in particular was said to be dreadful, so clearly Carl did not go there for his law studies. Perhaps he realized he could never be a big fish in his father's pond—at Frankfurt he conducted the collegium musicum—or perhaps as the second-favorite son he did not want to stay home when the favorite had managed to gain his freedom. Whatever his reason, his father cannot have been entirely pleased about his son's move to Frankfurt, and from the time Carl left home, there is no record of his coming home again until a few months before Bach died, when he returned to Leipzig to audition for his father's job.

The year after Bach's second son left him, so did his third. Gottfried Bernhard had got his father's old job in Mühlhausen, where he promptly ran up so many debts that Bach had to go to Mühlhausen, pay off all the creditors, and take his wayward son with him. He then helped Gottfried get the job in Sangerhausen that he himself had lost thirty years before, fresh out of St. Michael's Lyceum in Lüneburg. Bach even played on the council's guilt and embarrassment at having to turn him down for a favorite of the duke. Now, only months into that job, it seemed that Gottfried had run up such enormous debts that he had felt forced into hiding.

The burgomaster wrote to Bach to find out if he knew his son's whereabouts, and Bach responded with the only letter he ever wrote that spoke of such deeply personal matters.

With what pain and sorrow . . . I frame this reply, Your Honor can judge for yourself. . . . Upon my (alas! misguided) son I have not laid eyes since last year. . . . Your Honor is also not unaware that at that time I duly paid not only his board but also the Mühlhausen draft . . . but also left a few ducats behind to settle a few bills, in the hope that he would now embark upon a new mode of life. But now I must learn . . . that he once more borrowed here and there and did not change his way of living in the slightest, but on the contrary has even absented himself and not given me to date any inkling as to his whereabouts.

What shall I say or do further? Since no admonition or
even any loving care and assistance will suffice any more, I
must bear my cross in patience and leave my unruly son to
God's Mercy alone. . . .

Even so, he could not stop trying to protect his son.

I would not willingly have Your Most Noble Council bur-
dened with this request, but for my part would only pray
for patience until such time as he turns up, or it can be
learned otherwise whither he has gone. . . . I most obedi-
ently request Your Honor to have the goodness to obtain
precise information as to his whereabouts. . . .

For the year that followed there was no word from Gottfried
and no clue to where he was. The discovery that he had enrolled
at the University of Jena, intending to study law, was made only
when he turned up dead there, at the age of twenty-four. The
only cause of death ever given was "a hot fever." Bach had said
good-bye to many of his children, but this son, his last child with
Maria Barbara, was the only grown child he ever had to bury, and
the tone of his letter to the burgomaster of Sangerhausen leaves
no doubt that this was a crushing loss.

§

GOTTFRIED'S DEATH MARKS the beginning of Bach's last decade of life, a decade in which, although his quantity of work was
not as great as it had been before, its lucidity and sense of purpose
were never greater. Perhaps like his rejection by the Church authorities, the absence of his sons was a kind of liberation. Gottfried's death, as terrible as it was, at least spared him continued
heartbreak over an always unbalanced child, and the departure of

the other two meant that he did not have to live daily with the painful fact that they were in sympathy with the aesthetic theory articulated by Scheibe, even if they would not have approved the stridency or cruelty of his attack. Scheibe after all spoke very much for their generation when he criticized Bach's music as old-fashioned. Though perhaps not so categorically as Scheibe, Friedemann and Carl also saw that the "natural" in music was an easier pleasure than the "forced labor" of counterpoint; they too understood the value of feeling over rationality, *sensus* over *ratio,* simplicity over complexity. Perhaps his sons' departure freed Bach to pursue his own path without their unspoken doubts in mind. In any case that is what he did, with ever greater clarity, ambition, and force.

Bach never did respond to Scheibe, at least in words. He enlisted the aid of a colleague at the university, a professor of rhetoric named Johann Abraham Birnbaum, to compose a reply, in which he collaborated closely. When Scheibe got wind of what he was doing, he pressed the attack with a satiric letter to his own journal signed only "Cornelius" but whose author was supposed to be Bach himself.

I have never concerned myself with learned matters. . . . I have also read very few musical writings or books. . . . Since, however, I have firmly convinced myself [that] I am undoubtedly the greatest artist in music, I cannot forbear to warn you that you are in the future not to make bold to find fault with me or to condemn or make ridiculous the manifold counterpoints, canons, circular songs and all the other intricate forms of music writing that, as I have found, you have perversely called "turgid." All these things are particularly close to my heart. . . . I will not let such insult stand. Though I cannot write against you my-

self . . . one of my good friends . . . will protect me
against you, you may be sure. Don't let things come to
that, for you might very easily rue it.

After Scheibe's signed but no less mean-spirited response to
Birnbaum's long-winded defense, the professor inadvisably expanded his defense of Bach with an even more peevishly
grandiose display at much greater length than his first one. One
of Bach's students, who had a music journal of his own, issued a
somewhat more successful because shorter argument for Bach,
but at moments it too seemed to be a defense that proved the pros-
ecution's case. "If Mr. Bach at times writes the inner parts more
fully than other composers, he has taken as his model the music of
twenty or twenty-five years ago. He can write otherwise, however, when he wishes to."

Bach did seem to respond to Scheibe directly late in 1739, the
year of Gottfried's death, when he published the third volume of
his *Clavierübung*, this one a set of chorale preludes for organ. In
the middle of it were four "duets" that seemed entirely out of
place with the collection, even jarring. Bach's student-defender
saw in this volume of the *Clavierübung* "a powerful refutation to
those who have dared to criticize the composition of the Honor-
able Court Composer," and so it was perhaps intended to be. In
his book *Bach and the Meanings of Counterpoint*, David Yearsley
finds Bach arguing with Scheibe and his generation most clearly
in the F-major Duetto, which begins with a sweetly melodic, entirely pretty fugue (read: Counterpoint doesn't have to mean serious or complicated). As the piece progresses, though, our
melodic innocent is led into an ever deeper and more winding cat-
acombs of precisely wrought contrapuntal development, a very
unsettling passage from pastoral serenity into a scene out of
Brueghel. As if bound in chains, the melody is made to follow
counterpoint wherever it leads, even as what happens as a result

defies rather than courts any notion of good taste. Bach slams his point home when he returns to the sun of the opening section and shows us our sweet melody in a new light: as an empty amusement. "The piece's sprightliness now seems coy," as Yearsley puts it, "its pleasantness more like mockingly undemanding pleasantries." In music that is among the least pretty and most beautiful he ever composed, Bach had answered Scheibe and the aesthetic ideals of the Enlightenment in no uncertain terms, and not for the last time.

## XI

*WAR AND PEACE AND*

*A MECHANICAL DUCK*

FREDERICK COLLECTED PEOPLE THE WAY OTHERS COL-
lect napkin rings or yachting pennants. As soon as he took the
throne he began to recruit various eminent writers, scientists, and
philosophers to his court as members of a rejuvenated Prussian
Academy, for intellectual companionship and as trophies. During
his first week as king he brought back the Enlightenment philosopher Christian Wolff from the exile into which his father had banished him, and in no time he had also managed to recruit the
Swiss mathematician Euler and the French scientist Maupertuis,
who became head of the academy. The one he really wanted as a
jewel in his crown, though—or as featured attraction in his
celebrity zoo—was Voltaire. Frederick would not have dared
bring him to Prussia when his father was alive; he was, after all,
French. But not long after Fédéric became Frederick II, after four
years of the most fervent mutual admiration in the history of letters, they met.

The circumstances were a little awkward: Frederick was in
bed, wrapped in a shawl, shivering with fever; and, for all the pacific idealism of the *Anti-Machiavel,* there were two thousand
Prussian soldiers outside who were no escort. They were in the
town of Wesel to settle an old dispute over the nearby barony of

Herstal, which had been inherited by Frederick's father eight years before but ever since had rebuffed its Prussian overlords in favor of the prince-bishop of Liège. Since the bishop had the support of France and Austria, Frederick's ministers advised him against using force to regain Herstal, fearing the start of a wider war. Not for the last time, Frederick dismissed their advice. "The ministers are clever when they discuss politics," he said, "but when they discuss war it is like an Iroquois talking about astronomy." Just before Voltaire arrived Frederick had given the bishop an ultimatum and two days to think it over. Despite his own pacific ideas, Voltaire was delighted, joking that Frederick had engaged the bishop in theological debate "and brought two thousand good arguments with him."

Voltaire was always ambivalent about power, infatuated at one moment, disgusted the next. He once said that Virgil "had the weakness of paying Augustus an homage that no man should ever give to another man, no matter who he is"—which only proved, as Peter Gay cracked, "the Socratic maxim 'know thyself' was imperfectly realized in the Enlightenment."

Describing his first meeting with Frederick in a letter to a friend, Voltaire gushed:

> I saw one of the most amiable men in the world . . . a philosopher without austerity, full of sweetness, complaisance and obliging ways. . . . I needed an effort to remember that the man sitting at the foot of my bed was a sovereign with an army of 100,000 men.

Actually the bed, at least the first bed they met in, was Frederick's. A world-class hypochondriac, Voltaire was deeply at home in sickrooms, and no sooner were the formal introductions over than he was sitting next to the king in bed and taking his pulse. He

advised Frederick to take quinine: It had worked for the king of
Sweden, he said, and though Frederick was clearly nothing like
that militaristic land-grabber, their bodies presumably worked the
same way. Frederick said that if Voltaire's visit was not enough to
cure him, they should call for the confessor.

While they basked in their mutual worship, the Bishop of
Liège considered his options. As soon as the basking was over, in
the absence of a response, Frederick's troops moved against him.
(Finally Frederick decided simply to sell Herstal to the bishop for
an extortionate price.) At least when they were on good terms,
Voltaire justified Frederick's action against the Bishop of Liège
and even made excuses for his later, far more serious military exploits, but the fact is that he had seen the last of his philosopher-
king. And despite a lifelong regard for Voltaire's intelligence and
his gifts, Frederick had seen the last of his onetime idol as well.
The next time they saw each other, two months later, Voltaire
came to Potsdam as a spy.

§

DURING THE FIRST MONTHS of his reign, Frederick was
everything Voltaire could have wished for in an enlightened
monarch. The author of the high-minded *Anti-Machiavel* (whose
authorship was supposed to be a secret but was in fact widely
known and celebrated) announced a policy of absolute religious
toleration, enacted judicial reforms, abolished torture in criminal
cases other than treason and murder, and greatly curtailed newspaper censorship. He set up a new office for the poor. He let it be
known that he saw himself as "first servant of the state" and that
he considered it his job to make his subjects "comfortable and
happy." He set loose his father's giants, which made his senior officers happy, since they were relieved of the need to recruit them,
and he emphasized actual readiness for battle over parade-ground
beauty. ("The soldier polished his rifle . . . the cavalier his bri-

dle . . . the manes of horses were dressed with ribbons," he said. "If peace had lasted beyond 1740 we would probably now have rouge and beauty spots.") He demanded more discipline from his officers, forbidding the customary abuse of cadets, and he made examples of those who persisted in such brutality "so that everyone can see that I will tolerate no such excesses." He made it known that he disliked flatterers, and he treated those who had persecuted him years before without prejudice, allowing them to retain their rank and privileges. He did, however, give Katte's father a promotion, and he brought back his old tutor Duhan from exile and gave him the salary he had promised more than twenty years before. When Duhan asked what he was to do for it, Frederick wrote, "Live happily in Berlin, my dear Duhan, and enjoy in these later years all that you deserve."

Frederick knew his honeymoon would be short. He came to power determined to expand his territory and make Prussia a power in Europe at least equal to Austria and the Hapsburgs, and he did not underestimate the size or danger of that ambition. He knew—every European leader knew—that when this emperor, Charles VI, died, the map of Europe would change dramatically. For one thing, he was going to die without a male heir, and while most powers had signed on to the so-called Pragmatic Sanction, which would allow him to be succeeded by his daughter through her husband, everyone knew the empire was crumbling. The leaders of its parts were expected to wrest themselves free of it whenever they could, and Frederick, who had long thought his father was mistaken to think the emperor was his ally, was first among them. He knew he needed his independence—from the Hapsburgs and anyone else—to gain the territory that would give him a nation with secure boundaries, and he knew as well that accomplishing that would require the shrewd, not to say flagrantly deceitful management of alliances, among experts in that game.

But Frederick reveled in deception. Knowing very well that he was being closely watched for his intentions, he carefully advertised his unpredictability, offering alliance and war to all the pivotal antagonists. He sent an envoy to France, telling him that troops would be mobilized in Berlin while he was in Paris and the diplomat should use that fact to good effect. "The increase . . . in my troops during your stay at Versailles," he wrote, "will furnish you the occasion to speak lively and impetuously on my behalf; you may say that it should be feared that this increase would light a fire which would set Europe ablaze, that it was the way of the young to be daring. . . . You may say that by nature I am partial to France. . . ." At the same time, an envoy to London was to make a fuss over the fact that his counterpart was in Paris. "Mention with a show of jealousy that he is one of my intimates, that he possesses my confidence, and that he does not go to France to waste his time. . . . Speak a great deal of my inclination for [England]. . . ."

He was no less deceitful with his friends. When Charles died and his daughter Maria Theresa came to power, the author of the *Anti-Machiavel* wrote to Voltaire, as if confused by what had happened: "This death disturbs all my pacific ideas. . . ." To his close friend Algarotti at the same moment he wrote: "It is only a question of putting those plans into action which I have been hatching so long in my head."

§

EVERYONE KNEW THAT Prussia had long felt it had claims on the small provinces of Jülich and Berg, but Frederick's ambition was bigger than that. He wanted Silesia, Austria's most prosperous territory, a mineral- and trade-rich province, fifteen thousand square miles of fertile land with Poland and Hungary to the east, Bohemia to the south, Brandenburg and Saxony to the west and north. It brought in no less than a quarter of all the Hapsburg tax receipts, so Vienna could be expected to be more than a little unwilling to part with it. Frederick's ministers once again counseled caution, and once again he overruled them. He argued (correctly) that Maria Theresa, at twenty-three and new to command, was weak and almost completely ignorant of politics and that her treasury was depleted, her revenues mortgaged long into the future. Her army was not battle-ready, her generals were old and tired, and all the powers of Europe had aims for her territories, not just him; if he waited he would lose the advantage of surprise. Beyond that, Silesia's border with Brandenburg was completely undefended. The weakness of Prussia's claim to the territory hardly entered the discussion. When the legal argument for it was presented to him in a brief, he wrote in the margin, "Bravo! The work of an excellent charlatan."

The man in whom Frederick most confided, at this time and others, was Charles Étienne Jordan, a Lutheran minister who had lost his faith and abandoned his pastorate when his wife died. The affluent son of a banker, he absorbed himself in study and travel after her death, visiting such Enlightenment figures as Voltaire and Alexander Pope, and later wrote a memoir about this period entitled *Voyage littéraire*. Frederick could never make a courtier of him; he lived not at the palace but with his young daughter at his own home in town. Perhaps in part because Jordan never asked anything of him, Frederick gave him a real job when he became king, making Jordan his advocate for the poor, and his letters to Jordan reflect genuine affection and respect, one of the few friends of whom that can be said. His candor with Jordan was apparently complete, sometimes horribly so. He confessed to Jordan that he was driven to the invasion of Silesia by

> my age, fiery passion, the lust for glory, curiosity even
> [and] if I am to be perfectly frank . . . the satisfaction of
> seeing my name in the gazettes and thereafter in the pages
> of history.

Knowing Frederick's military ambition and anxious to know his plans, France's Cardinal Fleury thought he could use Frederick's weakness for Voltaire to find out the new king's intentions and so sent him to Potsdam as a spy. But Voltaire was a babe in these woods. Fleury had written Voltaire a letter in which he talked about France's peaceful intentions toward Prussia, and Voltaire later wrote Fleury coyly that he had "obeyed the orders your eminence did not give me" by showing the letter to Frederick. Of course, that gave Voltaire away to Frederick instantly; he knew Fleury well enough—and he knew that Fleury knew Voltaire well enough—to know this was no indiscretion. Later Voltaire excitedly told the French ambassador that Algarotti had shown him a letter in which the king was clearly "in the grip of the demon of war," but if that happened the disclosure was intentional. Frederick trusted very few people in this delicate period. Jordan was one, Algarotti was another. Voltaire could report to Fleury that Berlin was full of troops, that the river Spree was choked with boats carrying artillery and supplies, but he could not say where they were headed. Frederick's beloved old tutor Kalkstein asked him one day if the march was to Silesia. "Can you keep a secret?" Frederick asked. Of course, he said. "So can I."

Frederick, a lover of deception in all its forms, scheduled a masquerade party for the night he set for the beginning of the war—December 13, in the first year of his reign. When the party was over he rode to a rendezvous with his main force of twenty-four thousand men for the march on Silesia. Only after the invasion was under way did his minister in Vienna present Maria Theresa's government with his intentions and his proposal that she let him keep Silesia in return for reparations and a defense treaty. This poor minister was also saddled with the responsibility of arguing that Frederick was only taking Silesia for the good of the empire. The fact that she said no to Frederick's terms was not surprising, but the ferocity of her response shocked Frederick and all the rest of Europe. "Never, never will the queen renounce an inch of all her hereditary lands, though she resist with all that remains to her. Rather the Turks before Vienna, rather cession of the Netherlands to France, rather any concession to Bavaria and Saxony than renunciation of Silesia." She called Frederick the "heretic king . . . an enemy without faith or justice . . . that evil animal . . . that monster." She thus gave notice of a new force on the European stage—a woman armed, as one biographer put it, "with nothing but her character."

For the time being, however, her military's lack of readiness was decisive. Frederick's forces met almost no resistance in Lower Silesia, and in mid-January he wrote:

> My dear Mr. Jordan, my sweet Mr. Jordan, my quiet Mr. Jordan, my good, my benign, my peaceable, my most humane Mr. Jordan, I announce to Your Serenity the conquest of Silesia. . . .

So ended the first campaign of Frederick's First Silesian War, which, despite several pitched battles and many thousands of casualties, he would win decisively a year later.

§

DURING THE TWO YEARS after the First Silesian War, while the general European War of the Austrian Succession (which he had started) continued without him, Frederick resumed his recruitment of talent to Prussia for his rejuvenated academy, for his chamber music group, for the new Berlin Opera, and for his dinner table. Among his targets was an inventor and something of a charlatan named Jacques de Vaucanson, who in 1738 had presented to the Royal Academy of Sciences in Paris an astonishing thing: a six-foot-six-inch copy of a statue known as *The Marble Faun of Coyfevaux* that could play the transverse flute. This wooden statue of a shepherd had precisely movable lips, throat, tongue, and fingers connected to an intricate system of levers, pulleys, and bellows; and the great Fontenelle himself, secretary of the academy, certified in his abstract of the inventor's presentation that Vaucanson's faun could play twelve different tunes "with an Exactness which has deserved the Admiration of the Publick . . . imitating by Art all that is necessary for a Man to perform in . . . a Café." Even more amazing, in a way, was Vaucanson's mechanical duck. "It stretches out its Neck to take Corn out of your Hand," the inventor wrote in a letter to the Abbé de Fontaine, "it swallows it . . . [and the] Matter digested in the Stomach is conducted by Pipes, (as in an Animal by the Guts) quite to the Anus, where there is a Sphincter that lets it out." A later model could even fart. "The smell which now spreads through the room becomes almost unbearable," one happy witness wrote. "We wish to express to the artist-inventor the pleasure which this demonstration gave to us."

Vaucanson's duck was a fraud; the "excrement" was prepared and hidden in the works, to be expelled on cue, but the flute player was very real and by all accounts a creditable performer. This raised the specter—tantalizing to some, threatening to others— that a machine might one day actually play the flute with greater technical facility than any human. Frederick's flute teacher Quantz was cool to the idea. "With skill," he wrote,

a musical machine could be constructed that would play certain pieces with a quickness and exactitude so remarkable that no human being could equal it either with his fingers or with his tongue. Indeed it would excite astonishment, but it would never move you.

His student, however, found the flute-playing automaton captivating, and when Vaucanson declined his offer to move to Berlin, Frederick built a factory so he could make them for himself.

The relation between man and machine—which devolved to questions about the nature and existence of the soul—was very much au courant in the mid-eighteenth century, and it figured nowhere so prominently as in the debate over aesthetics. "Our manner of being is wholly arbitrary," Montesquieu wrote for his entry on "Taste" in Diderot's *Encyclopedia*.

> We could have been made as we were, or differently. But if we had been made differently, we would see differently; one organ more or less in our machine would have given us another kind of eloquence, another poetry; a different structure of the same organs would have produced still another poetry: for instance, if the constitution of our organs had made us capable of longer attention, all the rules which proportion the disposition of the subject to the measure of our attention would disappear.

Perhaps the ultimate statement of eighteenth-century materialism was *Man a Machine*, a monograph by the Dutch physician Julien Offroy de La Mettrie, who argued that there really is not much difference between people and animals. If we have a soul, it must be physical, because clearly our feeling states are affected by all sorts of physical things—disease, sleep, drugs, food, age, sex, the climate. We have five senses and we have imagination and reason, but they cannot tell us what if anything may lie beyond this single, physical dimension of existence, and we should stop pretending otherwise. "Man," he wrote, "is a machine that winds its own springs." Years later, in a eulogy for La Mettrie, Frederick commended his mechanistic worldview this way:

[H]e could clearly see that thought is but a consequence of the organization of the machine, and that the disturbance of the springs has considerable influence on that part of us which the metaphysicians call soul. . . . [H]e boldly bore the torch of experience into the night of metaphysics; he tried to explain by aid of anatomy the thin texture of understanding, and he found only mechanism where others had supposed an essence superior to matter.

La Mettrie claimed not to be an atheist. He thought there might be a God, but since one could not possibly know whether there was a God or not because of the limitations of the machine, it really did not matter one way or the other. Such an argument was little use against his enemies' charge of atheism, however, and La Mettrie's book proved so scandalous—and the scandal so delighted Frederick—that La Mettrie accepted the king's invitation to move to Prussia, where he spent the rest of his life.

§

RECRUITING PERFORMERS FOR his new opera house in Berlin was a great deal easier than recruiting intellectuals for the academy, and Frederick pursued them with the same avidity his father had shown for giants. One famous Venetian dancer signed and then canceled a contract to come to Berlin, and when authorities in Venice would not act to enforce the contract, Frederick had one of their ambassadors kidnapped and held until they did. (Frederick may have had an affair with her, or she may have been a beard. Voltaire cracked that if he did want her sexually, it was because she had boyish legs.)

Even during the war, Frederick had worked feverishly on plans for his opera company and the house itself. He had opinions on every singer and dancer, every detail of the house's decoration and sets, even rehearsal schedules. When it opened in December

1742 it was not yet finished, but it was a marvel. There was room in the square outside for a thousand carriages, and among its mechanical wonders was its provision for balls: After the opera, diners would adjourn to a building alongside the concert hall, whose floor would then be raised to stage level by pneumatic jacks. The stage scenery would be camouflaged by columns, and the torch-lit room would suddenly come alive with spouting-naiad fountains and statues of the immortals. It was said that Frederick spent a million thalers on the opera house. The fact that he spent most of that money while his treasury was being depleted by war is some measure of his commitment to it.

§

SOON ENOUGH, FREDERICK saw his attention to the arts diverted once again by diplomacy and the prospect of war. No one expected the peace that ended the First Silesian War to settle the matter. By the end of it, secret treaties had been made and broken among all the players, so although Frederick's last treaty was with Austria, it was considered very unlikely that Maria Theresa would sit quiet forever.

Fleury once more played to Voltaire's patriotism (but counted on his infatuation with Frederick and his love of the game of duplicity) to get him to go to Potsdam again as a spy. This time Voltaire was given cover: His new play *La Mort de Caesar* was "banned" in Paris to demonstrate a rupture with the court and so to make Frederick think he might actually move to Prussia. Voltaire wrote to Frederick inviting himself to Potsdam in a letter whose oozy deceit bears reading at length:

When I am ready to weep over the decadence of the arts I say to myself: There is a monarch in Europe who loves them and cultivates them and is the glory of his century. Then I say, I shall soon see him, this charming monarch, this King who is also a man, this crowned Chaulieu, this Tacitus, this Xenophon. . . . You, Sire, are my *grande passion*. I have much to tell Your Majesty. I will lay my heart at your feet, and you will decide if it is possible for me to pass my life at your side. You will be the arbiter of my destiny. . . . Do not forget me, my adorable sovereign.

In this "friendship" of vipers, Frederick had the nastier bite. In one of his letters Voltaire had jokingly referred to an old nemesis, the *ancien évêque de Mirepoix* (former Bishop of Mirepoix), as the *âne évêque* (the ass bishop). Frederick sent it to his envoy in Paris with a note:

Here is part of a letter of Voltaire, which I beg you to convey to the Bishop of Mirepoix by a roundabout way without you and me appearing in the matter. My intention is to make it so hot for him in France that he will have to come to Berlin.

He also forwarded some bad poetry of his own in Voltaire's name that referred to Louis XV as "the most stupid of kings." The poetry was so clumsy, though, that Voltaire was easily able to disown it.

In his attempts to act the spy, Voltaire was once again an abject failure. Frederick knew exactly why he had suddenly decided to come to Berlin and refused to discuss politics with him, which he said would be like a man "offering a glass of medicine to his mistress." Frederick wrote of Voltaire to Algarotti: "It is a pity that such a mean soul is mated to such a fine genius. But I shall say nothing, because I need him for my French studies." He meant that literally. The man he had called the very incarnation of Racine would remain in his menagerie as a French teacher.

§

FLEURY WAS RIGHT to suspect the king of Prussia would be up to something just now. Two years after the First Silesian War the situation in Europe was almost the reverse of the way Frederick had left it: Austria was newly ascendant, having recaptured Bavaria and Bohemia from an "emperor" who had been voted in by the German electors and supported on the battlefield by France to challenge Maria Theresa. Now France was in full retreat and the electors' would-be supplanter had no more money and no land. Most worrisome, Frederick discovered that Maria Theresa had secretly made a coalition with England, Holland, and his neighbor Saxony. One of his spies gave him a letter from "Uncle" George II to Maria Theresa that made a clear and disturbing reference to Silesia: "*Ce qui est bon à prendre est bon à rendre.* [What's good to take is good to give back.]" Saxony's siding with Austria was trouble even closer to home.

In the spring of 1744 Frederick attempted to regroup the German princes under the banner of their landless emperor, Charles Albert, formerly elector of Bohemia, but he had a hard time selling his plan. No one was buying his argument from German patriotism or his appeal to the assaulted dignity of their propped-up emperor. Even after promising that he would virtually carry the war himself, he could only get two of the electors to sign on with him in the "Union of Frankfurt," which pledged itself to get Bavaria and Bohemia back for Charles Albert. Frederick's motive for going to war, of course, had nothing to do with Charles Albert or his "empire" but lay in the absolutely correct insight that what was bad for Austria was good for Prussia and vice versa.

This would not be like the First Silesian War. Maria Theresa's now battle-hardened troops had been reinforced by twenty thou-

sand Saxon and sixty thousand Hungarian soldiers and a
bankroll from Frederick's not-very-avuncular uncle George. In
the fall and winter of 1743, Frederick's forces moved deep into
Bohemia, but his French allies, who were supposed to keep Austria's forces engaged, folded. Undaunted, Frederick moved on to
capture Prague, then farther south in terrible weather. In the process he overextended his forces, and this time he was not in
Protestant Silesia but in loyal Catholic, Hapsburg territory,
where the Prussians were despised. The forces against him had
perfect intelligence, and Frederick could recruit no spies. He was
chronically short of supplies, his troops were laid low by dysen-
tery and typhus, the weather was unremittingly cold, desertion
became epidemic, and finally Frederick was forced to retreat to
Silesia. "No general ever committed more faults than the king in
this campaign," he said. Later he told someone, "Good fortune is
often more fatal to princes than adversity. The former intoxicates
them with presumption, the latter renders them circumspect and
modest."

By the next spring he had rebuilt his forces, and this time when
the Austrian and Saxon armies came to meet him, near Hohenfried-
berg in Silesia, he was ready. Disarmed with false intelligence, they
were unprepared for the Prussian assault, and after two pitched battles, the Austrians and Saxons made a decisive retreat.

§

WITH THE AUSTRIAN RETREAT, the Saxon elector fled to
Prague, and the Prussian army occupied all of Saxony, including
Leipzig. The occupation was mercifully brief. Prussian troops
were filled with "an unparalleled hatred of the Saxons," Frederick had written approvingly before one especially bloody battle,
and they had grown no fonder of Saxons during the rest of the
war, in which they lost tens of thousands of their fellow soldiers.
During the occupation, Frederick made himself at home in Dres-

den, which had been heavily damaged by the Prussian bombard-ment. In the rubble, as it were, he gave dinner parties, enjoyed himself with the royal Kapelle, and did a little discreet looting. He sent sets of Meissen porcelain to friends—tokens, he said, of "the fragility of human fortunes"—and, in addition to some cash and other odds and ends, the spoils of war would come to include a few of Dresden's best musicians. At the elector's birthday two months before, the Dresden Kapellmeister Johann Adolph Hasse had put on a new opera in his honor titled *Arminio*. Frederick re-quested a repeat performance for himself. The Kapelle did sev-eral concerts for him, and he impressed them with some flute sonatas of his own. Hasse actually dedicated a new flute sonata to Frederick while he was there and accompanied him on the harpsi-chord when he played it. Frederick gave him a diamond ring in appreciation.

The pleasantries were cut short by a peace agreement, which was signed on Christmas Day 1745. Leipzig could not have got a better Christmas present—the occupation had been particu-larly harsh there—and Bach apparently conducted a new can-tata for the occasion, his *Gloria in Excelsis Deo* (BWV 191), which he drew directly from the *Gloria* of the short mass he had dedicated and presented to the Saxon elector a dozen years be-fore. Despite the fact that its lyrics were in Latin, the congrega-tion would have needed no translation, and the words—"Glory to God in the highest . . . and on earth, peace among people of goodwill"—would have rung resoundingly triumphant just then, as the Prussian soldiers withdrew. This is another of the moments in the course of this story when it makes wonderful sense to stop reading, to find an LP or CD of what would later become the B-minor Mass, and try to imagine what hearing Bach's "Gloria in excelsis Deo" and even more his "Et in terra pax" would have been like on that particular Christmas Day at St. Thomas's Church in Leipzig.

§

DESPITE APPEARANCES to the contrary during his triumphant coda in Dresden, the Frederick who made his way home to Berlin had been dramatically changed by the past two years of war. He had not obeyed the old soldier's axiom never to look at the faces of the dead. More than once he lingered in battlegrounds when the fighting was over, overseeing medical treatment for his forces and the enemy's alike, and these were unforgettably gruesome sights. At night after the worst of the battles, with thousands dead and thousands of others screaming in pain, fires mercilessly lit the scene, to help the surgeons continue their grisly work through the night and to roast dead cavalry horses for food. After one such scene, Frederick wrote his brother: "We have beaten the enemy, but . . . we are the most distressed victors that you can imagine. God preserve us from such another bloody and murderous affair." Many more were still ahead of him when he wrote that, and the war left him a bitterly despairing misanthrope. After another long and bloody battle, he wrote, "I regard [men] as a herd of stags in the park of a grand nobleman, with no other function than to breed and fill up the park." Since for him there was no principle attached to his cause but power, how could he have felt anything but despair at the ways of such a world? There is no evidence he ever reflected on the fact that it was a world he was making.

At home, two of his best friends had died, Keyserling and Jordan, and the war had given him no time to mourn. Jordan's last letter to Frederick reads like a last attempt to rescue him from his nihilism, and perhaps to recover in some measure the belief Jordan had himself lost with the death of his wife.

Sire,
My sickness has become so much worse that I can no longer hope for a cure. I have come to realize, in this situ-

ation, the necessity of a thoughtful, enlightened religion. Without that we are the most miserable beings in the universe. I hope that Your Majesty will remember, after my death, that as I fought superstition with all my strength, I always had at heart the interest of Christianity, however removed from the notions of theologians. As one cannot know the need for valor except in danger, one cannot know the consolation of religion except in suffering. . . .

But Frederick was beyond redemption. In a letter after news of Jordan's death reached him on the battlefield, he wrote, "I think the only really happy men are those who love no one." He wrote his tutor Jacques Duhan from the war that he was wrapped in "a heartrending grief more gloomy and grave than mourning clothes." He had been back in Berlin for less than a month when he sat on Duhan's deathbed as well.

Frederick's family and remaining friends felt the brunt of the change in him after the war. He began to abuse his brothers with the same contempt (though without the violence) that his father had visited on him. He became increasingly brutal with even his most senior ministers, and his court lost its life. He was even on bad terms with Wilhelmina. When she discovered that her husband had been unfaithful to her with one of her ladies-in-waiting and best friends, the daughter of a Prussian general, she decided the best way to get rid of her was to marry her off to someone far away. In the event she arranged a marriage to an officer in the Austrian army just as Frederick was about to enter the Second Silesian War against Austria. He was furious at what he perceived as her disloyalty at such a moment (as was the girl's father), and Wilhelmina could not bring herself to tell him why she had arranged the marriage. Their letters—his condemnations, her entreaties—crossed, and years passed before he discovered the truth. Even then it was years more before he could truly forgive her.

He still held his concerts in the evening, but increasingly he devoted himself to work. He seemed to be growing more and more like his father, who came to him in recurrent dreams, always accompanied by a phalanx of soldiers. He orders them to arrest Frederick, bind his hands, and take him into custody. His sister Wilhelmina is there, and he asks her why their father is doing this to him. "What is the charge?"

"It's because you don't love your father enough," she says.

He always awoke from this dream in a cold sweat, he said, "as if I had been swimming in a river."

One night the scene changed at the end of the dream, and this time he was back at the war, on a desolate battlefield, where his father came to him again, this time without the soldiers.

"Have I done well?" Frederick asks him, and his father says yes, he had done well.

"I am content then," Frederick tells him. "Your approval means more to me than that of the whole world."

Frederick actually worked even harder than his father. There was so much to be done, so many problems that had been neglected because of the war—not enough schools, not enough hospitals, and for the moment not enough money, thanks to the war, to do anything about them. To raise revenue, he devised and undertook reforms to increase commerce—draining marshes, luring émigrés to Prussia to settle and farm the reclaimed lands, promoting Prussian exports. He worked from four in the morning until midnight some nights, reading every bit of diplomatic correspondence and writing his own replies, supervising every ministry, personally adjudicating subjects' complaints, writing long discourses on matters from taxes to animal husbandry. People were awestruck by his dedication and his energy. He was tireless, relentless, reliable as a machine.

## XII.

## *THE NIGHT OF A*

## *MUSICAL OFFERING*

Frederick had hired Bach's son Carl even before he had become king, during the palmy years in Rheinsberg, and he kept Carl on for thirty years, despite the fact that he never quite liked him or his music. In his autobiography, Carl said he kept working for Frederick despite "one or two lucrative offers from elsewhere [because] His Majesty was gracious enough to increase my salary substantially each time this happened." The truth was not quite so pleasant. He was hired at the unimpressive salary of three hundred thalers, but as often as he made the request, and for all the many wonderful compositions he dedicated to the king, he could not get a raise. In 1755, seventeen years after he started playing in the Prussian court Kapelle, the king's chamberlain sent Frederick a memo about Bach's latest petition.

> His other complaints are too numerous [to list] but his principal grievance is that he can no longer survive on 300 Thalers. In every year of service he has needed to spend a further 600 Thalers—Nichelman and Agricola were his pupils, and they get 600 Thalers, he humbly requests Your Majesty to increase his salary, or else to release him from his duties.

Frederick contemptuously scrawled in the margin,

Bach is lying; Agricola gets only 500 Thalers. [Bach] once played in a concert here and now he's getting cocky. His pay will be increased, but he must wait for the next round of financial measures.

Seventeen years is a long time to wait for a raise. That he stayed is some indication of just how glamorous and promising he thought the job to be, and why not? The king, who was only two years older than Carl, was clearly serious about music. Even when Frederick was still hiding from his father the fact that he had any musicians at all, he had already hired the great flautist Quantz as well as the famous Benda brothers, and his Kapellmeister was no less than the eminent composer Graun, on whom Carl saw Frederick lavishing all praise and glory (he and Quantz both made two thousand thalers to Carl's three hundred). Carl was a composer of some accomplishment as well when he went to work for Frederick, at least he had been so recognized in Frankfurt, and he had reason to believe, at least at first, that it would be only a matter of time before the king similarly perceived and rewarded his gifts.

Fifteen months after Frederick took the throne, when Carl finally began to receive a regular salary, "old Bach" came to Berlin for a visit. There was no question of his meeting Frederick on that trip since the king was at the First Silesian War. Saxony was then still allied with Prussia, having even allowed Frederick to take his troops across its territory for the initial invasion of Silesia, so Bach was breaching no protocol by making the trip, which had the dual purpose of seeing his son settled in (as he had done with Friedemann in Dresden) and of bringing a recent commission, his "Aria with Different Variations," to its patron, Count Hermann von Keyserling.

A man of worldly wisdom and taste with a broad knowledge of music, Keyserling (an uncle of Frederick's beloved "Caesarion") was Russian ambassador to the Saxon court in

Dresden when he first met and became a patron of Bach (he also sent his daughter to study with Friedemann). He had been moved to Berlin when power shifted there on Frederick's accession. The story goes that Keyserling commissioned Bach's "Aria with Different Variations" because he was a chronic insomniac who wanted something for his keyboardist, a sometime student of Bach named Johann Gottlieb Goldberg, to play for him at night. As good as it is, the story is somewhat implausible, since Goldberg was only fourteen years old at the time, and the *Goldberg Variations* could hardly put anyone to sleep. The aria is peaceful enough, a wistfully melancholic French dance Bach had written for Anna Magdalena fifteen years before, but based on its simple, eight-note bass line, Bach contrived thirty variations of astonishing vigor and ingenuity, using virtually every style and device of European music. Perhaps his greatest masterpiece for keyboard, certainly among his most difficult, the Goldbergs may have been beyond even Bach's virtuosity by this time in his life. Passionate, bold, tender, playful, lyrical, and deeply introspective by turns, every movement of the work is full of fire and light, guaranteed to make Keyserling or anyone else bolt upright in bed and stay there.

Among the loveliest pieces in the set are canons. Every third variation is a canon—the first a canon at the unison (meaning that the second voice enters on the same note as the first), the second a canon at the second (the second voice is one whole interval higher than the first), the third a canon at the third, and so on. In place of the tenth canon, however, just before the final movement, which is a note-for-note repeat of the opening aria, he wrote a quodlibet, like the ones the Bach family used to sing at their re-unions, in which two folk songs play against each other. The first of these songs, "I haven't been with you for a long, long time, come here," was traditionally an evening's last dance, and here refers to the opening aria, which is an hour's worth of variations in the past by now and is coming back in the next movement to close off the work. The second song goes "Cabbage and beets have driven me away / Had my mother cooked meat I might longer have stayed." Bach was not above making a plain joke about flatulence, but given the character of the previous reference, it is just possible he was making self-effacing fun of his own contrapuntal extravagance: Having forsworn the "meat" of simpler composition, he would spare his audience any further complexity (the sort of thing Frederick William might have called "wind-making") and simply say a merciful good-bye. Whatever the literal joke may be, the winding together of these two folk tunes—over the same bass line as all the other variations, at the very end of this long, bravura display of every sort of counterpoint—is both a whimsical retort to those who denigrate canon as self-serious and itself a dazzling contrapuntal act. The aria's return at the end, precisely as it was stated at the outset, closes the circle: We have listened to an extravagantly various set of variations on a simple series of notes that represents a stunning demonstration of the ideal of identity in variety, analogue of the indivisible presence of God in the manifold, phenomenal world, a feat that was possible only in counterpoint.

The *Goldberg Variations*, which Bach published as the fourth and final volume of his *Clavierübung* (and for which Keyserling compensated him with a hundred *louis d'or*, about $4,000, in a golden goblet), was the first great work of his last decade, and there could have been no more pointed sign to where the rest of his work was headed. There would be no quarter given to the aesthetic imperatives and criticism of Scheibe, his sons, or anyone else.

§

EXACTLY WHAT CARL made of his father's music is ambiguous in the literature, perhaps because it may have been unclear to him.

On the one hand he expressed great respect for his father's genius and dedication, which he witnessed every day of his young life. On the other hand, as he admitted after his father was gone, he had needed to break away, to become himself as a composer and as a man, and that involved defining himself to some extent in opposition to his father's aesthetic ideals. Even at his most reverential, as in the obituary he wrote soon after Bach died, his praise had rejection in it: His father's melodies were "strange [but] always varied, rich in invention and resembling no other composer." His "serious temperament drew him to music that was serious, elaborate and profound." In Carl's mouth, these were not unambiguous compliments. Like all important musicians of his generation, Carl admired the *galant* work of his Berlin colleagues (the best of it anyway; his father's son, after all, he complained bitterly about the emptiest of it). His very popular *Essay on the True Art of Playing Keyboard Instruments* talked almost exclusively in terms of the *galant* and its dramatic child, the *empfindsamer Stil* ("highly sensitive style"). For Carl and his generation, the expression of feeling in music was all, and the affection that mattered was not a text or other object for depiction but the feeling state of the performer and composer. Carl was almost theatrically demonstrative when he played. "A player cannot move others unless he himself is moved," he wrote. "This cannot come off without corresponding gestures, which would only be denied by someone who is constrained by his lack of sensitivity to sit in front of the instrument like a carved image." When his father played even the most passionate or technically difficult passage, he barely moved.

While Friedemann, the first and favorite, performed Bach's works often on high feast days and rarely changed them except to correct mistakes in the score, Carl, even when he left Frederick's court for Hamburg and was desperate for material to fill the city's demanding schedule of music, performed his father's works infre-quently, and when he did he often replaced Bach's arias with his own. He also routinely lifted his father's works without attribution; every one of the twenty-one passions he wrote in his late life as musical director in Hamburg has one or more thefts in it (to be fair, he was not alone in doing that; Handel was infamous for stealing others' work, and Friedemann, whether for profit or expediency, once erased his father's name on a work and replaced it with his own).

Carl was clearly of two minds about canon as well. Even as he shared them in correspondence with colleagues, he was said to have disdained them. In a parlor-game stunt that emphasizes nothing so much as their mechanical, technical quality, he created an "Invention by Which Six Measures of Double Counterpoint Can Be Written Without a Knowledge of the Rules." The sheet on the facing page is one of four which come with instructions: First, pick six numbers at random (low numbers, to make it easy). Use the first to determine how many measures to count from the beginning to get the first note. Then count nine measures ahead to pick up the second, nine again for the third, and so on, until you have completed a full measure in 2/4 time (four eighth notes, two quarter notes, one quarter and two eighth notes, or one half note). Then do the same for the second measure—use the second random number to count forward for the first, count nine forward from there for the second, and so on; and likewise through all six measures. One table of notes will supply the upper voice, another the lower. Six measures of perfectly acceptable counterpoint result every time. A machine could do it.

According to Dr. Charles Burney, an itinerant music historian who visited with him late in his life, Carl wrote off canons as "dry and despicable pedantry" which demonstrated only "a total want of genius in anyone who was fond of such wretched studies." Carl's attitude toward canons was surely more nuanced than

that, but the position as Burney reports it was entirely in keeping with that of Carl's generation, very much including his onetime patron Frederick the Great.

§

AS BACH WENT his own way, the music journals continued their spirited debate. Scheibe in particular could not let go. As late as 1745, his *Critischer Musikus* rehashed the whole ugly argument he had started about Bach eight years before, reprinting his initial attack as well as Birnbaum's response, his response to Birnbaum's response, and then Birnbaum's endless defense of his response, which Scheibe now sprayed with 164 nasty-to-savage footnotes, some of them of great length. Both Birnbaum and Scheibe had by this time become very tiresome, and we need not join them in their mud wrestle, because in the end, the battle between Bach and the next generation was not so much their embrace of the *galant,* nor even their dismissal of counterpoint. What most divided him from them was their motive for making music at all, of whatever sort. The new "enlightened" composer wrote for one reason and one only: to please the audience. When he was Kapellmeister in Dresden, for example, Heinichen had written that the proper ambition of a composer "consists once and for all in the art of making his music, as a matter of course, popular and pleasing to the reasonable world." Mattheson went further: "Really we should follow not our own inclinations but those of the listener. I have often composed something that seemed to me trifling, but unexpectedly attained great favor. I made a mental note of this, and wrote more of the same, although it had little merit when judged according to its artistry." For Bach, of course, that statement was the coarsest philistinism, a musical blasphemy.

"[I]t hinders a preacher greatly if he wants to look around and concern himself with what people want to hear and not hear," Abraham Calov wrote in his commentary on Luther, another one of the passages that Bach double-marked for emphasis.

. . . RATHER, AS HE STANDS HIGH UPON THE MOUNTAIN AT AN OPEN SPOT AND LOOKS AROUND HIMSELF WITH A FREE MIND, SO HE SHALL ALSO SPEAK FREELY AND SHY AWAY FROM NO ONE, EVEN IF HE SEES A MULTITUDE OF PEOPLE AND FACES. HE NEED NOT GUARD HIS MOUTH NOR TAKE INTO VIEW GRACIOUS OR WRATHFUL LORDS OR NOBLEMEN, NOR CONSIDER MONEY, WEALTH, HONOR, OR POWER, SHAME, POVERTY, OR HARM; HE NEED NOT THINK ANY FURTHER THAN THAT HE SAYS WHAT HIS OFFICE DEMANDS.

We cannot know if that passage was on his mind as Bach traveled to the court of Frederick the Great. Perhaps Bach had marked these lines in his Calov for some other occasion. There had been more than one time in his life when he had acted in accordance with this advice of Luther's, sometimes with alarming force. In any event, his composition for Frederick would be no exception.

∫

THE TRIP TO Potsdam was to be, perhaps even primarily, a family reunion. Because of the war, Bach had not yet met Carl's new wife or the couple's first child, his first grandchild. Friedemann accompanied his father in part because he too had yet to meet his new nephew and sister-in-law, and in part because who would want to miss this matchup between his old Saxon-speaking, God-fearing patriarch and the godless young warrior-king of Prussia. Friedemann and his father traveled by coach from Leipzig to Potsdam, a long and bone-jarring trip. The roads were terrible, muddy in early spring and sometimes virtually indistinguishable as their coach wound through forest. If they stopped only to change horses and grease wheels at post houses along the way, the trip straight through would have taken at least two days and a night, during which sleep would have been all but impossible.

They arrived in Potsdam in the early evening of May 7, 1747, a Sunday. Summoned to the city palace virtually as soon as he arrived, Bach was still shaken by the coach ride and in the clothes he had worn for the journey. Ushered into the king's concert room, he must have made elaborate apologies to Frederick for his appearance and a brief bow to the many acquaintances, colleagues, and friends in the room who had assembled for the evening's concert: Quantz, with whom he had played more than once in Dresden, his friends the Benda brothers and the Graun brothers, one of whom had been Friedemann's teacher for a time. There could have been as many as forty musicians in the room for that night's concert, including, of course, the king's keyboardist, Carl.

Among Frederick's other objects for collection were prototypes of the modern piano, new keyboard instruments that, unlike the harpsichord, could be controlled for volume. Instead of plucking strings (harpsichord) or pressing against them with a metal tangent (clavichord), the new fortepiano (literally "loud-soft") had covered wooden hammers connected by a complex lever to the end of each key, thanks to which the performer's greater and lesser force could make itself felt in the music. The chief fortepiano manufacturer in Germany was the distinguished

organ builder Gottfried Silbermann, who had a decade before begun asking Bach to play and give his opinion of them. Bach's exact words are lost to history, but the first verdict was not good: He
said the treble was weak and the keyboard action was too stiff,
making it hard to play. Silbermann was offended but knew Bach
was right and went back to work, continuing to call on Bach's
opinion from time to time. Eventually he developed instruments
that Bach liked well enough to become a sales agent for them in
Leipzig. Frederick had become so infatuated with the new instrument that he wanted to collect them all, and by now he had fifteen
of them scattered around the Potsdam "city palace," some of
them marked for the move to his new home, "Sanssouci," which
had opened that very week.

So of course Frederick wanted to hear Bach play them, or he
wanted to say that Bach had played them, or he wanted Bach to
tell him how wonderful they were, perhaps all of the above. After
all the courtesies had been attended to, the king began to lead
Bach from one room to another, from fortepiano to fortepiano, all
of his musicians trailing after them as he asked Bach to try out
each instrument in its turn. So many fortepianos, so little time!
What could Bach have played as he went through them one by
one? Surely not an entire suite; that would have taken much too
long. Maybe only a movement, then, or a prelude and fugue set?
Perhaps there was only time for a fugue. Or would the king, mid-
piece, simply pull "old Bach" off the keyboard by the arm and
haul him off to the next one? Surely not. At least we hope not.
The fact is that we know nothing about what repertoire Bach used
to play his way through the king's collection of piano prototypes
that evening until one particular moment, when Frederick sat
down at one of the keyboards, played a tune of twenty-one notes,
and so presented Bach the most difficult improvisational challenge of his life.

These were not just any twenty-one notes (although any

twenty-one notes would have been several longer than one might wish for the improvisation of a fugue). These were twenty-one notes that, if they were not calculated to make the task as difficult as possible, had been thrown together in an accident of anticontrapuntal genius. Was Carl the author of a calculated test for his father? We simply cannot know. Others could have done it, one of the Grauns, or possibly Quantz, though nothing about them suggests they would knowingly have taken part in a meanspirited practical joke on an old friend and esteemed colleague. The theory that Bach was given such a contrapuntally resistant theme by benign chance, however, comes up against some withering images: Frederick's treatment of Voltaire, for example, so eerily like his father's treatment of the hapless Gundling or the professors of Frankfurt. It is not hard to see how such a trick could have appealed to Frederick. For one thing, Bach was a contemporary of Frederick's father, and he represented the backward, boorish, superstitious world on which Frederick had turned his back but which still haunted him in his sleep.

Carl too had a larger-than-life father hovering over him that evening, and in this sense he was, or may have felt he was, caught between two despots, both of whom, for different reasons, he wished both to escape and to embrace. We are far beyond known territory now. All we know is that Carl's authorship is at least a subject for plausible speculation, which is itself an unhappy fact.

§

A FUGUE IS not as strict as a canon. The subject of a fugue, like the Royal Theme, does not have to play over and against itself or be inverted or augmented or otherwise transformed in any particular way, but there are several things that are required for a piece of music to call itself a fugue: It must announce the complete subject at the outset; and the complete subject must be imitated in one or more additional voices, each voice layering on more harmonic complexity, until all the intended voices—Frederick asked for three—have entered. Thus ends the so-called exposition section of a fugue, and thus ends just about all one can say about what fugues have in common.

That should be enough, though, to understand the insidious ingenuity of this one:

Things get interesting after the third bar, when the signs in front of notes—first a sharp sign, then a natural, then another natural, then a flat, etc.—indicate that we are descending not in the nice, predictable whole and half steps familiar from every major scale but only in halftones, through all the notes the scale leaves out because they would make it longer, less "normal," more ambiguous, and more complex, otherwise known as chromatic. With a subject like this one, every statement after the first would have to be matched note for note with a complex series of harmonies that could accompany this snaky, anything but simple descent, and that accompaniment would also have to fit with whatever new passages Bach devised to keep each voice going after it had finished with the subject; these "secondary" motifs would have to fit together too, here and later. Once all the voices had finished stating the subject, there would be some breathing room in which he could loosen up and follow the piece where it led him, but there should be at least references to the theme and its countersubjects even there, and eventually he had to get back and accompany the subject and its imitations all over again, differently from the way he had done it the first time, of course, and end up in the key he started out in, with a final statement of the subject as close to the end as possible.

As difficult as it was to read that paragraph, imagine how difficult it was to do all that, and to do it *ad-lib!*

As Frederick slowly played this impossible theme at the keyboard, note by chromatic note, the musicians and particularly the composers in the room must have become increasingly alert with every new half step. Bach too would have been aware that the task being set before him was growing more difficult with each note. No one was better at working out problems like this than Bach, though, and after whatever time it took him to set the theme in mind and get his thoughts aligned, he was off.

By every account and by the evidence of the transcription Bach eventually published of that night's improvisation, which is the first movement of his *Musical Offering,* the result was dazzling, a fugue that surpassed all reasonable expectations. Few people of his time could have managed even a competent improvisation on such a theme, not to mention a brilliant one, but Bach was a famously ingenious improviser. A witness told Forkel that Bach could improvise on a single theme at the organ for hours at a time, often following a certain order: first a prelude and fugue based on the theme using the full organ; then with an evolution of movements with different configurations of stops and forms— duets, trios, quartets; then with the addition of one chorale tune or another as a *cantus firmus* and new various combinations of stops; and always finishing with one great fugue, for which he would literally pull out all the stops.

So perhaps it is not surprising but only wonderful that his improvisation of a three-part fugue on Frederick's Royal Theme had all the intellectual rigor of a finished work: a strict fugue, based entirely on statements of the Royal Theme, that paired his incomparable polyphonic and harmonic density with long passages in precisely the *galant* style which was then ravishing the music circles of Berlin and finding its highest expression in the very court and ensemble whose musicians were listening to him that night. While doing all that, he managed to incorporate the entire Royal Theme no fewer than twelve times (in a seven-minute piece), several more than were necessary to meet the challenge, the last very close to the end.

Given this achievement, it must have come as something of a shock when Frederick asked for more: He wanted Bach to do it all over again, this time improvising a fugue on the same theme for *six* voices.

How exactly might that have gone? Bach finishes the improvisation on this long and complex theme, so that his audience of star-caliber musicians is "seized with astonishment," in the newspaper account, prompting great applause, congratulations all around, as well as perhaps some relief among Bach's colleagues at his having met a very daunting challenge, and just as we're thinking about heading out for the next fortepiano, the king hangs back and says, Herr Bach, might we hear a six-part fugue, if you please? In what world or formulation could that be a polite question?

As we know, Bach demurred (he apologized in his dedication of the completed work for his "lack of necessary preparation," as if any were possible), and instead played a six-part fugue on a presumably shorter and less complex subject of his own. The fugue subject on which he improvised has not survived, and it may not have been an improvisation at all. There are exactly no six-voice fugues in all *The Well-Tempered Clavier*, which after all he had had the opportunity to *write*, and there is only one fugue of even five parts. As he played this six-voiced consolation fugue he had every reason to be infuriated at having been put in the position of having to admit a defeat which had no recorded precedent in his life. He had proved too much for the great Louis Marchand and for the even greater Georg Friedrich Handel, both of whose avoidance of Bach has no more plausible motive than intimidation. The image that comes to mind of Bach as he played for Frederick that evening—after two sleepless days bouncing around in a carriage for the pleasure of this moment—is of reddened face and burning anger, of a man who is only too aware that he has been shown up by a man not only decades younger, not only by far the lesser musician (understatement of understatements), not only the enemy of his Saxon elector and king, not only the not-very-appreciative employer of his son, but also by someone who plainly thinks of Bach as no more than Prussia's latest Royal Executor of Puzzles, someone about as important to him as a farting duck.

A night of sleep and a change of clothes later, Bach was summoned once more into the service of the king. Presumably from the same mix of motives he had for taking Bach from fortepiano to fortepiano—among which motives of course was the desire to hear a great virtuoso who would not be around much longer, this time on the instrument for which he was most famous—Frederick asked Bach for a performing tour of the organs of Potsdam. *All* the organs of Potsdam. At the time there were at least four major instruments scattered around town, and Bach of course had no choice but to oblige him. He actually gave his last known keyboard performance that day, though which of Potsdam's churches had that honor is unclear.

For all that, at the end of Bach's two very busy days in Frederick's court, there is no indication that the king sent him off with any reward for his pains, and if he had there would be a record of it, the accounts were kept that carefully. Neither is there a suggestion of any recognition later, even two months later, when Frederick received by courier from Leipzig an elaborately printed and musically extravagant suite which had been composed on his theme and dedicated to him. There is not even a note of thanks to "old Bach," either for his troubles on his visit or his work on the Royal Theme (not to mention a diamond ring like the one Hasse got in Dresden). This lack of response to one of Bach's greatest works—and the king was enough of a musician to recognize it as such—is the only reason we have to speculate that Frederick may actually have understood what Bach was saying to him in it, but no doubt the explanation is a great deal simpler than that. Sanssouci was ready! There were marshes to drain! Voltaire, always good for a bit of fun, could be arriving any day! Frederick would have stopped thinking about Bach and the Royal Theme as soon as they had ceased to amuse him.

§

BACH, ON THE OTHER HAND, seems to have thought of nothing else after he left Potsdam. Even during the long carriage ride home, according to Carl, he would have been thinking about what the possibilities were for this theme, how limited his options were, given all that chromaticism, what complementary themes he could deploy around it to fashion the finished work—and perhaps most important, of what forms and styles exactly he would use in the finished work.

He put himself to the task as soon as he was home in Leipzig, or as soon as he had recovered from the completely exhausting round-trip, and he could have focused on little else, because only two weeks later he emerged from his composing room with a suite of sixteen movements that was one of the great masterpieces of Western music—a work that, taken together, is at once sublimely graceful, brilliantly expressive, a bracing blast of learned counterpoint, and an intriguing set of mysteries. The first three attributes are relatively simple to explain, the last somewhat less so.

If the three-part fugue was impressive, the variety of new ways he had discovered to elaborate Frederick's torturous subject after giving it some thought was breathtaking, including a four-movement trio sonata that was not only the last but by far the best trio sonata he ever wrote. There too was the promised six-part fugue *(touché!)*, which may have been the last piece he ever wrote for keyboard, along with ten canons—count them, ten—on the theme, remember, that the great contrapuntist Arnold Schoenberg said would yield exactly zero canonic imitations. Schoenberg was right. Bach had to invent canons that could be placed *around* the Royal Theme, and this he did, royally: canons above it, canons beneath it, canons to both sides of it, canons going forward, backward, sideways, upside down, and upside down and backward at the same time. There has never been a volley of canons like it, and we will be coming back to them.

As for the sonata, the most generous superlatives seem only to scatter dust on it. On the most superficial level the trio for flute, violin, and keyboard is loveliness itself. Look deeper and every level drops away until its beauty seems bottomless, as perhaps it is. One of the most interesting pieces in it, obviously intended for Frederick to play, is the andante movement, which is built on "sighing" figures typical of the highest *galant* style. At first the almost cloying melancholy of it threatens insulin shock, but not to worry: The movement is bound and chained to the Royal Theme's chromatic descent, the rhetorical figure known to the Baroque composer as a *subjectum catabatum* and *passus duriusculus* (the sort of thing they used to suggest lowly, insignificant, and sorrowful, for those who do not remember their lesson in the musical-rhetorical figures on page 81). Voltaire said the essential mission of all things *galant* was "to be amusing." But listen to it: Does this movement amuse you? We will be coming back to this too.

As for the final fugue for six voices, it is not, played on the keyboard, the most transparently beautiful work Bach ever composed; its greatest virtues are sometimes barely audible. But for those willing to mobilize the concentration required to hear and read "eye music," a derisive term for music in its most formally rigorous aspect, the beauty of this ricercar is blinding. Most music is better when you close your eyes. This piece requires that sort of hearing, and yet all the eyes-wide-open or eyes-wide-shut attention you give it never seems to rob it of surprise. No more impeccably concise, structurally graceful, and intensely contrapuntal work was ever written, even by the man himself.

§

AS FOR THE mysteries, here are a few of the simpler ones: We do not know in what order Bach composed the *Musical Offering*, nor do we know in what order he wished it to be played, if he wished it to be played as a suite at all. Should both fugues come first, followed by five of the canons, then the sonata and then the other five canons, or should all ten canons go together at the end, or should the fugues bracket the sonata and the canons—*or what?* As Malcolm Boyd puts it in his wonderful biography of Bach, if someone who went to Bach's house and a paid a thaler to buy the score but then "had the misfortune to slip . . . and to scatter the pages of his copy over the cobbles of the *Thomaskirchhof*," he could forget about trying to get them back together again. There were no page numbers, most of the pieces had no performance instructions, some of the canons were enigmatically abbreviated, and there was no written clue to what instruments should play any of it except the trio sonata and two of the canons. Some of the pages that have survived are on large, fine paper stock, others on different sizes, shapes, and qualities of paper.

Everyone who ever owned a copy seems to have taken a tumble with it, because no intact copy has ever been found, and for a long time no one could make a terribly persuasive case for the "right" order. One musicologist supported her arrangement of the parts by showing how its thirteen movements follow precisely the oratorical model set forth in Bach's schoolboy textbook in rhetoric, the *Institutio Oratoria* of Quintilian, written in the first century A.D. Another said the work was arranged in order of increasing theological significance, which would put the canons (the Ten Commandments) together at the end. Christoph Wolff seemed finally to have put the pieces in their intended order when he discovered the only organization that made the originals' mélange of oblong, upright, heavy- and light-stock pages make sense: The two fugues are the work's bookends, the sonata is its centerpiece, and the canons flank it. (Wolff also concluded that Bach never meant the entire work to be played sequentially anyway, making the question of order somewhat irrelevant.)

Now begin the deeper mysteries, which require a bit of onion peeling.

In whatever order Bach finished it, the printed work was dated July 7, exactly two months after the evening in Potsdam—incredibly fast work for the printer as well as the composer. A few days after that an engraved copy of the work, titled *Musicalisches Opfer,* arrived at Sanssouci with an elaborate and somewhat odd dedication, in German, which began:

> To Your Majesty is hereby consecrated in deepest submission a Musical Offering. . . .

Translators have often rendered the German verb *weihen* in that sentence as "dedicated," because "consecrated" simply sounds wrong, but the meaning of *weihen* was then and is now clear, "to consecrate." No two ways about it: Bach said he was consecrating an offering to Frederick. Bach knew that Frederick had no patience for organized religion, especially Christianity, so why would he have made his dedication sound less appropriate for a piece of music than for a ritual slaughter? Bach was nothing if not painstaking to the point of obsession with every detail of a work, including the use of words with his music.

Consider, for example, his use on the title page of the word

*Opfer,* the largest word on the page by far, larger than *Musicalisches* by a factor of ten. As Arnold Schoenberg pointed out, *Opfer* is a loaded word. This was not the first time a composer had named his piece a "musical offering," but it was the first time the alternative meanings—"victim" and "sacrifice"—had been invoked with a consecration.

Bach goes on to say in his dedication that his work "has no other purpose than this sole irreproachable one: to exalt, although only in one small aspect, the glory of a monarch whose greatness and might, just as in all the sciences of peace and war, so also especially in music, everyone must admire and venerate."

But consider the work itself, starting with the three-part fugue. In the very first movement, just as he bows deferentially to Frederick's taste with *galant* gestures, he begins that downward modulation through the flat keys—the "distant tonal movement in the flat direction outside the ambitus" that Michael Marissen heard in his early *Capriccio* (page 86) when Bach wished to warn his departing brother of "various casualties that could befall him." The Royal Theme, of course, is itself darkly minor, including not only a *saltus duriusculus* ("hard leap," meaning "false"—see page 82) in the diminished seventh between the second and third bars but also the long chromatic *passus duriusculus* of the next nine notes. But here, just as later in the andante movement of the sonata, he does not use the *galant,* as he might easily have done, to mitigate the chromatic onslaught. Instead, he italicizes it by modulating so far down into the flat keys—all the way to six flats, the key of E-flat minor, below even the *extremum enharmonium* of B-flat minor, which was Christ on the cross—that one may be excused for wondering if he is working to let the king's glory shine forth or digging a deep dark pit for it.

Suggestively, he calls neither the three- nor the six-part fugue a fugue: He calls them both "ricercars," which by 1747 was an antique term for strict counterpoint. Never before or later did he call any composition of his a "ricercar," as many strict fugues as he wrote. One theory was that he only used the word because it was a neat Latin acronym for a phrase that could be applied to the whole work: *Regis Iussu Cantio et Reliqua Canonica Arte Resoluta* ("By order of the King the tune [the Royal Theme] and the remainder, resolved with canonic art"). Bach did love wordplay (see *Opfer*). The fact is, though, as Christoph Wolff pointed out, he chose the name for the fugues before he discovered that he could make *ricercar* an acronym, which is why the Latin phrase had to be inked in after the work was printed. As J. G. Walther derived the term in his *Musical Lexicon*, the word *ricercare* (which shares the Latin root of *recherché*) was an Italian verb meaning "to investigate, query, inquire, search out with diligence." That of course is what Bach was doing here, searching out the uses of the Royal Theme, but that is what all fugues do. Could the word suggest another sort of search?

Between the ninth canon and the tenth, both of them "puzzle" canons and so in enigmatic notation (page 117), there is a Latin epigram—*Quaerendo invenietis*, "Seek and ye shall find"—a quotation from the gospels of both Matthew and Luke, referring to the search for God's mercy. Bach would hardly have used a line of Scripture here, at the end of the work, only as a redundant indication that the puzzle canons were puzzle canons, for which, quite obviously, a solution had to be found. This too seems a suggestive hint that there may be something else to be sought and found in the work.

Bach left trails of bread crumbs everywhere. Between the fourth and fifth canons are two epigrams addressed to the king. The fourth canon is an augmentation canon in contrary motion, meaning that the second voice is an inversion of the first and in notes twice as long. The inscription reads: "As the notes increase, so may the fortunes of the king." The fifth canon is the one that Douglas Hofstadter, in his *Gödel, Escher, Bach,* appropriately nicknamed the "Endlessly Rising Canon" because each time it is played it leads to a higher key, one whole note above the last. Hofstadter likens this canon to the lithographs of M. C. Escher, like *Waterfall,* in which a stream of water seems to make a "Strange Loop," rising in cleverly designed steps from the pool below a mill wheel back to the top of the falls that turns the wheel, where it splashes to the bottom only to return to the top, and so forth. The fifth canon is the musical equivalent of such an optical illusion: Play it six times, and it will be back where it started, only an octave higher, and yet without seeming to have left its original key. This canon is inscribed, "As the notes ascend, so may the glory of the king."

As the musicologist Eric Chafe was first to point out, both inscriptions sort oddly with their respective works—in the fourth because this canon about the king's fortune is so relentlessly melancholy, in the fifth because despite the fact that the canon is supposed to reflect the king's ascendant glory, the magic of it is that it does not seem to rise at all. Chafe's conclusion is that Bach is commenting on the distinction between the apparent glory of the king and the fact of his humble human estate, bound to a world of flaw and sin just like the rest of us.

All sorts of the loveliest ripe fruit seem to drop and shrivel in the fallen world of the *Musical Offering.* Some of the elegantly melancholy passages of the trio sonata for Frederick are just this side of cheap in their *galant* sensitivity, guaranteed to make audiences swoon (though some of the sonata's passages would have left Frederick breathless too). But they are set in the form of *sonatas da chiesa,* four-movement "church sonatas," which always featured counterpoint. Their structure was to begin with a slow movement followed by a fast fugue, then another slow movement and another fast fugue. Frederick never played *sonatas da chiesa* since, as we know, he disliked any music that "smells of the church." He preferred the three-movement chamber sonata, which was most often made up of dances. In Frederick's vast music library, there was not a single *sonata da chiesa*.

Bach knew all about Frederick's aesthetic preferences. After all, his son was there to warn him of them, even if his friends in the Kapelle did not. His *Musical Offering* defied virtually every one of them. He would have known that a polite dedication would be in French, Frederick's language, rather than German, which Frederick not only did not speak but held in contempt. He would have known that, far from appreciating Bach's learned style of composition, Frederick specifically prohibited his court composer from writing in it. Of the four hundred or so flute-sonata movements that Frederick himself is supposed to have written, only one could be considered even in fugal style.

Canons in particular had an uncomfortable role in Frederick's thinking and repertoire, and Bach, as we have seen, presented him with ten of them. That took some doing since, as Schoenberg pointed out, he could not make a single canon of the Royal Theme itself: "All the miracles that the *Musical Offering* presents are achieved by countersubjects, counter-melodies and other external additions." For all that, he managed to give Frederick all sorts of canons with the Royal Theme tucked inside them one way or the other: a crab canon and puzzle canons, a canon at the unison for two violins, a canon in contrary motion (backward), a canon in contrary motion and augmentation (backward with one voice in double-length notes), the upwardly modulating canon, a four-voice canon—all of these are "perpetual" canons—as well as a canonic fugue.

Just one more thing and this onion will be peeled to the core:

That he went to the trouble to make ten canons means, as we know (page 115), that he wished to invoke the Law. Sometimes he meant specifically the Ten Commandments, but always the number ten was associated with the Law of the Old Testament, particularly in connection with canon, one of whose original meanings was "law."

Putting these onion peelings, bread crumbs, and dried fruit together brings us to the musical-rhetorical stuffing that Bach cooked into his *Musical Offering*. All of the oddities contained in the work—the harrowing descent in *galant* passages, the melancholy fate of the king's fortune, the song to glory that goes nowhere, the German dedication, the Scriptural invocation to "seek and find" God's mercy rather than the harsh, eternal judgment of God's own canon law, the setting of a church sonata—all of these were of a piece, and this is what they say: Beware the appearance of good fortune, Frederick, stand in awe of a fate more fearful than any this world has to give, seek the glory that is beyond the glory of this fallen world, and know that there is a law higher than any king's which is never changing and by which you and every one of us will be judged. Of course that is what he said. He had been saying it all his life.

If this seems a foolhardy message to have sent an absolute monarch and his son's employer, it was entirely in keeping with past practice. Bach would no more have held back, trimmed, or censored his musical and theological beliefs for Frederick than he would have shrunk from telling the young Saxon prince, grandson of his king Augustus and the son of his elector, to choose Virtue over Vice. He did not hesitate to side against his own superior in Mühlhausen, or to tell the town fathers there that *God Is My King*, or to defy repeatedly and roundly both the consistory of Arnstadt and the council of Leipzig. If he could press his patron-elector about a student prefect, what would he draw back from addressing with a monarch he did *not* like? He had nothing to be afraid of, or, more precisely, what he feared was far more powerful than any monarch. As a composer, for a congregation or a king, he stood always on that terrible earthly battlefield, fifer to the corps of angels in Uncle Christoph's oratorio as they fought off the monster with Saint Michael, and perhaps never more so than at this time in his life, when he knew very well that death was stalking him. See Roland Bainton's Luther, back on page 19. "The most intrepid revolutionary is the one who has a fear greater than anything his opponents can inflict upon him."

§

IN ALL THE very good records and written memoirs of people around Frederick, there is no suggestion that he ever played the *Musical Offering* or that he ever heard it. He gave his copy of it away. Eventually it ended up in the library of one of his younger sisters, an organist who collected Bach's music. Many years later, Frederick told the story of their meeting to a friend, Baron von Swieten, once an Austrian diplomat in Frederick's court, now back at home in Vienna, where he held a salon at which Mozart then reigned. In his memoirs, von Swieten wrote that, twenty-seven years after the event, Frederick told him the story of Bach's visit and sang the Royal Theme for him. Sang the Royal Theme? How would he have remembered it for so many years? A better question: Why? He did not mention to von Swieten any published work Bach wrote that had been based on it. Why would he have forgotten that (if he had ever known it) but remembered the theme? Any answer to these questions, suggestive as they are, would only be speculation. According to the baron's memoir Frederick said Bach had been able to improvise not only a three-part fugue, but then one in six parts and finally one in eight! Here Frederick gave something of himself away: that he did not know the work Bach gave him, and that, despite being a composer, there was a great deal he did not know about improvisation or fugue. (This would have surprised no one. Many of Frederick's compositions were "filled in" by his teacher Quantz and others. As Brahms would say later, "Never criticize the composition of a king. You never know who may have written it.") For Michael Marissen, the von Swieten story suggests that Frederick was interested in fugue mainly "as spectacle," and what we know of him supports that conclusion. He seems to have looked at Bach the same way, as some kind of circus act.

Would it have mattered had he played the *Musical Offering*, or if he had studied the score and understood its meaning? Surely not. Even the letter from Charles Jordan, the last plea of a dying intimate, had made no difference to him; still less would the cautionary notions of an old Lutheran cantor embedded in a church sonata. But of course Bach had not put the message there to change Frederick anyway, as some sort of Salvation Army come-to-Jesus pitch; it was simply another declaration of faith in a lifetime of such declarations. Given Frederick's neglect of his work, it is comforting to remember that Bach would not have cared whether Frederick liked the *Musical Offering* or not, and to remember as well that Bach's indifference to Frederick's opinion was not stubborn or arrogant but rooted in his character too deeply even to be considered a matter of principle.

Bach's masterpiece was obviously a great deal more than a message to Frederick the Great. Most important, it is a work of incomprehensibly comprehensive intellectual and sensual beauty, ranging from the tightest of tight canons to the melancholy, dance-happy profundity of the French-Italian-contrapuntal-*galant* sonata to the wedding cake of counterpoint that is the six-voiced ricercar: a feast of inexpressibly delicious delights. Having said that, we come once more to the speed bump of the unspeakable.

The reason so much of the Bach literature, like this book, focuses on "extra-musical" issues—the frame rather than the painting, as it were—is that what is greatest about Bach's work is literally impossible to talk about, a characteristic that perhaps more than any other distinguishes his music from the *galant*. In a discussion of the nineteenth-century standard of artistic greatness in his book *The Roots of Romanticism*, Isaiah Berlin might as well have been talking about Bach's music versus that of his sons' generation:

> In the case of works of art that are beautiful but not pro-
> found . . . I can explain to you, say, about some musical
> work of the eighteenth century, well constructed, melodi-
> ous, agreeable, even perhaps a work of genius, why it is
> made in the way it is, and even why it gives pleasure. I can
> tell you that human beings feel a particular kind of plea-
> sure in listening to certain kinds of harmonies. I can de-
> scribe this pleasure, perhaps quite minutely. . . . But in the
> case of works which are profound, the more I say the more
> remains to be said.

We can find the words Bach was speaking, the "point" he was trying to make in his works, but in doing so we can only discover something less than what he did. His way of writing had indeed stressed the figurative expression of words at first, Luther's words and the Bible's, and then the more thematic and a bit less literal interpretation of the cantata librettos with which he worked. He had spent his entire career, from his first day in Arn-stadt, writing messages into his music, making messages *of* his music, and his musical "lexicon" had developed early—back to his late twenties in Weimar and the *Orgelbüchlein*, where Schweitzer discovered it, and actually before that, as early as the *Capriccio* for his brother. What sets Bach so far apart from other composers, though, are not specific skills and devices but the heights and depths he could reach from the security of the ground on which he stood.

Bach's work was not simply the product of his devotion, of course; maybe devotion was the least of it. He attributed his achievement to hard work, and surely it was that at least in part: He had an almost obsessively stubborn insistence on mastering the most difficult forms and ideas in the music of his time, and he worked with constant, riveted concentration. No composer has ever been more diligent. But he was also a hardheaded, hot-tempered man, just like his father's twin with "the Wieneren girl" whom he refused to marry, and it was in part this unequal temperament that protected his character and his music from fickle tastes, from the pleasure and displeasure of an audience. He could thank his ancestors for that—his stubborn father and his Ana-baptist mother alike—and he could thank the writings and example of the notoriously, triumphantly intemperate Martin Luther for inspiring in him not only a love of God but, perhaps more important to his music, a sense of certainty rooted in something deeper than approval or respect.

In many ways Bach was not a man of his time at all. At a moment in history when the composer was a craftsman in service to town or church or court, charged with making music for every occasion, he forcefully, almost madly declared his independence. Such a stance was unheard of at the time, and presaged not the attitude of his sons' generation but that of their sons and their sons' sons. In a way, Bach was the first "genius," if by that we mean the Romantic notion of an individual seized by and expressing his own singular creative power. Having the core of his musical thinking entirely in himself rather than in his audience or his peers, not to mention in Enlightenment theory, is precisely what allowed Bach to deconstruct and dominate rather than simply use or be influenced by what he studied, to make his music the sum and pinnacle of all the music of his time and so to prepare the way not just for a distinctively German musical language but for all of Western music.

∫

BY THE TIME he met Bach, Frederick's best years were behind him, and his worst were ahead. Eventually his prayer for Voltaire to move to Potsdam was answered, and the result was predictably ugly, ending after a couple of years in mutual recriminations and a scathing "secret" memoir from Voltaire about scandalous goings-on in Potsdam that was widely read and tittered at. A few years later they renewed their correspondence, which continued until Voltaire's death, but the two men, both of whom survived to old age, never saw each other again.

Frederick left whatever vestige of youthful vigor remained in him on the battlegrounds of his Seven Years War. He had always been a gambler in war, thanks to the fatalism that came with his belief in predestination, but the gamble he took this time, starting a preemptive war against a threatening new alliance among Austria, France, and Russia, was the costliest he ever made, in a cause so often hopeless that he spoke several times of suicide. During one particularly horrific battle, after two horses were shot from under him, he cried for the bullet that would kill him. By the time his nearly miraculous victory came it was wholly cheerless: He had lost more than a hundred fifty thousand soldiers and at least half a million Prussian civilians. Berlin was in ruins, the whole country was in ruins. A triumphal reception awaited Frederick on his return to Berlin, but he found his way to the palace through side streets to avoid it. "I am returning to a city where only the walls are still familiar," he wrote, "where endless labor awaits me, and where soon my bones will find refuge which will never again be disturbed by war, misfortune or human meaninglessness." He gave no victory speeches, not even to praise the soldiers who had fought and died for him, and the people of Berlin especially never forgave him for the trials he had brought upon them.

The war seemed to have bent him over physically. He had lost several teeth, and in his shabby and faded blue uniform, smeared with snuff, he looked a sorry remnant of himself—except for those enormous blue eyes, which could still run a knife through his ministers. The day after his return from the war he gave an audience to a group of regional officials who wished to congratulate him on his victory. He brought them up short. "Be silent and let me speak. You have something to write with? Very well, write this down: The gentlemen must draw up a list of how much wheat for bread, how much seed, how many horses, oxen and cows are immediately needed in their counties. Think it over carefully and come back the day after tomorrow." As the distinguished biographer Reinhold Koser put it, Frederick returned from the Seven Years War "gloomy, cold, hard, like a sunless winter day," an old man of fifty-one.

The old and good friends who had not died before died now, and though their chairs were occupied at dinner, they were not replaced. His remote and hostile family relations never improved. Even Wilhelmina, during their estrangement, wrote a memoir of her life with him almost as pitiless as Voltaire's. There is no record that Frederick ever knew of it, however, and years after she wrote it they reconciled. "I have kissed your dear letter a thousand times," he wrote her when she had fully convinced him of her remorse for what had appeared to be disloyalty at a time of trial for him. "My heart speaks a language that I cannot put into words. It is full of you, owes everything to you, is entirely yours."

He never wrote his sister more movingly than during the Seven Years War, when her health was deteriorating along with his fortunes on the battlefield. "You are the only person left who is attached to me," he wrote. "My friends are dead; I have lost everything." When she wrote that a longtime illness appeared to have turned fatal, he was inconsolable. "Life would be unbearable without you," he wrote. "These are not phrases but the truth." Two days before his most disastrous defeat, at Hochkirk, he wrote: "I am so full of you, of your dangers and my gratitude, that, awake or in my dreams . . . your image reigns in my heart and shapes all my thought. May heaven hear my appeals for your recovery!" She was dead before the letter arrived in Bayreuth, and as Frederick's biographer G. P. Gooch put it, "the last touch of romance vanished from her brother's stormy life."

Even in his last years he managed to add to Prussian territory, though, first managing by diplomatic guile to divide up a third of Poland among Russia, Austria, and himself, and later with a bloodless war that kept Austria from annexing Bavaria, a successful campaign for which he rewarded himself two more provinces.

Gradually the two sides of his life that had come together all those years ago in Neuruppin—the military and the arts—came down to one. By the end of the war over Bavaria he had lost several more teeth, his fingers had so stiffened with gout that he could no longer play the flute, and at that he lost interest in music completely. In his last years he begrudged every penny that went to his once-beloved Berlin Opera, and the performances there became so widely ridiculed that Frederick, onetime champion of free speech, issued a ban on press comment about them. Eventually he had to order soldiers to fill the house during performances just to keep it warm. Suspicious and cruelly dismissive of everyone who worked for him, he gave his only affection to a pair of greyhounds and his only devotion to his duties as king, which he carried out with mechanical regularity to the very end.

The Enlightenment went on without him. He was blind and deaf even to the new generation of German artists. He thought Goethe wrote "disgusting platitudes" that parodied the worst of the "ridiculous . . . bizarre" Shakespeare. Italian music was "dumb stuff," French music "childish." Haydn's music was "a racket that hurts the ears" and Mozart's was "caterwauling." "New music," he wrote in 1777, "has degenerated to mere noise, bludgeoning our ears rather than caressing them. Noble song is lost. . . ."

Frederick did a great deal for the people of Prussia. He enforced religious toleration, established the first German code of law, reduced censorship, encouraged free speech (within limits), greatly expanded access to education, and assured his subjects of markets for their products when times were good, freedom from starvation when times were bad, and help from the state in times of natural disaster, promises that brought a steady influx of settlers from countries without such enlightened policies. Frederick was, in fact, an enlightened leader by the standards of his day, especially in his domestic policies, when he sounds most like his obsessively practical father. "The ill custom prevails among us that both in town & country the servant-girls make the best rags into tinder to like light the fire," he wrote to one of his ministers during a cotton shortage. "We must try to break people of it, and therefore the rag collectors must be provided with touch-wood, which is just as good tinder for lighting fire, to give to the girls in exchange for rags."

At the same time, Frederick's cynical and bellicose diplomacy cost untold misery, and his inability to trust anyone—though who could blame a person for lack of trust whose mother was filled with treachery and whose father seriously considered killing him?—led to a world of pain for himself, for most of the people around him, and ultimately for his country. His obsessive control of every aspect of government created a system that could not survive without him, and his autocracy was responsible for how easily Prussia adjusted to Napoleon's rule twenty years later, one dictator being very like another. Twenty years after he died, when French troops had securely occupied Berlin, Napoleon visited Frederick's grave with some of his officers to pay tribute to a dauntless wartime general, which finally is the greatest part of what he was. "Hats off, gentlemen," Napoleon said. "If he were still alive, we would not be here."

§

RACKED BY GOUT, asthma, a chronic lung disease, and possibly chronic malaria, Frederick lived through many more sleepless nights than he had any wish to before he died. After he finished his history of the Seven Years War, he sent a letter to an old friend that showed just how deep and despairing his cynicism had become: "[T]o write history is to compile the follies of man and the blows of fate. Everything runs on these two lines, and so the world has gone on for eternity. We are a poor race, which is very restless during the little time it vegetates on this atom of mud called the earth. Whoever passes his days in quietness and repose until his machine decomposes, is perhaps more sensible than they who, by so many torturous circles, spiked with thorns, descend to the grave. In spite of that, I am obliged to go round like the wheel of a water mill, because one is dragged by one's fate." He lived for another twenty years after he wrote that.

By the time he died, the world was fast passing by him. In 1785, the marquis de Lafayette paid the old king a visit. He was twenty-eight years old, Frederick's age when he had taken the throne. After the meeting, Lafayette sent his impressions to General George Washington:

[I] could not help being struck by that dress and appearance of an old, broken, dirty Corporal, covered all over with Spanish snuff, with his head almost leaning on one shoulder, and fingers quite distorted by the gout. But what surprised me much more is the fire and some times the

softness of the most beautiful eyes, which can give as
charming an expression to his physiognomy as he can take
a rough and threatening one at the head of his troops.

The American Revolution had been won at that point—
Frederick had even signed a trade agreement with the new nation—
but revolution in Europe was still aborning, threatening every
monarch in Europe but Frederick, who was convinced that
American-style democracy could never take hold there. One evening at dinner, when Lafayette spoke glowingly of elected government, constitutions, the rights of man, Frederick cut him off.

"I once knew a young man who . . . decided to defend these
principles in his own country. Do you know what happened to
him?"

"No, sire."

"He was hanged."

Fittingly, perhaps inevitably, Frederick's excess of bile led to
the illness that finally killed him. He had so insulted one Silesian
regiment during their review that he was obliged to review them
personally the next year, despite a crippling attack of gout and
dyspepsia. That morning, from the time the drill began at 4 A.M.
until it ended six hours later, the seventy-three-year-old king sat
defiantly on his horse in a cold, pouring rain without a coat. He
never recovered.

He wanted to be buried with his greyhounds—the two with
him now were the last of eleven, each of which still has a grave
marker at Sanssouci—but the new king, Frederick's nephew
Henry, decided he should be laid to rest instead next to his father
in the Garrison Church. In his own years of waiting at Rheinsberg, Prince Henry had taken so much abuse from his uncle that
by the time he got the throne he had heard enough about Frederick the Great. Among his first acts was to build an obelisk
to honor all those soldiers who had served Frederick so well,

"about whom his fucking memoirs say nothing." One of those was Henry's father, Frederick's brother, who had died in disgrace not long after Frederick relieved him of his command during the Seven Years War and publicly denigrated him as a coward. Few mourned Frederick. One poignant exception was his wife, who had never set foot inside Sanssouci and who was having a party at her palace the night he died, unaware that he was ill, but who, during a very lonely life, had never stopped missing him.

Only an orderly and his last pair of greyhounds were with him at the end, and in most of his country the news of his death was met with indifference. In his biography of 1904, William Reddaway ends his introduction with the conclusion reached by all students of Frederick's life:

> Through all his life—in his councils, in his despair, in his triumph, and in his death—Frederick, almost beyond parallel in the record of human history, was alone.

§

BACH LIVED ONLY three years after his meeting with Frederick, but during those three years he devoted himself over and over again to proving the range and eloquence of counterpoint. The *Musical Offering* is entirely in keeping with the content and intention of all his late works. *The Art of the Fugue,* the *Goldberg Variations,* and his *Variations on Vom Himmel hoch* were all monothematic, like the *Musical Offering* all variations on a theme, and all of them bent to the same purpose: to demonstrate more bountifully than anyone had ever done before, whatever the critical reception might be for such a project, the most sublime reaches of learned counterpoint. In these works of his last years, all of them in sublime defiance of the aesthetic theory and taste of his time, were mirror canons, crab canons, augmentation and diminution canons, canons at every interval, double, triple, and quadruple fugues, and canonic fugues. In his own copy of the *Goldberg Variations* Bach wrote fourteen more canons, all of them perpetual, all of them based on the theme's simple eight-note bass line.

The last great achievement of his life, which he finished over the course of his last two years, was the B-minor Mass—everyone in the family knew it only as "the great mass"—and for this work, which he knew would be his final masterpiece, he pulled material from every corner of his life's work. He had been doing this for the last decade, reaching back to his beginnings—back to his work with his cousin in Weimar, back to his word painting for Luther, back to the beginnings of Western music itself—as if he were trying to make one complete and perfect work of everything he had ever written and from the whole of music history. The *Kyrie* and *Gloria* of the B-minor Mass were from the mass he had dedicated to his elector in 1733. The *Sanctus* was based on a *Sanctus* he had written for the Christmas of 1724, the *Hosanna* on a piece dated 1732, the *Agnus dei* on a cantata movement of 1725. For the *Crucifixus* of the mass he reached back to the mournful descending figure he had used in *Weinen, Klagen, Sorgen, Zagen,* the figure that had roots in his cantata for the town council of Mühlhausen (page 95) and even earlier, in his time with Buxtehude. This appeared next to the very last choral composition of his life, the most modern section of the mass, the *Et incarnatus est,* a boldly experimental and entirely successful evolution of contrapuntal part writing. Perhaps the most glorious movement of the mass, maybe the ultimate declaration of his life in music, reaches back beyond even his own life to the Renaissance style of Palestrina. The only choral work he ever wrote in *stile antico* is the mighty *Credo in Unum Deum,* a fugue whose subject is the priest's intonation in the Roman Catholic mass, a single phrase of Gregorian chant developed into one of the most spectacular polyphonic statements of all time, a work almost physically robust, glowing with passion for its subject—"I believe."

In reaching back to the Renaissance at the end of his life and in the explosion of rigorous counterpoint that characterized his last decade, he was pursuing more plainly than ever before his ultimate goal for music: a demonstration of "identity in variety" that would embody "insight into the depths of the wisdom of the world." Those are the words Bach put into the mouth of his advocate Johann Adam Birnbaum to describe his mission to Scheibe's and his sons' generation. Put into the language of Baroque music theory with which Bach would have been more comfortable, he was attempting to come as close as anyone had come before to the celestial music of a divinely ordered universe, the very music of Creation. He was still working on his masterpiece of counterpoint, *The Art of the Fugue*, having just woven the figure B-A-C-H into its nineteenth fugue,\* when he embarked on the "health care" that would ultimately kill him.

§

HIS EYES HAD been progressively weakening for more than a year by the time, in the spring of 1750, he turned for help to a "famed oculist," a self-promoting quack named Dr. John Taylor, who traveled with ten servants in two coaches painted all over with eyes. Handel survived an operation by Taylor to improve his vision and lived for seven more years in almost total blindness. Bach was less lucky. After a first operation he briefly regained his sight, but the procedure had to be repeated. After that he was left completely blind, and the postoperative treatment seemed to drain him of all his remaining resources. One afternoon ten days before he died, he could suddenly see again, but the reprieve lasted only for a few minutes before he had a stroke, and after that he did not leave his bed.

---

\*   The letter *H* is b in German. The letter *B* is b-flat.

One day in late July, as Carl told the story (though like his brothers he was not there during his father's final days, so he could only have got the story secondhand), Bach called one of his students to his deathbed and asked him to play, on the pedal harpsichord in his room, an organ chorale he had written decades earlier in Weimar for the *Orgelbüchlein*. He had later elaborated his original twelve-bar setting of "When we are in the greatest distress" (BWV 641, *Wenn wir in höchsten Nöten sein*) into a full-scale work (BWV 668a) that took its place in the collection of organ chorales written during his last decade in Leipzig, the "Great Eighteen," which in effect was an homage to his teachers Buxtehude and Böhm, late masters of the form. Listening now to his prelude on this chorale tune, one of those handed down by Luther himself, Bach heard an older text to which it had once provided the setting, an intimate, personal plea entirely appropriate to this moment in his life, when he knew that he was dying.

> *Before Thy throne, my God, I stand,*
> *Myself, my all, are in Thy hand;*
> *Turn to me Thine approving face,*
> *Nor from me now withhold Thy grace. . . .*

> *Grant that my end may worthy be,*
> *And that I wake Thy face to see,*
> *Thyself for evermore to know!*
> *Amen, amen, God grant it so!*

Now, sightless, he set about composing a quietly eloquent variation in counterpoint for this text, *Vor deinen Thron*. The result was one of the most beautiful chorales he ever wrote (BWV 668). Set to the medieval *integer valor*—the tempo that of the

human heart, each bar the length of one deep breath in and out—
it is also in every other way a work of human scale and sympathy.
Bach manages the remarkable feat of making each of the
melody's four sections into its own fugue, each time using the in-
verse of the subject as his countersubject, and as the work proceeds the counterpoint becomes ever more complex, "moving
ever farther from the body into the domain of the spirit," as
David Yearsley puts it. "It is in this way a representation of the
act of dying." And yet even as it unfolds as a tour de force of the
most intellectually demanding contrapuntal art, there is no aesthetic sacrifice to this technical achievement, no hint of "eye music." From beginning to end, "Vor deinen Thron" is a song of
hope and courage, with all of the elaborate ornamentation of the
earlier version stripped away. Whether the story is true as Carl
told it is unclear—as great a contrapuntist as Bach was, the idea
that he dictated this work from his deathbed in his last week
somewhat stretches credulity—but the music itself almost justi-
fies Albert Schweitzer's account of its creation:

> In the dark chamber . . . the tumult of the world no longer
> penetrated through the curtained windows. The har-
> monies of the spheres were already echoing round the dy-
> ing master. So there is no sorrow in the music; the tranquil
> quavers move along on the other side of all human pas-
> sion; over the whole scene gleams the word, "Transfigura-
> tion."

In Leipzig at this time was a young theologian who hated
Vaucanson's mechanical flute-playing shepherd and all that it
represented almost as much as he loved Bach. After Bach died,
he wrote angrily, "No one has ever invented an image that
thinks, or wills, or composes, or even does anything similar,"

and he cited this chorale prelude as the best possible answer to Enlightenment skeptics like La Mettrie: "All that the advocates of Materialism could bring forward must collapse before this one example."

Bach died on July 28, 1750, some minutes after eight in the evening. A note about it was placed in the Leipzig burial register: "A man, 67 years, Herr Johann Sebastian Bach, Kapellmeister and Cantor to the school of St. Thomas's; died at the school and was buried, with a hearse, July 30, 1750."

§

THE AUTHORITIES OF St. Thomas's and Leipzig made no secret of their relief. At the first word of an illness, a year before he died, they had auditioned and all but proclaimed a successor, so that Bach's last months had to be spent in part in the attempt to upset that choice in favor of Friedemann or Carl. The very day after his death, even before he was buried, the council met and once again expressed its favor for this previously auditioned non-Bach, who had friends in the Dresden court. He was clearly the musical inferior of both Bach sons, but he was willing to be "what the school needs," as one of the councillors disdainfully put it, "a cantor, not a Kapellmeister."

Bach's lifelong friend Georg Philipp Telemann, godfather of Carl, wrote a valedictory poem for Bach by way of epitaph. It was not much of a poem, but it began lavishly enough.

> . . . Departed Bach! Long ago thy splendid organ playing
> Alone brought you the noble title "Great,"
> And what your pen had writ, the highest art displaying,
> Did some with joy and some with envy contemplate.

At the end, though, the poem took a strange turn.

*Prepare your future crown of glory brightly glowing.*
*Your children's hands adorn it with jewels bright,*
*But what shall cause your worth to be judged aright*
*Berlin to us now in a worthy son is showing.*

This was surely an odd occasion for a paean to Carl, especially since, despite Frederick's coolness toward him, he was fast becoming the It Boy of the Berlin music scene, ranking exponent (along with the ever trendy Telemann himself) of that sort of music his father had stood so forthrightly against. ("Prussian blue," he reportedly cracked. "It fades.") Bach was outspokenly proud, not at all resentful of his sons' successes, and godfatherly pride excuses Telemann's thoughtlessness to some extent. But the fact remains that Telemann had declared, in his last words to an old friend, that Carl was a greater musician than his father had been and that this son, not his own music, would be Bach's greatest legacy.

Unfortunately, Telemann's poem was in keeping with other aspects of Leipzig's farewell to Bach. His grave outside the city walls was unmarked, no mention was made of him in Reverend Ernesti's annual address that year, and his successor at St. Thomas's Church, who of course was expected to compose and perform his own music, rarely performed works by Bach. Friedemann and Carl took most of the music manuscripts from their father's estate before it could be probated, leaving Anna Magdalena less than what was rightfully hers, and for unknown reasons they declined to help her financially when, all too soon, she was left without means. She died an almswoman ten years after her husband. Friedemann sold most of the scores he took from his father's estate to support a less than responsible life. Carl preserved most of what he had got from the estate but not all of it. Just after Bach died he cobbled together what was finished of *The Art of the Fugue* and slapped the "deathbed chorale" on the end to make up for the last unfinished movement, but when it failed to find an audience he sold the plates for scrap.

Bach never got to hear his Mass in B minor, and for practical purposes it was forgotten for decades, as in a sense he was. More than a century would pass before the B-minor Mass or the *Passion According to St. Matthew* would be heard again. No silence in music could be quite as deafening as this.

# XIII.

*AFTERLIVES: AN EPILOGUE*

FOR A LONG TIME IT SEEMED THAT TELEMANN'S POEM had been right about Carl. Though undervalued by Frederick, he was a flamboyant virtuoso and prolific composer with an eye fixed on business. During his time off from court duties, he managed to become not only the most successful keyboard teacher in Germany but also among the best-known composers in Europe, standard-bearer of the *empfindsamer Stil*. Eventually his fame and fortune grew so great that he overshadowed his father completely in the public mind.

Of course he did. His popularity and his father's disfavor were both ordained by the Enlightenment's cramped mission for music. Still, Carl had enough of his father in him to save him from writing music that was merely popular. Until Haydn rediscovered "old Bach" in his last years, he said Carl was the only composer who had ever taught him anything, and Carl's keyboard works especially were much admired by Mozart.

Mozart of course was the ultimate composer for the Enlightenment. A good way to break up any dinner party is to claim Bach's superiority to Mozart, but there it is: Spend any serious amount of time listening to Bach, and most of Mozart's work, however wantonly gorgeous, will seem to be . . . missing something. One measure of his genius is that he could write masterpieces even in a time of such limited expectations for music, but lightweight music was beginning to lose its appeal even in his youth, and he drew himself away from it in part by studying Bach, whose influence can be heard especially in such late works as the *Requiem*.

*The Magic Flute*, another work clearly influenced by Bach, also contains one of the best and most beautiful declarations of rationalist self-confidence, when Tamino arrives at the Temple of Wisdom, flanked by the Temple of Reason and the Temple of Nature, and Sarastro sings:

> *The rays of the sun*
> *Drive away the night;*
> *Destroyed is the hypocrites'*
> *Surreptitious power.*
> *Hail to the initiates!*
> *You have penetrated the night.*

For Mozart, as for Frederick the Great and for C. P. E. Bach, the happy day had finally dawned when superstitious myth was shown for what it was. As Newton had long since demonstrated, the universe displayed a perfect order, the Great Design, of which humanity and human society were very much a part. The task of empiricism was simply to discover that order. The mind and universe being of the same orderly structure, and our brains now freed of religious nonsense, the answers to all questions and cures to all ills could now be discovered through the clear, unfettered exercise of reason.

An age unfamiliar with such certitude can only be confounded by the terrible shock that afflicted Enlightenment intellectuals in 1755, when an immense earthquake and tidal wave struck Lisbon, Portugal, killing many thousands of people. It was no worse than several other earthquakes in recorded history, including one in the Apennines only fifty years before, and the world was hardly unfamiliar with other natural disasters. But they had not occurred during a wave of optimism like the one perhaps best expressed by Alexander Pope's *Essay on Man* of 1733:

> *All Nature is but Art, unknown to thee;*
> *All Chance, Direction, which thou canst not see;*
> *All Discord, Harmony not understood;*
> *All partial Evil, universal Good;*
> *And, spite of Price, in erring Reason's spite,*
> *One truth is clear, Whatever is, is right.*

Or, as Leibniz had put it, this was "the best of all possible worlds."

Voltaire had always been a little suspicious about that, but after the Lisbon earthquake he was finished with it. "What! Would the entire universe have been worse without this hellish abyss, without swallowing up Lisbon?" he wrote in his *Poème sur le désastre de Lisbonne.* "Are you sure that the eternal cause that makes all, knows all, created all, could not plunge us into this wretched world without placing flaming volcanoes beneath our feet? Would you limit thus the supreme power? Would you forbid it to show mercy?" By the time he wrote his caricature of Leibniz as Dr. Pangloss in *Candide,* his outrage with optimism had turned to savage ridicule. Having been robbed, cheated, kidnapped, and beaten, the hapless Candide observes as he watches a noose being lowered about the neck of his beloved Pangloss: "If this is the best of all possible worlds, what are the others like?"

But this was not funny. If reason could not be trusted and faith was discredited, how could the world be understood? How could we understand ourselves? All over Europe, in pamphlets and books about Lisbon that expressed a desperate, rising pessimism, the question arose, as if for the first time: What if the order of nature is not perfect after all, what if it is chaotic and indifferent, likely as not to kill us all? Suddenly the reliability of reason—part of nature, after all, since it was a product of the human mind—was itself in doubt. Increasingly in the years and decades that followed, those who continued to claim their trust in reason did so more in hope than confidence, almost as an article of faith (of all things). Everyone else faced a dead end. At the close of *Candide*, Voltaire suggested that, lacking any better option than skepticism, we should "cultivate our garden," work for the betterment of individuals and society. But that was not much of an answer, and a better one did not come along.

What did, at least in Germany, was a period and movement aptly named Sturm und Drang, or "Storm and Stress," whose signal expression was the first novel of a young writer, Johann Wolfgang von Goethe, who had just been jilted by his sweetheart. He turned his agony into *The Sorrows of Young Werther*, an autobiographical novel about a young man who also had lost his head in love but who, instead of writing a novel, blew his brains out. Goethe averts God's eyes from this sight by ending his novel with Werther's secular burial, a rite in which "no clergyman attended him." An immediate best-seller in this world bruised by a sense of its own pitilessness, the novel inspired a generation of Werther wannabes and a widely reported (if perhaps exaggerated) rash of real-life suicides. When the novel was reissued some years later, Goethe felt moved to write a preface declaring that he had not meant to recommend suicide as a solution to unrequited love. In any case, Goethe's first novel clearly gave notice that to be "pleasing" or "amusing" was no longer much of an ambition for an artist, and his hero proved decisively that rationalism had completely lost its grip. The subsequent disaster of the French Revolution—untold bedlam and terror set loose in the pursuit of the loftiest Enlightenment ideals—put a very fine point on that.

In such a time, all things were up for reconsideration. Some years after his own disillusion with the Revolution, Beethoven was visited by an old Thuringian harp maker, one Johann Andreas Stumpff. When Stumpff mentioned his landsman Sebastian Bach, Beethoven thought to ask, "Why is he dead?"

§

THE ROMANTIC MOVEMENT was conceived and spent its prenatal period in Frederick's East Prussia, home to two exceedingly smart, well-educated, and socially oppressed young men named Johann Gottfried Herder and Immanuel Kant, the sons of Pietists and the men largely responsible for dynamiting what was left of the Enlightenment's optimistic trust in reason. Herder's contribution was to undermine the certainty that all questions are in theory answerable by reason and that truth is singular, that one truth could never contradict another. Herder did not set out to refute this fundamental notion, but his powerful assertion of the fact that different cultures have very different "truths," all of them valid in their different contexts, inevitably had that effect. Kant likewise was in no way trying to prepare the way for a movement with his *Critique of Pure Reason*, but the notion that order was a quality of the mind rather than the universe, that the mind was capable of many different metaphysical conceptions of the world, dashed any hope of cosmic certainty, though it comported nicely with the evidence of Lisbon and the bloody mess in the Place de la Révolution.

After Lisbon, the French Revolution, Herder, and Kant, no one could argue for an orderly universe or for the ultimate triumph of empiricism. If only the mind knew order, and if various intellectual constructions of order could be equally valid, every human being would now be, like it or not, the maker of his own world, every person responsible for her own Creation, and the progress toward human fulfillment that had once been the project of the church would now be the province of the creative self. Every life would be a work of art, and the ultimate task of finding a source of meaning in the world would belong to the artist.

The young Beethoven who had thought to ask after the music of Sebastian Bach had admired his works from childhood, but he liked Carl's music as well. This was not the Bach-intoxicated Beethoven of the Ninth Symphony and the *Missa Solemnis*, but he was on his way. Born a crucial fourteen years later than Mozart, Beethoven did not have to learn but began with the knowledge that music had to be more than a nobleman's entertainment, more than a depicter of this or that element of the natural or even supernatural world, and eventually he devised a new job for music: exploring and expressing the newly emergent creative self, the life of the mind. There were no words for this world yet, no talk about frustration and gratification, tension and relaxation, conflict and resolution, not to mention neurosis and psychosis (though there had been quite a bit of talk about one of music's best means of communicating such psychic dynamics in the arguments over consonance and dissonance; when Scheibe charged there was entirely too much "affected dissonance" in Bach, what he was really saying was that composers demonstrated bad taste by trying to endow music with meaning). Freud was born almost thirty years after Beethoven died, but Beethoven beat him to the unconscious, and he did so in large part by listening to Bach, who can practically be heard singing in the background of the late quartets. Bach was never really lost to composers, not at least to good ones.

Carl too in his last years seemed to turn away from the lightweight pieces that had made him a star, drawn back in both his late choral and keyboard music toward the profundity of his father's work. (It was too late to rescue his reputation from the Romantics, who would turn viciously on light music. E. T. A.

Hoffmann described Carl's concertos unkindly as "laughable and empty," and Mendelssohn said of his place in the Bach line, "It was as if a dwarf had appeared among the giants." Thus was the indignity of the father's late life visited on the reputation of the son.) In fact the works of Carl's last decade were among his most challenging and introspective, and at the end of his life he spoke of his father's music with only unambiguous esteem. He even copied out the canonic fugue from the *Musical Offering*, presumably for a performance. At the same time, despite all his achievements, he seems never to have quite got over the mixed feelings of the second son. When Charles Burney visited him in Hamburg toward the end of his life (he had become music director of the city on the death of the incumbent, his godfather Telemann), Carl proudly brought out his original manuscript of the *Well-Tempered Clavier*. Carl told Burney that, just as his father had written the notebook for Friedemann, the *Well-Tempered Clavier* was written for him. There is no evidence beyond his statement that this is true.

∫

IN 1825, FOR THE fourteenth birthday of her grandson Felix, Fromet Mendelssohn gave him a copy of J. S. Bach's *Passion According to St. Matthew*. To get it transcribed, she had to pry loose the original temporarily from Felix's music teacher, Carl Friedrich Zelter, who years before, so the story goes, discovered the manuscript at a cheese shop, where it was being used to wrap butter.*

Bach was already making a comeback of sorts by this time.

---

\* Actually, though Bach's manuscripts were not well kept, particularly by Friedemann, this version of events, especially given the Romantics' infatuation with scorned geniuses, seems too good to be true. More likely Zelter inherited the manuscript from one of Bach's former students, with whom he had made it his business to keep in touch.

Even before Napoleon occupied them, the Germanic cities, provinces, and principalities were discovering a sense of common national history and identity, and at the same time experiencing a spiritual resurgence, a combination of forces that makes Bach's rediscovery by a large public seem inevitable in hindsight. Still, even among cognoscenti, he was more admired than heard until the now nineteen-year-old Felix Mendelssohn got his teacher to agree to let him perform the *St. Matthew Passion* with Zelter's Singakademie in Berlin. By the time of the performance, on March 11, 1829, exactly a hundred and two years after its first performance (though they thought it was the centenary), word had got out that it was to be an extraordinary concert, and Berlin turned out for it in force.

What they heard was not exactly what Bach had written. As if preparing Quasimodo for his first blind date, they apparently felt it needed a bit of cosmetic work. In letters to his friend Goethe, Zelter said he had always been put off by the work's "atrocious German chorale texts" and their "dense fumes of belief, which is what no one really wants anymore." He also thought Bach "as a son of his age . . . could not escape French influence. We can, however, dissociate him from this foreign element, it comes off like thin froth." (Goethe, whom Zelter had made a fan of Bach by this time, knew enough to wonder about that: "You might give me a serious exposition of what you call the French froth which you take it upon yourself to separate from the basic German element.") In the words of Edward Devrient, the singer who helped Mendelssohn produce the work and who sang the role of Christ, all involved felt the need in various ways "to make the antiquated work modern, vivid, and alive by carefully selecting the most appropriate means to this end."

Mendelssohn did the work. Among other things, he cut the *Passion* by a third, from three hours to two. We only know what he took out of the work as he conducted it at St. Thomas's Church

264 ·· J A M E S   R .   G A I N E S

twelve years later, when he had restored quite a bit of it, but even for that performance he had cut six arias, four recitatives, and six chorale movements. He replaced the plaintive oboes with sweeter clarinets. He replaced the organ with a piano. He modified the orchestration in various other ways, changed some cadences from major to minor, reordered passages, gave alto parts to sopranos, and put dynamic markings all over Bach's score that had the effect of making the work a demonstration of Romantic passion as well as Christ's, especially so since he performed the work with a huge orchestra and a chorus of four hundred! (Bach's orchestras were not much larger than chamber music ensembles, his choirs usually not more than twenty or thirty voices.)

Whatever he did, though, the performance had the desired effect. Mendelssohn's sister Fanny wrote in her diary that the audience was awestruck, "filled with the most solemn devotion; one heard only an occasional involuntary ejaculation that sprang from deep emotion." Even the grumpy Hegel, whose lectures on aesthetics Felix had attended at the university, seemed visibly moved. Fanny said the concert hall that day had the feeling of a church.

This is the concert that brought Bach back to life, but in a new home. Just as the concert hall felt that day like a church, future performances would make churches feel like concert halls. Before Mendelssohn's concert version, it had always been part of a Good Friday Vespers service, the two halves of the passion divided by a sermon. This time it was presented only as itself, as a work of art, and given the setting that must have seemed in one way odd. It is, after all, the story of the Passion, which ends before the Resurrection, with Christ in the tomb. As part of a Good Friday service no one expected it to have an emotionally satisfying end, since the Resurrection would not be celebrated until the Easter service two days later. Heard in concert, though, the *St. Matthew Passion* seems to end at the edge of a cliff. The anticlimactic minor chord at the end, the irresolution, the lack of a triumphant final cadence, means that the last thing one can imagine is applause. This was a new problem: How can you leave the performance of such a work without clapping. But how can you applaud a crucifixion?

It would have taken a few bold people to begin, but after the initial oddness wore off, the applause must have grown to a roar, because this *St. Matthew Passion*, liberated from the context of worship, had been heard that day in a way it could never have been heard before, not as a call to devotion but as one of the most complex and gorgeous pieces of music ever written. Never mind what Mendelssohn had done to it: Deploying every style and form, along with two choirs and two orchestras, Bach had created what could now clearly be heard as the masterpiece it was, a work far more elaborate and intricately plotted than the most ambitious opera of its time, embracing music for stage, court, and church—polyphonic motets, chorales, choirs in counterpoint, arias for solo and duet, arias with chorus, the whole work ranging through all twelve chromatic keys and even beyond that, to the six-flats key of E-flat minor. It was an almost insanely ambitious mix of dances and dirges, passages of *galant* song and Renaissance madrigal, free-verse arias and Gospel recitatives, the bold concision of Italian melody and the ravishing filigree work of France, all brought into perfect coherence in a profound and staggeringly beautiful work of art. Having been given a sort of spiritual asylum in the modern concert hall, Bach proceeded in death to find the audience and the glory that had been denied him during his life.

§

WITH ITS RENEWAL of interest in German myth and history, its recovery of a respect for mystery, and its exaltation of the Heroic Artist, the lonely, singular soul in pursuit of an inner vision heedless of poverty, scorn, or neglect, Romanticism had every reason to love the ever-faithful-visionary Bach. As Wagner put it, Bach was "himself the history of the German spirit through that horrible century during which the light of the German people was completely extinguished."

> Look then upon this head, disguised in its absurd French full-bottomed wig, this master—a wretched cantor and organist wandering from one little Thuringian village to another, hardly known even by name, dragging out his existence in miserably paid posts, remaining so unknown that it took a whole century for his works to be retrieved from oblivion.

As a Romantic figure, Bach was in every way perfect.

To Frederick's reputation, though, the Romantic movement was a great deal less kind. Romanticism was all very well for painting, literature, and music, but it had no business in politics. The empowerment of the individual to create his or her own world led easily to the enshrinement of the will, which had perverse consequences. Given political power, the Romantic hero became a demigod whose exercise of will was a positive virtue, at a time when the notion of virtue was otherwise unrooted and unclear, and the movement that had sent out its first tender shoots under Frederick's thumb in East Prussia eventually rose to strangle him.

Brahms once said that the two greatest events of his lifetime were the formation of the Bach-Gesellschaft, founded in 1850 to undertake an edition of Bach's complete works, and twenty years later the declaration of the German Reich, which drew the Germanic provinces into a state. (This would be known as the Second Reich, the first having been the remnant Roman empire.) These two events were intimately connected: The coalescence of a nation and a national identity made Bach a German hero (interesting, since he would never have called himself a German; he would have said Eisenacher, Saxon, or Thuringian). It also doomed Frederick's Prussia to oblivion. In one of the greatest series of unintended consequences in history, Bismarck's success in making Germany a nation—which was really an attempt to save Prussia by placing it at the head of a German state—actually killed the entity that neither Frederick nor his forebears had had any wish to create. They were proprietors of hereditary lands, no more a "nation" than any other collection of real-estate parcels. The only motto Prussia ever had was what Frederick's Sun King–aping grandfather had chosen when he invented the Order of the Black Eagle, the decidedly unstirring "To each his own." Nevertheless, in one of several strange posthumous roles prescribed for him, Frederick too became a hero of this new German nation, reincarnated as a cross between knight and burgher, speaking folksy German and drinking beer. Only a few decades later, as part of the most perverse enactment of German Romanticism, Adolf Hitler—to the hijacked music of Wagner and in a cape stolen from Nietzsche's Superman—made Frederick his collaborator as he willed into being the darkest night of modern history.

The formal proclamation of the Third Reich took place at Frederick's tomb, where Hitler laid an elaborate garland. In *Mein Kampf* he called Frederick's Prussia "the germ cell of the Reich," and all through the war Nazi Germany invoked Frederick in every way it could. There were Nazi posters of the Teutonic trinity featuring Frederick alongside Bismarck and Hitler. At Hitler's enormous desk in his enormous office, the little Führer sat under Frederick's portrait. "The spirit of Frederick the Great is living in the Third Reich," Wilhelm Wolfslast wrote, "and it will continue to live as long as the swastika waves over Germany."

As the Allies advanced on Berlin, Göring ordered Frederick's remains, precious Teuton relics now (how he would have laughed at that), to be moved into the Harz mountains, where they were hidden in a mine. In the bunker at the end, Goebbels fanned the Führer's dwindling hopes and kept him in tears reading Carlyle's accounts of Frederick's triumphant recovery from devastating defeats during the Seven Years War.

To associate Frederick with Hitler is not entirely unfair. His most important legacy to Germany, after all, lay not in his enlightened domestic reforms but in Prussia's military culture and conquests, as he followed perhaps to a fault the advice of his father and the Great Elector. He would have worn no brown shirt, he was not a barbarian, but with the forcible disarmament of Germany after World War II, Frederick's greatest legacy was destroyed along with Nazism, no less decisively than his once-beloved Berlin Opera was leveled by Allied bombs.

After the war Frederick's corpse was sent into the safekeeping of the last of the Hohenzollerns, who had withdrawn to a castle in one of the family's former principalities. There he rested for half a century, until the post-reunification summer of 1991, when Chancellor Helmut Kohl created something of a stir by attending Frederick's reinterment where he had always wished to be buried, next to his dogs at Sanssouci. Among the many protests surrounding the ceremony (one sign along the route of the cortege read "Old Fritz's bones today, yours after the next war"), gay demonstrators in Baroque costume handed out leaflets with unsubtle references to Frederick's sexuality. A poll conducted during the controversy over his reburial found that most Germans could not say when Frederick the Great had lived or what he had ever done.

§

BACH'S BONES HAD a ride to their final interment almost as wild as Frederick's, beginning with a very messy dig nearly a century after his death around the area where his grave was thought to be (in the vicinity of everyone else who had been buried in Leipzig for the past two centuries, more than a thousand people in 1750 alone). The search was aided by the fact that he had been buried in a casket made of oak, an unusual extravagance, and eventually the bones of a not improbable skeleton-candidate were recovered from one such casket. Enthusiastically shown around, prodded, measured, and dissected, these bones and casts made from them were shipped from this laboratory to that one until finally, based on vaguely scientific speculation and a variety of more or less racist conclusions about what the skull and physique of a German genius would look like, the remains were certified as Bach's and eventually entombed in an appropriately dignified sarcophagus in the chancel of St. Thomas's in Leipzig, just in time for the gala bicentennial of his death in 1950.

By then Bach was an exalted figure in music, one of the most revered figures in Western civilization, and in the bicentennial year St. Thomas's Church was teeming with tourist-pilgrims. For months Bach's tomb was covered with wreaths, and lines wound out the church door down the street. Most of the world's great living composers paid their respects, in person or in print, in a sense fighting over his remains. Paul Hindemith, whose many neo-Baroque works identified him as a devoted student of Bach, gave a speech—widely distributed and argued about later—in which he lamented the fact that Bach had been elevated into oblivion. "In the two hundred years since his death," he declared, "each rising generation has seen him differently; his creations have been analyzed and criticized, performed and deformed, used and abused; books and pamphlets, paintings and plaster busts have made him a common household article; in short he has finally been transformed into a statue."

In his speech, Hindemith took as his task to revivify this cultural *objet* that had been handled to death, but in the end he only seemed to add evidence to his point: He spoke in favor of authenticity in the performance of Bach's music, of small-scale orchestras and choruses and the use of original instruments tuned to the historical rather than the modern standard. This reactionary protectiveness was quite new for Hindemith, who in his youth took the C-minor Fugue from the first book of the *Well-Tempered Clavier* and made a version of it for four hands—in ragtime! "Do you suppose Bach is turning in his grave?" he wrote gleefully on the score. "He wouldn't think of it! If Bach were alive today, perhaps he would have invented the shimmy. . . ." Hindemith had done a lot of apologizing in the years since then (though perhaps he had it right the first time).

Before the bicentennial year was out, the Marxist critic Theodor Adorno wrote an inflamed rebuttal charging Hindemith with trying to make Bach into "a composer for organ festivals in well-preserved Baroque towns." He did not say so, but Adorno was speaking in defense of works like Anton Webern's orchestral version of the six-part ricercar from the *Musical Offering* (1935), a gorgeous if somewhat eccentric arrangement that was a breakthrough in making each of the contrapuntal voices come alive, in making some of the work's most challenging ideas audible. In a letter to a colleague Webern wrote that he had wanted to liberate the ricercar from the narrow compass of the keyboard, to score it "the way I feel it. . . . Isn't the point to awaken what is still sleeping in the secrecy of Bach's abstract rendering?" Adorno certainly thought so. Bach's heritage, he argued, "falls to the act of composing, which remains faithful to him by being unfaithful, and identifies that heritage's content by recreating it for itself."

No one was wrong in this debate: Adorno was correct in observing that the most ingenious use of Bach's musical legacy was made by composers like Webern, and his teacher Schoenberg, who also wrote an encomium to Bach in 1950, calling him only half in jest "the first twelve-tone composer."* And the surpass-ingly beautiful recordings of the complete cantatas by Nikolaus Harnoncourt and Gustav Leonhardt, completed by the 250th an-niversary of his death in the year 2000, more than vindicated the musical vitality of "authentic" performance.

Ultimately, though, in the tide of history, the only direction available is forward. Even Harnoncourt and Leonhardt would not claim that a modern audience can hear Bach as he was heard in the eighteenth century. Just as Bach influenced all the music and history that came after him, all that music and history changed him, or changed at least how his music could be heard. For this reason and others, no matter how "original" the instru-ments or groupings of choristers, however "authentic" a perfor-mance strives to be, Bach can never again be heard as his contemporary audiences heard him. On the other hand, his music can speak to new audiences in ways that neither the eighteenth-century parishioners of St. Thomas's Church nor even the com-poser himself could ever have imagined.

§

THE MODERN WORLD is a creature of both the Enlightenment and Romanticism but completely the offspring of neither. The Enlightenment, which set out to rid the world of its superstitious credulity, still usefully instructs us to find and tear down veils of illusion wherever they exist, to be just to one another, and to keep studying; even if empiricism could not find a perfect order hidden

---

* The twelve-tone or serial method of composition developed by Schoenberg and his dis-ciples of the Second Viennese School utilized many of the contrapuntal devices Bach used, such as inversion, retrograde motion, augmentation, diminution, etc. Schoenberg also made the point that, unlike sixteenth-century counterpoint, which used the seven notes of the common diatonic scale, Bach used all twelve notes of the chromatic scale.

in the universe, after all, it took us to the moon. The Romantics, who came to the rescue when trust in reason failed, suggest that we embrace the world, imperfect as it may be, that we listen to the stirrings of the unconscious and remember that, whether we wish to be or not, we are the creators of our lives and our world. Yet these two postures stand opposed, one warning of the danger that the light of reason can blind us to a deeper kind of illumination, the other pointing out what can happen, what has happened, when we entrust ourselves to myth.

There being no settled agreement between them, the tension continues between reason and faith, *ratio* and *sensus*, Frederick and Bach. In this struggle, Frederick usually seems to have the upper hand. The world of the early twenty-first century has no trouble knowing Frederick: that mocking, not-really-self-effacing skepticism, the head-fake toward principle during a headlong rush toward the glamour of deeds. His mask and his loneliness are all too familiar. Bach is more of a stranger, a refugee from "God's time" displaced to a world where religion can be limited to a building and a day of the week, or dispensed with altogether. The chasm that opened with the Enlightenment between the secular and the sacred has grown only wider, to the point of making a commonplace of what would have been un-thinkable for Bach: a sense of the world as something unremit-tingly solid and factual, La Mettrie's self-winding, spring-loaded machine. Modern history has shown what such objectification can do—without it, how could there have been concentration camps?—but the history of ideas has, at least so far, provided no clinching argument against it.

The beauty of music, of course, what sets it apart from virtu-ally every other human endeavor, is that it does not need the lan-guage of ideas; it requires no explanation and offers none, as much as it may say. Perhaps that is why music coming from a world where the invisible was palpable, where great cosmic forces played their part everywhere and every day, could so deeply move audiences so far from Bach's time. Whether in the thrilling exuberance of his polyphonic *Credo* or in the single voice of an unaccompanied cello, in works extravagantly expressive and as intimate as a whisper, Bach's music makes no argument that the world is more than a ticking clock, yet leaves no doubt of it.

NOTES ON SOURCES

In addition to those signal influences cited in the acknowledgments and in the text, several authors' works have been especially important to me and would be for anyone else setting out on this territory. Every student of Bach is of course deeply indebted to Christoph Wolff, whose scholarly achievement in this field (and others) is breathtaking and whose biography of Bach is definitive. The best English-language biography of Frederick, aside from Carlyle's deeply researched but eccentric eight-volume monologue, is that of Robert Asprey. For Frederick's youth, the work of Ernest Lavisse is unmatched, and Ernest Helm's *Music at the Court of Frederick the Great* remains the most useful work on the subject. Most of the primary-source material I have used in languages other than English has been taken from the translations cited, but for some documents in German I turned to a translator, Dr. Ursula Sautter, and for those in eighteenth-century German to her mother, Dr. Elisabeth Sautter. Both of them have my gratitude especially for translating 164 long, ranting footnotes in Scheibe's last attack on Bach, not one of which made it verbatim into this book but which at least put the finishing touches on my portrait of their author. In the interest of space I have annotated only facts and quotes that would otherwise be difficult to locate. All quotations from Bach and his contemporaries are, unless annotated, in the translation of the indispensable *New Bach Reader (NBR)*. Unannotated statements by Frederick or his correspondents should be understood to be in his *Oeuvres* (which begin with letters he wrote as a boy), translated either in one of the major English-language sources cited here or by me. Anyone wishing the source for facts, details, or sources of translation not given here may contact me through the publisher at 4thestate@harpercollins.com (FourthEstate, 10 East 53rd Street, New York, NY 10022) or at my e-mail address, jg@jimgaines.com.

I. THEME FOR A PAS DE DEUX

3     **could not even spell** *Deutschland*   Ergang, 40.

5     **One Sunday . . . in his voice**   Forkel, *NBR*, 429*ff*.

6     **Frederick had been hinting**   *NBR*, 429.

6     **Carl's letters home**   *Idem*.

7     **warring values**   For his insight into the array of conflicts between Bach and Frederick, I am indebted to Marissen, *Bach Studies* 2.

7     **Frederick, a bisexual**   See discussion in Chapter IX.

7     **"never read a German book"**   The quote is from a letter of October 22, 1757, to Cölestin Christian Flottwell from Johann Christoph Gottsched reporting on a conversation with Frederick; cited in Marissen, *Bach Studies* 2, 89.

7     **weavers of the cosmic tapestry**   The most comprehensive discussions of the esoteric in Baroque music theory are in Yearsley's *Bach and the Meaning of Counterpoint* and in his dissertation. Bukofzer, Bartel, and Leisinger are also very useful.

8     **"smells of the church"**   Burney, Vol. 2, 92.

8     **Bach's chorales . . . "dumb stuff"**   Georg Thouret, *Friedrich der Grosse als Musikfreund und Musiker* (Leipzig, 1898), 29; cited in Helm, 75.

9     **"One hears from Potsdam"**   *Spenersche Zeitung* (Berlin, May 11, 1747); *NBR*, 239.

9     **"one single canonic imitation"**   See Schoenberg. All quotations from Schoenberg, in this and later chapters, are in *Style and Idea*.

11    **" 'making fun of you' "**   Voltaire, *Mémoires pour servir à la vie de M. de Voltaire écrits par lui-même, suivis de lettres à Frédéric II*, Jacques Brenner, ed. (Paris, 1988); cited in Macdonough, 224.

## II. BIOGRAPHY OF A TEMPERAMENT

16 **wood nymphs, mermaids, and goblins** Bainton, 19.

16 **"if a stone be thrown"** For this quotation, those that immediately follow, and the detail on Frederick's relics, I am indebted to Bainton.

17 **"so why are you standing about idly?"** Oberman, 188.

19 **"the water [running] with so mighty a force"** A *Wonderful and most Lamentable Declaration of the great hurt done, & mighty losses sustained by Fire that hapned; & mighty stormes of Winde, Thunder, Lightning, Haile & Raine*, etc. (London, 1613); cited in Young, 22.

21 **Thus was born the College** For the information of the musicians' union after the Thirty Years War, see Spitta, I, 144–151.

21 **"to sue for"** *Ibid.*, 29.

22 **"There may be conditions"** *Ibid.*, 31.

22 **"perhaps the only [twins]"** "Origin of the Musical Bach Family," by J. S. Bach (c. 1735). This passage was added by Carl. *NBR*, 288.

24 **"Both parties appeared"** For documents in the dispute between Johann Christoph Bach and Anna Cunigunda Wieneren, see Spitta, I, 159–162.

25 **several keepers of the town clocks** Composition of the town council is in Young, 64.

26 **"a simple creature"** Spitta, I, 174.

26 **he could have bought** Wolff, *Johann Sebastian Bach, The Learned Musician* (hereafter Wolff, *JSB*), Appendix 3, 539–541.

## III. THE HOHENZOLLERN REAL ESTATE COMPANY

27 **a baptismal gown made of silver** For details of the baptism and previous crown princes see Carlyle, I, Book I, Chapter 3, 20*ff.*; Asprey, 3; Lavisse, 3*ff.*

28 **trouble with teething** Lavisse, 2.

28 **a funny bunch** For early Hohenzollern history, see Carlyle, Fay, Haffner, Reddaway.

30 **twelve thousand ducats** The negotiation between Albert and the pope is in Bainton, 57.

33   **Albert was a secret admirer**   For the story of Albert, Luther, and the
     Teutonic Knights, see Fay 32–33.

36   **"Alliances . . . are good"**   *Ibid.*, 66.

38   **"our good master is dead"**   Baron Karl Ludwig von Pöllnitz, *The*
     *Memoirs of Charles-Lewis, Baron de Pöllnitz*, 4 vols., translated from the
     French (London, 1745); Macdonough, 17.

## IV. A SMALL, UNREADY ALCHEMIST

40   **"farmers . . . know their instruments"**   Georg Michael Pfefferkorn,
     *Merkwürdige und auserlesene Geschichte von der berühmten*
     *Landgrafschaft Thüringen* (1685); cited in Oesner, 37.

40   **"They sang popular songs"**   *NBR*, 424.

41   **the two men did not get along**   Marshall, *MQ*, 507.

41   **One of Sebastian's favorite works**   Wolff, *JSB*, 29.

42   **severely punished**   For this and several other insights, in particular
     related to Bach's feelings about being orphaned, I am indebted to
     Marshall.

42   **eighty-one children**   *NBR*, 32.

43   **"You will find that from the beginning"**   *Music in the Western World:*
     *A History in Documents*, edited by Piero Weiss and Richard Taruskin
     (New York: Schirmer, 1984), 101. Hereafter referred to as *MWW*.

44   **Pietism, an influence that took hold of him here**   For Bach's
     attachment to Pietism, see Schrade.

45   **he finished his first year**   Bach's class placements in Ohrdruf are in
     *NBR*, 34.

46   **Walther complains that his teacher**   Yearsley, *Bach*, 66.

46   **the practice of learned counterpoint and that of alchemy**   *Ibid.*, 42*ff*.

47   **"One day he was out walking"**   Godwin, 9–10.

49   **"I waver between the danger"**   Saint Augustine, *Confessions;*
     *MWW*, 32.

49   **"we have become deaf"**   Yearsley diss., 164.

49   **Kepler gave Luther's**   *Ibid.*

49   **"Now one will no longer"**   Godwin, 221–234.

51   **a prophecy in musical code**   Kees van Houten and Marinus
     Kasbergen, *Bach en het getal* (Zutphen, 1985); Tatlow, 1.

51    "powerful, ever-living Agent"    Gay, *Science*, 141.

51    "We marvel when we hear music"    Walter Buszin, *Luther on Music*,
        edited by J. Riedel, Pamphlet Series no. 3 (St. Paul: Lutheran Society
        for Worship, Music and the Arts, 1958), 6; cited in Bartel, 4.

51    "The heavens are now revolving"    Yearsley diss., 180; *Bach*, 20.

52    "beginning and end bound together"    Bokemeyer in *Critica Musica*,
        I, 328; cited in Yearsley, *Bach*, 24.

53    "consistence, oleosity and aquasity"    Paul Monroe, *History of
        Education* (New York: Macmillan, 1933), 487; cited in Chiapusso, 10.

56    dukedom of Celle    Wolff has raised doubt about Carl's assertion that
        Bach went to Celle, arguing that his education in French music came
        mainly at the castle in Lüneburg.

56    Like everything else at Versailles    For the substance and details of this
        discussion of music in the court of Louis XIV, I am indebted to
        Isherwood.

57    "knew perfectly well the necessity"    Isherwood, 333.

58    "This hero triumphs"    *Ibid.*, 230.

58    "I declare quite frankly"    *Ibid.*, 240.

## V. GIANTS, SPIES, AND THE LASH: LIFE WITH "FATTY"

61    fifty horses . . . 2,547 thalers    Fay, 91.

61    "Every day his majesty"    Diplomatic dispatch cited by *ibid.*, 92.

62    "The General Directory"    Lavisse, 57–58.

62    "A king needs to be strong"    *Ibid.*, 45.

62    Powerful nations . . . "will always be obliged"    *Ibid.*, 94.

63    "Fatty's heart is in my hands"    Diplomatic dispatch cited but not
        annotated in Simon, 69.

63    "The variable moods of the King"    Diplomatic dispatch cited in
        Lavisse, 77.

63    "Follow the example of your father"    Recalled by Frederick William
        in conversation with French minister La Chétardie; cited by Lavisse, 88.

66    "[Frederick] is to rise at seven"    Memo from Frederick William titled
        "Regulations for Schooling," September 3, 1721; cited in Carlyle, I,
        Book 4, Chapter 8, 395–396.

66    convinced it would lead to desertions    Ergang, 34.

66  They must "infuse into my son"  In *Oeuvres*, I; cited in Carlyle, I, Book IV, Chapter 8, 390.

71  **dispatch from the Saxon minister**  Diplomatic dispatch from Ulrich von Suhm cited in Asprey, 22. See also Lavisse, 128.

72  **"The people are greatly discontented"**  Diplomatic dispatch from Rothenberg cited in Lavisse, 120.

73  **Augustus's greatest gift**  Wonderful detail on Frederick's teenage romp in Dresden is in the memoirs of Pöllnitz and Wilhelmina, both referred to in Carlyle, II, Book VI, Chapter 3, 115–116.

74  **"For a long time"**  *Ibid.*, II, Book VI, Chapter 4, 134–135; this translation is Simon's, 60.

74  **"You know very well"**  *Ibid.*

75  **The king came unexpectedly**  The source of the story, according to Carlyle (II, Book VI, Chapter 7, 187–189) was Quantz.

76  **Augustus gave a dinner**  *Ibid.*, II, Book VII, Chapter 3, 157–258; Lavisse, 215.

76  **"Had I been so treated"**  Ranke, *Neun Bücher Preussischer Geschichte*, 3 vols. (Berlin, 1847), Vol. 1, 297; cited by Carlyle, II, Book VII, Chapter 3, 253; Reddaway, 31.

76  **"I have reason to believe"**  Diplomatic dispatch in Reinhold Koser, *Friedrich der Grosse als Kronprinz* (Stuttgart, 1886); cited in Asprey, 43.


VI. THE SHARP EDGES OF GENIUS

77  **promising to hang his tutors**  Ergang, 25.

79  **a hint of self-dealing**  For the irregularities surrounding Bach's hiring in Arnstadt, see Glöckner.

79  **"much incorrectness"**  *Ibid.*, 52.

79  **"the affairs and dealings of the world"**  See Leaver, *Calov Bible Commentary.*

81  **"the Holy Spirit was at work"**  *MWW*, 105.

82  **"through which something ascending"**  Walther, *Musical Lexicon*; cited in Bartel, 180.

82  **"through which lowly, insignificant"**  *Ibid.*, 215.

82  **"meant to express sorrowful"**  Yearsley diss., 235.

83  **"by the spirits which are contained"**  *MWW*, 214.

83    **bells that rang themselves**   For amusing detail on Kircher's background and theories, see Chiapusso, 125*ff.*

83    **"Music is nothing other"**   *Ibid.,* 129.

84    **Kircher invoked the four humors**   See chart, Bartel, 37.

84    **This animal-spirit-gas flows into the nerves**   Bartel, 36*ff.*

84    **"When the *harmonic numerus"***   Leisinger, 190.

85    **"With nothing more than gigue"**   *MWW,* 219.

85    **Far from being anachronistic**   Bartel, 33–34.

85    **"It cannot be otherwise"**   *Ibid.,* 16.

87    **"They have no respect for their masters"**   Diakonas Weissgerber, *Johann Sebastian Bach in Arnstadt* (Arnstadt, 1904), 5; Terry, 64.

88    **According to the consistory's account**   "Excerpts from the Proceedings of the Arnstadt Consistory," *NBR,* 43*ff.*

88    **"might very well have refrained"**   *Ibid.*

88    **"[Bach] must get along"**   *Ibid.*

89    **"Handel arrives from Hamburg"**   Spitta, I, 262.

90    **Extra security was required**   Details on Buxtehude's *Abendmusiken* are in Young, 79; Snyder, 69–70; and Schweitzer, I, 77.

90    **several thriving musical lives**   Wolff, *Bach Studies* 2, 196–199; Wolff, *JSB,* 95. Also see Snyder.

90    **music . . . could seem to be from different continents**   Wolff, *Bach Studies* 2, 196.

92    **its subject is time**   For this interpretation I am indebted to Chafe, *Tonal Allegory,* 91–123.

97    **eighteen bushels of wheat**   Bach's Weimar compensation is in Konrad Küster, *Der Junge Bach* (Stuttgart, 1996), 186*ff.; NBR,* 59.

## VII. WITNESS TO AN EXECUTION

100    **Frederick . . . put in writing a secret promise**   The letter is translated in full in Carlyle, II, Book VII, Chapter 2, 241.

101    **"The Crown Prince is loading me with favors"**   Diplomatic dispatch cited in Asprey, 27.

101    **"I pretend never to speak to the prince"**   Diplomatic dispatch cited in Lavisse, 166.

101 **"[Frederick William] is absolutely hated"** Diplomatic dispatch cited in Asprey, 29.

101 **"Profit by the relations"** Diplomatic dispatch cited in Lavisse, 169.

101 **"The other day the King asked the Prince"** Diplomatic dispatch cited in Carlyle, II, Book VI, Chapter 8, 191.

102 **"I am in the utmost despair"** *Ibid.*

102 **Frederick and Katte acted like lovers** Asprey, 51; Pöllnitz, cited in Macdonough, 49.

103 **The escape attempt in Mühlberg** See Carlyle, II, Book VII, Chapter 3, 253*ff.*

103 **Frederick said, "I prefer to go to France first"** Diplomatic dispatch from British envoy Guy Dickens cited in Lavisse, 223.

103 **in a smashing new red cape** Macdonough, 62.

104 **"I thought you would be in Paris"** Carlyle, II, Book VII, Chapter 6, 308.

104 **his first interrogator** The interrogation is similarly translated but not attributed in either Lavisse, 242–243, or Gooch, 114.

105 **"He said he wished to go incognito to Landau"** Diplomatic dispatch quoted in Lavisse, 235.

105 **"Fritz has attempted to desert"** Carlyle, II, Book VII, Chapter 7, 317.

106 **"The door [to his cell] must be well closed"** Letter from Frederick William to the governor general of Küstrin, cited in Lavisse, 244.

106 **"What does he deserve"** Wilhelmina, 215.

107 **with the daughter of a cantor** Carlyle, II, Book VII, Chapter 8, 329–330.

107 **"If the King of Prussia persists in these sentiments"** Lavisse, 249.

108 **"This little knave"** *Ibid.*, 259.

108 **"They must judge according to the law. . . ."** Details and quotations relating to the various appeals for Katte and Frederick are from *ibid.*, 272*ff.*

109 **"Oh my prince"** De Catt, I, 61–62.

110 **"burghers of a respectable standing"** Letter to the governor-general of Küstrin from Frederick William, cited in Lavisse, 291.

111 **"The king thinks he has taken Katte"** See Wilhelmina, 245*n.*, letter from the governor of the Küstrin fortress to Frederick William; also Lavisse, 292; Simon, 100.

## VIII. SONG OF THE ENDLESSLY ORBITING SPHERES

112    **as if he was marrying back**    For this insight I am indebted to Marshall, *MQ*, 512.

113    **a second Pachelbel**    Mattheson, *Critica Musica*, II, 175; Spitta, I, Book III, 383.

114    **Carl told the story in a letter**    Forkel; *NBR*, 435.

116    **"a heavenly-philosophical . . . science"**    J. G. Walther, *Praecepta der musicalischen Composition*, MS. 1708, new edition, edited by P. Benary (Leipzig: Breitkopf & Härtel, 1955), cited in Bartel, 10.

116    **Leibniz received a letter**    Leisinger, 82.

116    **"Perfection is the harmony of things"**    *Ibid.*

117    **"the hidden arithmetical exercise"**    Translation of Leibniz in Mizler, *Musikalische Bibliothek*; Butt, "A Mind Unconscious," 60.

117    **most famous in his lifetime**    Yearsley, *Bach*, 42–43.

118    **Houdemann canon looks like this**    The illustrations and realizations of the Houdemann canon are from Timothy Smith's illuminating and smart Web site on the Bach canons, http://jan.ucc.nau.edu/~tas3/bachindex.html.

122    **"Many an honest bore"**    Friedrich Erhardt Niedt, *Musicalischer Handleitung dritter und letzter Theil*, edited by Johann Mattheson (Hamburg, 1717); translated by Pamela Poulin and Irmgard Taylor as *The Musical Guide* (Oxford, 1989); cited in Yearsley, *Bach*, 263.

123    **"There are doubled"**    Niedt, *Musical Guide*; cited in Yearsley diss., 43–44.

123    **"could hardly eat"**    Johann David Heinichen, *Der General-Bass in der Composition* (Dresden, 1728), reprint (Hildesheim, 1969); cited in Yearsley diss., 82.

123    **"Do not expect that after all that quill-chewing"**    *Critica Musica*, II, 39; Cannon, 146.

123    **"Rules are valid as long as I consider it well"**    *Critica Musica*, I, 338; cited by Neumann, 258.

123    **One particularly incendiary article**    Yearsley, *Bach*, 53*ff.*

124    **"When I look at my old ideas"**    *Ibid.*, 55.

126    **he was more than "influenced"**    For insight into Bach's absorption of other composers' work, I am indebted to Dreyfus, *Patterns*.

126    **best hotel in town**    Glöckner, 65.

126   thirty quarts of beer   Wolff, *JSB*, 152.

127   Bach had never been seriously considered   Glöckner, 66.

128   "I tried to get a word with Mr. Handel"   Terry, 129.

128   "On November 6, [1717] the quondam concertmaster"   *NBR*, 80.

128   a passing reference by one Ernst Ludwig Gerber   Wolff, *NBR*, 321.

129   "like a surly foreigner"   Dreyfus, 42.

131   the orchestra, representing the collective society   For this discussion of
      the politics of the concerto, I am indebted to McClary.

134   a dedicatory poem by himself   *NBR*, 129.

135   "the earliest regular summer festival"   Wolff, 210–211.

135   no realm of neutrality or middle ground for action   For this discussion
      of Bach's relation to the Enlightenment I am indebted to Pelikan,
      Schrade, and Stiller.

136   "How good a bit of smooching"   Pelikan, 64.

136   Martin Luther . . . hymnal of 1524   Stiller, 208.

136   "the restoration of the heart"   The German phrase *Recreation des
      Gemüths* is usually translated differently, often as "recreation of the
      soul." While perhaps less precise as a direct translation, this translation
      from Stiller, 208, seems to evoke more fully the intended meaning of
      the phrase.

136   even in his filing system   Stiller, 208.

137   his *tombeau* or epitaph for Maria Barbara   Herbert Glossner, "The
      Most Arcane Secrets of Harmony," and Helga Thoene, "A Secret
      Language—Hidden Chorale Quotations in J. S. Bach's 'Sei Solo a
      Violino,'" articles (translated by J. Bradford Robinson) accompanying the
      CD entitled *Morimur*, Christopher Poppen's interpretation of the
      *Chaconne* from the solo violin sonata in D minor.

137   paper he had bought at a mill near Karlsbad   Thoene, 50.

137   numerological evidence in all six   Glossner, *Ibid.*, 39.

137   hidden in a cryptograph   Thoene, 50.

138   Leopold was being pressed so hard for funds   Glöckner, 74.


IX. A CHANGELING AMONG THE SWANS

139   when the event was "right fresh"   Lavisse, 291.

139   Müller brought . . . poison   From an account by Pastor Müller's son;
      translated in Carlyle, II, Book VIII, Chapter 1, 343–344.

139 **both men cried as they read**   Asprey, 75.

140 **"I know his wicked heart"**   Lavisse, 296.

140 **he tearfully made Grumbkow the gift**   *Ibid.*, 301.

140 **"happy as a lark"**   *Ibid.*, 303; Asprey, 78.

141 **"Frederick knows perfectly Aristotle's poetry"**   Variously translated from Koser by Lavisse, 312, and Asprey, 79.

142 **predestination, a tenet he quickly renounced**   Lavisse, 307.

142 **visit to the crown prince**   Grumbkow's first-person account is in Carlyle, II, Book VIII, Chapter 5, 375–378; also see Lavisse, 314–318; Asprey, 81–82.

143 **"My dear son Fritz"**   Complete letter is translated in Carlyle, III, Book IX, Chapter 1, 12–13.

145 **there were tears in his eyes**   Lavisse, 388.

147 **men before a bonfire**   Carlyle, III, Book IX, Chapter 2, 30.

147 **he . . . bombed the pastor's home**   *Ibid.*, III, Book IX, Chapter 2, 30–31.

149 **Frederick William was furious**   Asprey, 108.

151 **he did repay as king**   *Ibid.*, 128n.

152 **"ways not pleasant to his Father"**   Carlyle, VI, Book VI, Chapter 3, 119.

157 **The scholar Adrienne Hytier**   "Frédéric II et les Philosophes Recalcitrants," *Romantic Review* 57 (1966); cited in Asprey, 116.

157 **"a secret dialogue with himself"**   Friedrich Meinicke, "Ruler Before Philosopher," translated by Douglas Scott, in Peter Paret, ed., *Frederick the Great: A Profile* (London: Macmillan, 1972).

158 **"true desire is for fame"**   Diplomatic dispatch cited in Asprey, 129.

158 **Seckendorff . . . "begin with a thunderbolt"**   Quoted in Koser; cited by Asprey, 130.

159 **asked the general to choose**   Carlyle, III, Book X, Chapter 7, 271–272.

159 **"As soon as I am dead"**   Ergang, 245–246.

159 **That done, he was ready**   The scene with his pastors is in Carlyle, III, Book X, Chapter 8, 265*ff.*

159 **"Death, I fear thee not!"**   Wolfgang Venohr, *Friedrich der Grosse: Porträt einer Doppelnatur* (Bergisch Gladbach, 1988), 100; cited by Macdonough, 131.

160 **Dessauer came to console**   This and following details of Frederick's behavior immediately after his accession are from Carlyle, III, Book XI, Chapter 1, 278*ff.*; Jacob F. Biefeld, *Letters of Baron Biefeld*, 4 vols., translated by Mr. Hooker (London, 1768–70); Venohr, cited in Macdonough, 131; Asprey, 147*ff*; and Simon, 160–161.

286 ·· NOTES ON SOURCES

## X. THE ARTIST IN A PAINT-BY-NUMBERS WORLD

163    **age at which his father . . . mother . . . older brother . . . died**
Marshall, 506.

164    **"I, I, I, I"**  *NBR*, 325.

164    **Bach was near the bottom**  Siegele, 22–23.

164    **At the crucial meeting**  "Deliberations Excerpted from the
Proceedings of the Town Council," April 23, 1723, *NBR* 101, as
translated in Blume, 20.

164    **very different ideas for the job**  For the appointment process in
Leipzig, see Siegele, "Bach and the Domestic Politics of Electoral
Saxony."

165    **"a very sad state of things"**  Spitta, II, 201–202.

165    **"fast going to ruin"**  *Ibid.*, 202.

167    **Friedemann was clearly the favorite**  "Bach on His Sons," by Carl
Friedrich Cramer, *NBR*, 413.

167    **sons spoke . . . of having to distinguish themselves**  Blume, 16.

168    **Carl remembered his father's home**  *NBR*, 400.

168    **at his desk, where there were stacks of paper**  For details of the
description of Bach's working space I am indebted to Wolff, *JSB*.

169    **"not intended to be works"**  Friedrich Smend, *Bach-Studien*, 163;
cited in Pelikan, 26.

169    **In 1733 he bought a three-volume version**  Leaver, 21.

169    **the attic of a farmhouse**  Leaver, 16.

173    **"God help us! It's an opera-comedy!"**  C. H. Bitter, *Johann Sebastian
Bach*, 4 vols. (Berlin, 1881), Vol. 2, 58; cited in Terry, 197.

174    **"little inclination to work"**  This and following quotes are in Wolff,
*JSB*, 346.

178    **"a short and easy road to happiness"**  Quotations from the story "The
Choice of Hercules" are from Joseph Addison's translation in *The
Tatler*, no. 97, November 22, 1709.

179    **Six hundred students**  Details of the performance of *Preise dein
Glücke* for the Saxon elector are in Riemer, *Chronicles*, *NBR*, 164–167.
See also Crist.

179    **No fewer than six movements from *Hercules***  Pelikan, 137; Wolff, 364*ff*.

180    **The battle with Ernesti**  All of the many memos dealing with the
"affair of the prefects" are in *NBR*, 172*ff*.

182 **"Whereas Our Court Composer"** *Ibid.*, 195.

182 **the real issue between the rector and his cantor** The best general sources for Bach's confrontation with Ernesti as it demonstrates his posture toward the Enlightenment are "Rationalism and *Aufklärung* in Bach's Career," in Pelikan, 29*ff.*; "Bach's Quarrel with the Rector of St. Thomas School," in Stevenson, 67*ff.*; and Minnear.

182 **"the training of men toward God"** Quote from Luther in Stiller, 209.

183 **"Greater weight in exegesis"** Minnear, 136.

183 **"He began to quiver and quake"** Pelikan, 90.

184 ***Kritische Dichtkunst* of 1730 . . . dry, pedantic** Gay, *The Science of Freedom*, 247–248; Gagliardo, 205–206.

184 **Bach showed Gottsched what he thought** Dreyfus, *Patterns*, 232–242.

185 **"the equality of its divisions"** *Ibid.*

185 **"Your Saxony and dismayed Meissen"** Translation is in Dreyfus, *ibid.*, 235.

186 **"would be the admiration of whole nations"** Johann Adam Scheibe in *Der Kritische Musikus*, May 14, 1737, *NBR*, 338.

187 **"How can a man be faultless"** Spitta, III, 253–254.

188 **Bach had taken Communion** Stiller, 203.

188 **otherwise only twice or three times a year** *Ibid.*

188 **a strange and abrupt move** Ottenberg, 23.

188 **"Sensible Thoughts on Fools and Folly"** *Ibid.*, 24.

189 **audition for his job** Wollny, *Bach Studies* 2, 215; Wolff, 446.

189 **"With what pain and sorrow"** Letter to Johann Friedrich Klemm, May 24, 1738; *NBR*, 200.

190 **"a hot fever"** Insertion in Johann Walther's personal copy of his *Lexicon*; *NBR*, 295.

191 **"I have never concerned myself with learned matters"** A satire by "Cornelius" (Scheibe) in his *Der Kritische Musikus*; *NBR*, 351.

192 **"If Mr. Bach at times writes"** *NBR*, 350.

## XI. WAR AND PEACE AND A MECHANICAL DUCK

194 **The circumstances were a little awkward** Details of the story of Frederick's first meeting with Voltaire are in Carlyle, III, Book XI, Chapter 4, 345*ff.*

195 **Describing his first meeting with Frederick**  Voltaire, letter to M. de Cideville, October 18, 1740; in Carlyle, III, Book XI, Chapter 4, 357.

197 **Katte's father a promotion**  Macdonough, 140.

199 **"Bravo! The work of an excellent charlatan"**  Ritter, 82.

200 **he had "obeyed the orders"**  Besterman, 259.

201 **"Never, never will the queen renounce"**  C. A. Macartney, *Maria Theresa and the House of Austria* (London, 1969), 34; cited in Macdonough, 156.

201 **"with nothing but her character"**  Edward Crankshaw, *Maria Theresa* (London: Longmans, 1969); cited in Asprey, 155.

201 **a charlatan named Jacques de Vaucanson**  For this discussion of Vaucanson I am indebted to Richards.

202 **"with an Exactness"**  Fontenelle, "Abstract of the register of the Royal Academy of Sciences," appended to *Le Mécanisme du fluteur automate* (Paris, 1738), 21; translated by J. T. Desaguliers as "An Account of the Mechanism of an Automaton, or Image Playing on the German Flute," 23; see also Yearsley, *Bach*, 174*ff.*, and Richards.

202 **"It stretches out its Neck"**  "Mr. Vaucanson's Letter to the Abbé de Fontaine," appended to "Account"; *ibid.*, 21.

202 **"The smell which now spreads"**  A. Chapuis and E. Droz, *Automata* (Neuchâtel, 1958); cited in Richards, 381.

202 **"a musical machine could be constructed"**  Quantz, 131; Richards, 383.

203 **Frederick built a factory**  Richards, 382.

204 **When it opened in December 1742**  Description of the opera house is from Helm, 97*ff.*

208 **Frederick made himself at home in Dresden**  Detail from the contemporary account by Lorenz Mizler in his *Musikalische Bibliothek* (Leipzig, 1739–54), III, 366–368, is in Yearsley, *Bach*, 135–136.

209 **"the fragility of human fortunes"**  Asprey, 347.

209 **the occupation had been particularly harsh**  From Johann Salomon Riemer's handwritten *Chronicles of Leipzig*, November 19–December 18, 1745, courtesy Bach-Archiv Leipzig, translated by Sautter.

210 **these were unforgettably gruesome sights**  See Asprey.

212 **recurrent dreams**  Duffy, 17.

212 **the scene changed**  The second part of the dream is related in De Catt, I, 72; Ergang, 253.

## XII. THE NIGHT OF A MUSICAL OFFERING

213    **never quite liked him or his music**   Charles Burney, *A General History of Music*, 4 vols. in 2, Dover facsimile edition of the modern edition of the work originally published from 1775–82, Vol. 2, 961; Macdonough, 187; Lavisse, 72, 175; Ottenberg, 62; Burney, II, 262; *New Grove*, 846.

213    **"one or two lucrative offers"**   Carl Philipp Emanuel Bach, "Autobiography," translated by W. S. Newman, *Musical Quarterly* 51 (1965), 363*ff.*; cited in Ottenberg, 33.

213    **"His other complaints"**   H. Miesner, "Aus der Umwelt Philipp Emanuel Bachs," *Bach-Jahrbuch* 34 (1937), 139; Ottenberg, 57.

214    **"Bach is lying"**   *Ibid.*

214    **he . . . made two thousand thalers**   *New Grove* article on Carl, vol. 1, 845.

216    **Having forsworn the "meat"**   The interpretation is Yearsley's. See *Bach*, 121.

217    **"A player cannot move others"**   Carl Philipp Emanuel Bach, *Essay on the True Art of Playing Keyboard Instruments*, translated by William J. Mitchell (New York and London: W. W. Norton & Company, 1949), 152; as translated by Blume, 16; also see discussion in Ottenberg, 68.

217    **rarely changed them**   Wollny, *Bach Studies 2*, 202*ff.*

218    **[Carl] replaced Bach's arias with his own**   *Idem.*; Stauffer, 206.

218    **lifted his father's works**   Ottenberg, 175–176; Blume, 25.

218    **"Invention by Which Six Measures"**   C. P. E. Bach, *Einfall*, as printed in F. W. Marpurg, *Historisch-kritische Beyträge zur Aufnahme der Musik*, vol. 1 (1755); Yearsley, *Bach*, 185.

218    **"dry and despicable pedantry"**   Burney, II, 252.

218    **Carl's attitude toward canons**   Yearsley, "C. P. E. Bach's Canons," in *C. P. E. Bach Studies*, edited by Annette Richards (Cambridge University Press, forthcoming).

220    **"consists once and for all in the art"**   Heinichen, *Der General-Bass in der Composition* (Dresden, 1728); cited in Yearsley, *Bach.*, 94.

220    **"Really we should follow"**   Johann Mattheson, *Critica Musica*, 2 vols. (Hamburg, 1722–25), I, 346; cited in Yearsley diss., 94.

222    **the trip straight through**   Burney describes a carriage ride from Leipzig to Potsdam in *Present State*, vol. 2, 84.

222    **Summoned to the city palace**   NBR, 429.

223 a sales agent for them   Wolff, 413–414.

223 wanted to collect them all   NBR, 25n. 429n.

223 by now he had fifteen,   Ibid.

226 Bach could improvise . . . for hours at a time   NBR, 440.

228 performing tour of the organs   NBR, 430.

231 One musicologist supported   Ursula Kirkendale, "The Source for Bach's Musical Offering," Journal of the American Musicological Society 33:1 (Spring 1980), 88ff.

231 order of increasing theological significance   Marissen, Bach Studies 2.

232 Christoph Wolff seemed finally   Wolff, "New Research on the Musical Offering," Essays, 239ff.

232 Translators have often rendered   Marissen, Bach Studies 2.

234 ricercar an acronym   Wolff, "Apropos the Musical Offering: The Themum Regium and the Term Ricercar," Essays, 324ff.

235 Hofstadter likens this canon   Hofstadter, 10.

235 Eric Chafe was first to point out   Chafe, Tonal Allegory, 22–23, 213–215.

235 set in the form of sonatas da chiesa   Marissen, Bach Studies 2.

236 a polite dedication would be in French   Ibid.

236 Frederick specifically prohibited   Ibid.

236 Of the four hundred   Ibid.

238 Frederick . . . sang the Royal Theme   NBR, 366–367.

239 "Never criticize the composition"   A. W. Thayer, The Life of Ludwig van Beethoven, translated by H. E. Krehbiel, III, 20; cited in Helm, 28.

240 "In the case of works of art"   For his insights into the Romantic movement and the relation of Romanticism to both the Enlightenment and fascism, I am indebted to Berlin.

243 "gloomy, cold, hard"   Reinhold Koser, Geschichte Friedrichs des Grossen, 4 vols. Darmstadt, 1963. Quoted in Ritter, 185.

244 his fingers had so stiffened   Helm, 37.

244 lost interest in music completely   Ibid., 47, 76, 138.

244 he had to order soldiers   Ibid., 138.

244 "disgusting platitudes"   Pierre Gaxotte, Frederick the Great, translated by R. A. Bell (New Haven: Yale University Press, 1942), 379; cited in ibid., 76.

244 "ridiculous . . . bizarre" Shakespeare   Macdonough, 370.

244 Italian music was "dumb stuff"   Helm, 73.

245 French music "childish"   Ibid., 74.

245   "a racket that hurts the ears"   *Ibid.*, 71.

245   Mozart's was "caterwauling"   *Ibid.*, 76.

245   "The ill custom prevails"   Reddaway, 316.

246   "Hats off, gentlemen,"   Mitford, 196.

246   Lafayette paid the old king a visit   Olivier Bernier, *Lafayette: Hero of Two Worlds* (New York: E. P. Dutton, Inc., 1983), 161–163.

247   "about whom his fucking memoirs"   Macdonough, 385.

248   "Through all his life"   Reddaway, 2.

250   "the depths of the wisdom of the world"   Wolff, *Bach Studies* 2; Wolff, *Essays*, 389; *NBR*, 338*ff.*

250   a self-promoting quack named Dr. John Taylor   A. K. Kubba, "Johann Sebastian Bach's Disastrous Operation," *International Journal of Clinical Practice* 51:5 (July–August 1997).

251   "Before Thy throne, my God"   Translated by Terry, 136.

252   "moving ever farther"   Yearsley, *Bach*, 36.

252   "In the dark chamber"   Schweitzer, I, 223–224.

252   No one has ever invented   Johann Michael Schmidt, *Musico-Theologico*, 1754; *NBR*, 361; Richards, 383.

253   "A man, 67 years"   Terry, 265*n* (German); Spitta, III, 276 (translation); *NBR*, 244.

253   "what the school needs"   Terry, 265.

253   "Departed Bach! Long ago"   Telemann's valedictory, "Let Italy go on her virtuosi vaunting," *NBR*, 313.

254   no mention was made   Terry, 266.

254   rarely performed works by Bach   Blume, 26.

254   he sold the plates for scrap   Ottenberg, 56.

## XIII. AFTERLIVES: AN EPILOGUE

256   he said Carl was the only composer   Blume, 29.

258   All over Europe, in pamphlets and books   Besterman, 357.

260   "Why is he dead?"   *NBR*, 490.

260   The Romantic movement was conceived   For this discussion I am indebted to Berlin.

261   expressing the newly emergent creative self   See Peckham, 148*ff.*

262    "laughable and empty"   E. T. A. Hoffmann, *Schriften zur Musik*
       (Munich, 1963); cited in Ottenberg, 201.

262    "It was as if a dwarf had appeared"   Ottenberg, 203.

262    He even copied out   Yearsley "C. P. E. Bach's Canons."

262    Carl proudly brought out   Burney, II, 273.

263    "atrocious German chorale texts"   Blume, 44–45.

263    "could not escape French influence"   *Ibid.*, 45.

263    "You might give me a serious exposition"   *Ibid.*, 45.

263    "to make the antiquated work modern"   *Ibid.*, 51.

264    for that performance he had cut   Mendelssohn's cuts for the 1841 per-
       formance of the *St. Matthew Passion* are from Christopher Spering,
       "Affekt and Emotion: Comments on Felix Mendelssohn-Bartholdy's
       Arrangement of the St. Matthew Passion by J. S. Bach," translated by
       John Sidgwick, an article accompanying Spering's recording of
       Mendelssohn's 1841 arrangement.

265    the most ambitious opera of its time   See Wolff, 300*ff*.

266    "Look then upon this head"   Richard Wagner, *Was ist deutsch?*
       (1865–78), in *Gesammelte Schriften und Dichtungen von Richard
       Wagner* (Leipzig, 1871–83), Vol. 10, 51*ff*.; *NBR*, 505.

266    the Romantic hero became a demigod   For this discussion of
       Romanticism and fascism I am indebted to Berlin and Peckham.

267    Hitler . . . made Frederick his collaborator   For Frederick's
       appropriation by the Third Reich, see Macdonough, 5–9.

267    "as long as the swastika flies over Germany"   Duffy, 324.

268    Kohl created something of a stir   *Der Tagesspiegel*, Sunday, August 18,
       1991.

268    "Old Fritz's bones today"   *Ibid.*

268    gay demonstrators in Baroque costume   *Ibid.*

268    A poll conducted . . . controversy   Macdonough, 9.

268    Bach's bones had a ride   For the "authentication" of Bach's skeleton,
       see Yearsley, *Bach*.

270    "Do you suppose Bach is turning in his grave?"   Hinton, 134.

270    "the way I feel it"   Letter from Anton Webern to conductor Hermann
       Scherchen, 1938, quoted in Herbert Glossner, "Shadows of Death,
       Signs of Life," translated by Steven Lindberg, an article accompanying
       Christoph Poppen's recording of Webern's orchestration of the six-part
       ricercar.

# A SELECTED BIBLIOGRAPHY

Adorno, Theodor. *Introduction to the Sociology of Music*. Translated by E. B. Ashton. New York: The Seabury Press, 1976.

———. "Bach Defended Against His Devotees." In *Prisms*. Translated by Samuel and Shierry Weber. Cambridge, Mass.: MIT Press, 1981.

Althaus, Paul. *The Theology of Martin Luther*. Translated by Robert C. Schultz. Philadelphia: Fortress Press, 1966.

Asprey, Robert B. *Frederick the Great: The Magnificent Enigma*. New York: History Book Club, 1986.

Attali, Jacques. *Noise: The Political Economy of Music*. Translated by Brian Massumi. Minneapolis and London: University of Minnesota Press, 1985.

Bach, C. P. E. *Essay on the True Art of Playing Keyboard Instruments*. Translated by William J. Mitchell. New York: W. W. Norton & Co., 1949.

Bainton, Roland H. *Here I Stand: A Life of Martin Luther*. New York and London: Penguin Books, 1950.

Bamford, Christopher, ed. *Homage to Pythagoras: Rediscovering Sacred Science*. Hudson, N.Y.: Lindisfarne Books, 1994.

Barraclough, Geoffrey. *The Origins of Modern Germany*, revised edition. Oxford: Basil Blackwell, 1979.

Bartel, Dietrich. *Musica Poetica: Musical-Rhetorical Figures in German Baroque Music*. Lincoln and London: University of Nebraska Press, 1997.

Becker, Carl L. *The Heavenly City of the Eighteenth-Century Philosophers*. New Haven: Yale University Press, 1932.

Benjamin, Walter. *The Origin of German Tragic Drama*. Translated by John Osborne. London and New York: Verso, 1998.

Berlin, Isaiah. *The Crooked Timber of Humanity: Chapters in the History of Ideas*. New York: Alfred A. Knopf, 1991.

——. *The Power of Ideas*. Edited by Henry Hardy. Princeton: Princeton University Press, 2000.

——.*The Roots of Romanticism*. Princeton: Princeton University Press, 1999.

——. *Three Critics of the Enlightenment: Vico, Hamann, Herder*. Edited by Henry Hardy. Princeton: Princeton University Press, 2000.

Besterman, Theodore. *Voltaire*. New York: Harcourt, Brace & World, 1969.

Biermann, Berthold. *Goethe's World as Seen in Letters and Memoirs*. New York: New Directions, 1949.

Blume, Friedrich. *Renaissance and Baroque Music: A Comprehensive Survey*. Translated by M. D. Herter Norton. New York and London: W. W. Norton & Company, 1967.

——. *Two Centuries of Bach: An Account of Changing Tastes*. New York: W. W. Norton & Company, 1950.

Boyd, Malcolm. *Bach*. New York: Vintage Books, 1987.

——. "The Bach Family." In John Butt, ed. *The Cambridge Companion to Bach*. Cambridge, U.K.: Cambridge University Press, 1997.

——. *Bach: The Brandenburg Concertos*. Cambridge, U.K.: Cambridge University Press, 1993.

——, ed. *Oxford Composers Companions: J. S. Bach*. New York and Oxford: Oxford University Press, 1999.

Breig, Werner. "The Instrumental Music." In John Butt, ed. *The Cambridge Companion to Bach*. Cambridge, U.K.: Cambridge University Press, 1997.

Brokaw, James A. II. "The Perfectibility of J. S. Bach, or Did Bach Compose the Fugue on a Theme by Legrenzi, BWV 574a?" In Russell Stinson, ed., *Bach Perspectives*, Vol. 1, Lincoln and London: University of Nebraska Press, 1995.

Browning, Robert M. *German Poetry in the Age of Enlightenment: From Brockes to Klopstock*. University Park and London: Pennsylvania State University Press, 1978.

Bruford, W. H. *Germany in the Eighteenth Century: The Social Background of the Literary Revival*. Cambridge, U.K.: Cambridge University Press, 1965.

Buelow, George J., and Hans Joachim Marx, eds. *New Mattheson Studies*. Cambridge, U.K.: Cambridge University Press, 1983.

Bukofzer, Manfred F. *Music in the Baroque Era: From Monteverdi to Bach*. New York and London: W. W. Norton & Company, 1947.

Burney, Dr. Charles. *The Letters of Dr. Charles Burney, Volume I: 1751–1784.* Edited by Alvara Ribeiro, S. J. Oxford: Clarendon Press, 1991.

———. *The Present State of Music in Germany, the Netherlands and United Provinces,* a facsimile of the 1775 London edition, Vol. 2. New York: Broude Brothers, 1969.

Butler, Gregory. *Bach's Clavier Übung III: The Making of a Print.* Durham and London: Duke University Press, 1990.

———. "J. S. Bach's Reception of Tomaso Albinoni's Mature Concertos." In Daniel Melamed, ed. *Bach Studies 2.* Cambridge, U.K.: Cambridge University Press, 1995.

Butt, John. *Bach: Mass in B Minor.* Cambridge, U.K.: Cambridge University Press, 1991

———. "Bach's Metaphysics of Music." In John Butt, ed. *The Cambridge Companion to Bach.* Cambridge, U.K.: Cambridge University Press, 1997.

———. "J. S. Bach and G. F. Kauffmann: Reflections on Bach's Later Style." In Daniel Melamed, ed. *Bach Studies 2.* Cambridge, U.K.: Cambridge University Press, 1995.

———. *Music Education and the Art of Performance in the German Baroque.* Cambridge, U.K.: Cambridge University Press, 1994.

Cannon, Beekman C. *Johann Mattheson: Spectator in Music.* New Haven: Yale University Press, 1947.

Carlyle, Thomas. *Frederick II of Prussia, Called Frederick the Great.* 8 vols. London: Chapman and Hall, 1897.

Chafe, Eric. *Analyzing Bach Cantatas.* New York and Oxford: Oxford University Press, 2000.

———. *Tonal Allegory in the Vocal Music of J. S. Bach.* Berkeley and Oxford: University of California Press, 1991.

Chiapusso, Jan. *Bach's World.* Bloomington and London: Indiana University Press, 1968.

Clark, Stephen L., ed. *The Letters of C. P. E. Bach.* New York and Oxford: Oxford University Press, 1997.

Cox, Harvey, ed., *The Calov Bible of Bach.* In George Buelow, series ed. *Studies in Musicology* 92. UMI Research Press, 1985.

Cragg, Gerald R. *The Church and the Age of Reason 1648–1789.* New York: Penguin Books, 1990.

Cristensen, Thomas. "Bach Among the Theorists." In Michael Marissen, ed. *Bach Perspectives, Vol. 3: Creative Responses to Bach from Mozart to Hindemith.* Lincoln and London: University of Nebraska Press, 1998.

David, Hans T. *J. S. Bach's Musical Offering.* New York: G. Schirmer Inc., 1945.

——, and Arthur Mendel, eds. *The New Bach Reader: A Life of Johann Sebastian Bach in Letters and Documents.* Revised and expanded by Christoph Wolff. New York: W. W. Norton & Company, 1998.

De Catt, Henri. *Frederick the Great: The Memoirs of His Reader Henri De Catt.* 2 vols. London: Constable and Company Ltd., 1916.

Dreyfus, Laurence. *Bach and the Patterns of Invention.* Cambridge and London: Harvard University Press, 1996.

——. *Bach's Continuo Group: Players and Practices in His Vocal Works.* Cambridge and London: Harvard University Press, 1987.

Dudley, Underwood. *Numerology or, What Pythagoras Wrought.* Washington, D.C.: The Mathematical Association of America, 1997.

Duffy, Christopher. *The Army of Frederick the Great.* Second edition. Chicago: The Emperor's Press, 1996.

Edler, Arnfried. "Organ Music Within the Social Structure of North German Cities in the Seventeenth Century." In Paul Walker, ed. *Church, Stage and Studio: Music and Its Contexts in 17th-Century Germany.* Ann Arbor & London: UMI Research Press.

Elias, Norbert. *The Civilizing Process: The History of Manners.* Translated by Edmund Jephcott. New York: Urizen Books, 1978.

——. *The Court Society.* Translated by Edmund Jephcott. New York: Pantheon Books, 1983.

Eliot, T. S. "Tradition and the Individual Talent." In *Selected Essays.* New York: Harcourt, Brace & World, 1960.

Ergang, Robert. *The Potsdam Führer: Frederick William I, Father of Prussian Militarism.* New York: Columbia University Press, 1941.

Eyck, Frank. *Religion and Politics in German History: From the Beginnings to the French Revolution.* New York: St. Martin's Press, 1998.

Fay, Sidney B. *The Rise of Brandenburg-Prussia to 1786.* Revised edition edited by Klaus Epstein. New York: Holt, Rinehart and Winston, 1964.

Finscher, Ludwig. "Bach's Posthumous Role in Music History." In Michael Marissen, ed. *Bach Perspectives, Vol. 3: Creative Responses to Bach from Mozart to Hindemith.* Lincoln and London: University of Nebraska Press, 1998.

Forkel, Johann Nikolaus. *Johann Sebastian Bach: His life, Art and Work.* Translated by Charles Sanford Terry. New York: Vienna House, 1974.

Frédéric le Grand. *Oeuvres Historiques.* 30 vols. Edited by J. D. E. Preuss. Berlin: Prussian National Archives, 1846–57.

Friedenthal, Richard. *Goethe: His Life and Times.* London: Weidenfeld and Nicolson, 1963.

Frisch, Walter. "Bach, Brahms and the Emergence of Musical Modernism." In Michael Marissen, ed. *Bach Perspectives, Vol. 3: Creative Responses to Bach from Mozart to Hindemith.* Lincoln and London: University of Nebraska Press, 1998.

Fux, Johann Joseph. *The Study of Counterpoint, from Gradus ad Parnassum.* Translated and edited by Alfred Mann. New York and London: W. W. Norton & Company, 1965.

Gagliardo, John G. *Germany Under the Old Regime, 1600–1790.* London and New York: Longman Inc.: 1991.

Gawthrop, Richard L. *Pietism and the Making of Eighteenth-Century Prussia.* Cambridge, U.K.: Cambridge University Press, 1993.

Gaxotte, Pierre. *Frederick the Great.* Translated by R. A. Bell. New Haven: Yale University Press, 1942.

Gay, Peter. *The Enlightenment: The Rise of Modern Paganism.* New York and London: W. W. Norton & Company, 1969.

———. *The Enlightenment: The Science of Freedom.* New York and London: W. W. Norton & Company, 1969.

Geiringer, Karl and Irene. *Johann Sebastian Bach: The Culmination of an Era.* New York and Oxford: Oxford University Press, 1966.

Glöckner, Andreas. "Stages of Bach's Life and Activities." In Christoph Wolff, ed. *The World of the Bach Cantatas.* New York and London: W. W. Norton & Company, 1995.

Godwin, Jocelyn, ed. *The Harmony of the Spheres: A Sourcebook of the Pythagorean Tradition in Music.* Rochester, Vt.: Inner Traditions International, 1993.

Goethe, Johann Wolfgang von. *The Sorrows of Young Werther.* Translated by Michael Hulse. New York: Penguin Books, 1989.

Gooch, G. P. *Frederick the Great: The Ruler, the Writer, the Man.* New York: Alfred A. Knopf, 1947.

Haffner, Sebastian. *The Rise and Fall of Prussia.* Translated by Ewald Osers. London: Phoenix/Orion House, 1998.

Hayes, Malcolm. *Anton Webern.* London: Phaidon Press, 1995.

Helm, Ernest Eugene. *Music at the Court of Frederick the Great.* Norman: University of Oklahoma Press, 1960.

Hindemith, Paul. *Johann Sebastian Bach: Heritage and Obligation.* New Haven: Yale University Press, 1952.

Hinton, Stephen. "Hindemith and the Melancholy of Obligation." In Michael Marissen, ed. *Bach Perspectives, Vol. 3: Creative Responses to Bach from Mozart to Hindemith.* Lincoln and London: University of Nebraska Press, 1998.

Hofstadter, Douglas R. *Gödel, Escher, Bach: The Eternal Golden Braid.* New York: Basic Books, 1979.

Hytier, Adrienne. "Frédéric II et les Philosophes Récalcitrants." In *Romantic Review* 57 (1966).

Isherwood, Robert. *Music in the Service of the King: France in the Seventeenth Century.* Ithaca and London: Cornell University Press, 1973.

Jacob, Heinrich Eduard. *Felix Mendelssohn and His Times.* Translated by Richard and Clara Winston. Englewood Cliffs, N.J.: Prentice-Hall, 1963.

Jones, Richard D. P. "The Keyboard Works: Bach as Teacher and Virtuoso." In John Butt, ed. *The Cambridge Companion to Bach.* Cambridge, U.K.: Cambridge University Press, 1997.

Kerry, Paul E. *Enlightenment Thought in the Writings of Goethe: A Contribution to the History of Ideas.* Rochester, N.Y.: Camden House, 2001.

Kinderman, William. "Bachian Affinities in Beethoven." In Michael Marissen, ed. *Bach Perspectives, Vol. 3: Creative Responses to Bach from Mozart to Hindemith.* Lincoln and London: University of Nebraska Press, 1998.

Kirkendale, Ursula. "The Source for Bach's *Musical Offering.*" In *The Journal of the American Musicological Society* 33 (1980): 88–141.

Klingensmith, Samuel John. *The Utility of Splendor: Ceremony, Social Life, and Architecture at the Court of Bavaria, 1600–1800.* Edited by Christian F. Otto and Mark Ashton. Chicago and London: The University of Chicago Press, 1993.

Koopman, Ton. "Aspects of Performance Practice." In Christoph Wolff, ed. *The World of the Bach Cantatas.* New York: W. W. Norton & Company, 1995.

La Mettrie, Julian Offroy de. *Man a Machine.* LaSalle, Ill.: Open Court, 1912.

———. *A Natural History of the Soul.* La Salle, Ill.: Open Court, 1912.

Lang, Paul Henry. *Handel.* New York: W. W. Norton & Company, 1996.

Lavisse, Ernest. *La Jeunesse du Grand Frédéric.* Paris, 1891. Translated as *The Youth of Frederick the Great* by Mary Bushnell Coleman, Chicago: S. C. Griggs and Company, 1892.

Leaver, Robin A., ed. *J. S. Bach and Scripture: Glosses from the Calov Bible Commentary.* St. Louis: Concordia Publishing House, 1985.

Leichtentritt, Hugo. *Music, History and Ideas,* Cambridge, Mass.: Harvard University Press, 1950.

Leisinger, Ulrich. "Affections, Rhetoric, and Musical Expression." In Christoph Wolff, ed. *The World of the Bach Cantatas.* New York: W.W. Norton & Company, 1995.

———. "Forms and Functions of the Choral Movements in J. S. Bach's *St. Matthew Passion.*" In Daniel Melamed, ed. *Bach Studies 2.* Cambridge, U.K.: Cambridge University Press, 1995.

Little, Meredith, and Natalie Jenne. *Dance and the Music of J. S. Bach.* Bloomington: Indiana University Press, 1991.

Lodge, Sir Richard. *Great Britain and Prussia in the Eighteenth Century.* Oxford: Oxford University Press, 1923.

Longyear, Rey M. *Nineteenth-Century Romanticism in Music.* Englewood Cliffs, N.J.: Prentice-Hall, 1973.

Macdonough, Giles. *Frederick the Great: A Life in Deed and Letters.* New York: St. Martin's Press, 1999.

Mann, Alfred. *The Study of Fugue.* New York: W.W. Norton & Company, 1965.

Marissen, Michael. "Concerto Styles and Significance in Bach's First Brandenburg Concerto." In Russell Stinson, ed. *Bach Perspectives, Vol. 1.* Lincoln and London: University of Nebraska Press, 1995.

———. *Lutheranism, Anti-Judaism, and Bach's St. John Passion.* New York and Oxford: Oxford University Press, 1998.

———. *The Social and Religious Designs of J. S. Bach's Brandenburg Concertos.* Princeton: Princeton University Press, 1995.

———. "The Theological Character of J. S. Bach's *Musical Offering.*" In Daniel Melamed, ed. *Bach Studies 2.* Cambridge, U.K.: Cambridge University Press, 1995.

Marshall, Robert Lewis. "Bach and Mozart's Artistic Maturity," In Michael Marissen, ed. *Bach Perspectives, Vol. 3: Creative Responses to Bach from Mozart to Hindemith.* Lincoln and London: University of Nebraska Press, 1998.

———. *The Compositional Process of J. S. Bach: A Study of the Autograph Scores of the Vocal Works.* 2 vols. Princeton: Princeton University Press, 1970.

——. "Toward a Twenty-First-Century Bach Biography." In *Musical Quarterly* 84:3 (2000), 497*ff*.

Mattheson, Johann. *Der Vollkommene Capellmeister: A Revised Translation with Critical Commentary.* 2 vols. Edited by Ernest C. Harriss. Ann Arbor: UMI Research Press, 1981.

McCarthy, George E. *Romancing Antiquity: German Critique of the Enlightenment from Weber to Habermas.* New York: Rowman & Littlefield Publishers, Inc., 1997.

McClary, Susan. "The Blasphemy of Talking Politics During Bach Year." In Richard Leppert and Susan McClary, eds. *Music and Society.* Cambridge, U.K.: Cambridge University Press, 1987.

Melamed, Daniel R. *J. S. Bach and the German Motet.* Cambridge, U.K.: Cambridge University Press, 1995.

——. "A Thirty-six Voice Cannon in the Hand of C. P. E. Bach." In Daniel Melamed, ed. *Bach Studies 2.* Cambridge, U.K.: Cambridge University Press, 1995.

——, and Michael Marissen, eds. *An Introduction to Bach Studies.* New York and Oxford: Oxford University Press, 1998.

Mendelssohn-Bartholdy, Dr. Karl. *Goethe and Mendelssohn.* Translated by M. E. von Glehn. London: Macmillan, 1872.

Menhennet, Alan. *Order and Freedom: Literature and Society in Germany from 1720 to 1805.* New York: Basic Books, 1973.

Minnear, Paul. "J. S. Bach and J. A. Ernesti: A Case Study in Exegetical and Theological Conflict." In John Deschner, Leroy T. Howe, and Klaus Penzel, eds. *Our Common History as Christians: Essays in Honor of Albert C. Outler.* New York: Oxford University Press, 1975.

Mitford, Nancy. *Frederick the Great.* London: Penguin Books, 1973.

——. *Voltaire in Love.* New York: Carroll & Graf, 1957.

Neumann, Frederick. "Mattheson on Performance Practice." In *New Mattheson Studies.* Cambridge, U.K.: Cambridge University Press, 1983.

*New Bach Reader: A Life of Johann Sebastian Bach in Letters and Documents.* Edited by Hans T. David and Arthur Mendel; revised and enlarged by Christoph Wolff. New York: W. W. Norton & Company, 1998.

Norton, Richard. *Tonality in Western Culture: A Critical and Historical Perspective.* University Park and London: The Pennsylvania State University Press, 1984.

Oberman, Heiko A. *Luther: Man Between God and the Devil.* Translated by Eileen Walliser-Schwarzbart. New York: Doubleday, 1992.

Oesner, Claus. "Musical Life of the Towns and Courts in Central Germany Around 1700." In Christoph Wolff, ed. *The World of the Bach Cantatas*. New York: W. W. Norton & Company, 1995.

Oleskiewicz, Mary. "The Trio in Bach's *Musical Offering*: A Salute to Frederick's Tastes and Quantz's Flutes?" In Russell Stinson, ed. *Bach Perspectives, Vol. 1*. Lincoln and London: University of Nebraska Press, 1995.

Ottenberg, Hans-Günter. *Carl Philipp Emanuel Bach*. Translated by Philip J. Whitmore. Oxford: Oxford University Press, 1987.

Parker, Mary Ann, ed. *Eighteenth-Century Music in Theory and Practice: Essays in Honor of Alfred Mann*. Stuyvesant, N.Y.: Pendragon Press, 1995.

Parry, C. Hubert H. *Johann Sebastian Bach: The Story of the Development of a Great Personality*. New York and London: G. P. Putnam & Sons, 1909.

Peckham, Morse. *Beyond the Tragic Vision: The Quest for Identity in the Nineteenth Century*. New York: George Braziller, 1962.

Pelikan, Jaroslav. *Bach Among the Theologians*. Philadelphia: Fortress Press, 1986.

Pirro, André. *J. S. Bach*. New York: The Orion Press, 1957.

Quantz, Johann Joachim. *On Playing the Flute*. Translated by Edward R. Reilly. London: Faber & Faber Limited, 1966.

Radandt, Friedhelm. *From Baroque to Storm and Stress, 1720–1775*. London: Croom Helm, 1977.

Ranke, Leopold von. *Neun Bücher Preussischer Geschichte*. Berlin, 1847.

Reddaway, William Fiddian. *Frederick the Great and the Rise of Prussia*. New York and London: G. P. Putnam & Sons, 1904.

Richards, Annette. "Automatic Genius: Mozart and the Mechanical Sublime." In *Music & Letters* 80 (1999): 366–389.

Rifkin, Joshua. "Some Questions of Performance in J. S. Bach's *Trauerode*." In Daniel Melamed, ed. *Bach Studies 2*. Cambridge, U.K.: Cambridge University Press, 1995.

Ritter, Gerhard. *Frederick the Great: A Historical Profile*. Translated by Peter Paret. Berkeley: University of California Press, 1970.

Roehr, Sabine. *A Primer on German Enlightenment*. Columbia and London: University of Missouri Press, 1995.

Rosenberg, Hans. *Bureaucracy, Aristocracy and Autocracy: The Prussian Experience 1660–1815*. Boston: Beacon Press, 1958.

Sadie, Stanley, ed. *The New Grove Dictionary of Music and Musicians*, 26 vols. New York: Macmillan, 1980.

Sainte-Beuve, C. A. *Monday Chats*. Fourth edition. Translated by Dr. William Matthews. Chicago: S. C. Griggs and Company, 1882.

Schneider, Theodor. *Frederick the Great*. Translated by Sabina Berkeley and H. M. Scott. London and New York: Longman, 2000.

Schoenberg, Arnold. *Style and Idea: Selected Writings of Arnold Schoenberg*. Edited by Leonard Stern. Translated by Leo Black. London: Faber and Faber, 1975.

Schrade, Leo. *Bach: The Conflict Between the Sacred and the Secular*. New York: Da Capo Press, 1973.

Schulenberg, David. "Composition and Improvisation in the School of J. S. Bach." In Russell Stinson, ed. *Bach Perspectives, Vol. 1*. Lincoln and London: University of Nebraska Press, 1995.

———. *Music of the Baroque*. New York and Oxford: Oxford University Press, 2001.

———. *The Keyboard Music of J. S. Bach*. London: Victor Gollancz Ltd., 1993.

Schulze, Hans Joachim. "Bach the Composer." In Christoph Wolff, ed. *The World of the Bach Cantatas*. New York: W. W. Norton & Company, 1995.

Schweitzer, Albert. *J. S. Bach*. 2 vols. Translated by Ernest Newman. London: Adam & Charles Black, 1911.

Siegele, Ulrich. "Bach and the Domestic Politics of Electoral Saxony." In John Butt, ed. *The Cambridge Companion to Bach*. Cambridge, U.K.: Cambridge University Press, 1997.

Simon, Edith. *The Making of Frederick the Great*. Boston: Little, Brown & Co., 1963.

Smend, Friedrich. *Bach in Köthen*. Translated by John Page. St. Louis: Concordia Publishing House, 1985.

Snyder, Kerala J. *Dieterich Buxtehude: Organist in Lübeck*. New York: Schirmer Books, 1987.

———, ed. *The Organ as a Mirror of Its Time: North European Reflections, 1610–2000*. Oxford and New York: Oxford University Press, 2002.

Snyder, Louis, ed. *Great Lives Observed: Frederick the Great*. Englewood Cliffs, N.J.: Prentice-Hall, 1971.

*Source Readings in Music History*. Edited by Oliver Strunk. Revised edition edited by Leo Treitler. New York: W. W. Norton & Company, 1998.

Spitta, Philipp. *Johann Sebastian Bach: His Work and Influence on the Music of Germany, 1684–1750*. 3 vols. Translated by Clara Bell and J. A. Fuller-Maitland. London: Novello & Co., Ltd.

Stapert, Calvin R. *My Only Comfort: Death, Deliverance and Discipleship in the Music of Bach*. Grand Rapids, Mich.: William B. Eerdmans Publishing Co., 2000.

Stauffer, George B. "Bach as Organist." In Christoph Wolff, ed. *The World of the Bach Cantatas*. New York: W. W. Norton & Company, 1995.

——. "Changing Issues of Performance Practice." In John Butt, ed. *The Cambridge Companion to Bach*. Cambridge, U.K.: Cambridge University Press, 1997.

Stevenson, Robert. *Patterns of Protestant Church Music*. Durham, N.C.: Duke University Press, 1953.

Stiller, Günther. *Johann Sebastian Bach and Liturgical Life in Leipzig*. Translated by Herbert J. A. Bouman, Daniel F. Poellot, and Hilton C. Oswald. Edited by Robin A. Leaver. St. Louis: Concordia Publishing House, 1984.

Stolzenberg, Daniel, ed. *The Great Art of Knowing: The Baroque Encyclopedia of Athanasius Kircher*. Stanford: Stanford University Press, 2001.

Swack, Jeanne. "J. S. Bach's A Major Flute Sonata BWV 1032 Revisited." In Daniel Melamed, ed. *Bach Studies 2*. Cambridge, U.K.: Cambridge University Press, 1995.

Taruskin, Richard. *Text and Act*. New York and Oxford: Oxford University Press, 1995.

Tatlow, Ruth. *Bach and the Riddle of the Number Alphabet*. Cambridge, U.K.: Cambridge University Press, 1991.

Terry, Charles Sanford. *Bach: A Biography*. London: Oxford University Press, 1928.

*The New Oxford History of Music*. 10 vols. London and New York: Oxford University Press, 1974.

"The World-Famous Organist, Mr. Johann Sebastian Bach, Royal Polish and Electoral Saxon Court Composer, and Music Director in Leipzig." 1750. The only contemporary obituary of Bach, it first appeared in L. Mizler, *Musikalische Bibliothek*, IV (Leipzig, 1754. *NBR*, 297ff.).

Treitschke, Heinrich von. *The Life of Frederick the Great*. Translated by Douglas Sladen. Honolulu: University Press of the Pacific, 2001.

Voltaire, François-Marie Arouet de. *Philosophical Dictionary*. Translated by Theodore Besterman. New York: Penguin Books, 1972.

Walker, Paul, ed. *Church, Stage and Studio: Music and Its Contexts in 17th Century Germany*. Ann Arbor: UMI Research Press, 1990.

———. "Fugue in the Musical-Rhetorical Analogy and Rhetoric in the Development of Fugue." In Russell Stinson, ed. *Bach Perspectives*, Vol. 1. Lincoln and London: University of Nebraska Press, 1995.

———. "Rhetoric, the Ricercar and J. S. Bach's *Musical Offering*." In Daniel Melamed, ed. *Bach Studies* 2. Cambridge, U.K.: Cambridge University Press, 1995.

Webber, Geoffrey. *North German Church Music in the Age of Buxtehude*. Oxford: Clarendon Press, 1996.

Weiss, Piero, and Richard Taruskin, eds. *Music in the Western World: A History in Documents*. New York: Schirmer, 1984.

Werckmeister, Andreas. *Erweiterte und verbesserte Orgel-Probe in English*. Translated by Gerhard Krapf. Raleigh, N.C.: Sunbury Press, 1976.

Wilhelmina, Margravine of Bayreuth. *The Misfortunate Margravine: The Early Memoirs of Wilhelmina, Margravine of Bayreuth, Sister of Frederick the Great*. New York: St. Martin's Press, 1970.

Wolff, Christoph. *Johann Sebastian Bach: The Learned Musician*. New York and London: W. W. Norton & Company, 2000.

Wollny, Peter. *Bach: Essays on His Life and Music*. Cambridge, Mass.: Harvard University Press, 1991.

———. "Bach's Pre-Leipzig Cantatas: Repertory and Context." In Christoph Wolff, ed. *The World of the Bach Cantatas*. New York: W. W. Norton & Company, 1995.

———. "Cantatas, Arias and Recitatives." In Christoph Wolff, ed. *The World of the Bach Cantatas*. New York: W. W. Norton & Company, 1995.

———. "Choir and Instruments." In Christoph Wolff, ed. *The World of the Bach Cantatas*. New York: W. W. Norton & Company, 1995.

———. "Dietrich Buxtehude and Seventeenth-Century Music in Retrospect. In Paul Walker, ed. *Church, Stage and Studio: Music and Its Contexts in 17th-Century Germany*. Ann Arbor & London: UMI Research Press.

———. "Genres and Styles of Sacred Music Around and After 1700." In Christoph Wolff, ed. *The World of the Bach Cantatas*. New York: W. W. Norton & Company, 1995.

———. "J. S. Bach and the Legacy of the Seventeenth Century." In Daniel Melamed, ed. *Bach Studies* 2. Cambridge, U.K.: Cambridge University Press, 1995.

———. "Wilhelm Friedemann Bach's Halle Performances of Cantatas by His Father." In Daniel Melamed, ed. *Bach Studies* 2. Cambridge, U.K.: Cambridge University Press, 1995.

Yearsley, David G. *Bach and the Meanings of Counterpoint.* Cambridge, U.K.: Cambridge University Press, 2002.

———. "Ideologies of Learned Counterpoint in the North German Baroque." Unpublished doctoral dissertation. Stanford University, 1994.

Young, Percy M. *The Bachs, 1500–1850.* New York: Thomas Y. Crowell Company, 1970.

Zenck, Martin. "Bach Reception: Some Concepts and Parameters." In John Butt, ed. *The Cambridge Companion to Bach.* Cambridge, U.K.: Cambridge University Press, 1997.

*A   VERY   SELECTIVE*

*D I S C O G R A P H Y*

To recommend a few recordings of the works of Bach is to commit many terrible acts of omission, and so at the outset I disclaim the notion that the recordings suggested below are in any sense a list of "best performances." What follows is simply a collection of favorites and familiars of mine, chosen for a variety of reasons, both musical and nonmusical. I have in certain cases favored a recording because it is commonly available or because of other works on the same CD; and in some cases I have chosen performances simply because they would be most accessible to people unfamiliar with many of Bach's works (favoring piano over harpsichord in the performance of keyboard works, for example), on the theory that those with a more advanced familiarity with Bach would have no use for a discography as tightly circumscribed as this one. All that having been said, anyone wishing to become better acquainted with the works mentioned in this book will enjoy the following:

*Actus Tragicus* (Cantata, BWV 106). Ton Koopman and the Amsterdam
   Baroque Orchestra and Choir. Erato, 1995.
*Art of the Fugue* (BWV 1080). Reinhard Goebel with Musica Antiqua Köln,
   1979–1984. (The three-CD set includes his *Musical Offering* and many

canons, including the Houdemann canon, the canon for J. G. Walther's
son, and the fourteen canons based on the Goldberg ground.)

*Brandenburg Concertos* (BWV 1046–1051). Neville Marriner with the Academy
of St. Martin in the Fields. Philips, recorded 1980, reissued 1990.

*Capriccio on the Departure of a Beloved Brother* (BWV 992). Wanda Landowska.
RCA, 1945–1957, reissued 1992. (Includes her *Goldberg Variations*, the
Two- and Three-Part Inventions, and the Partita in C minor—taken
together, a wonderful introduction to Bach on the harpsichord.

*Chamber Music of Frederick the Great.* Richard Auldon Clark with Emily
Newbold. Helicon Records, 1997. (Includes works by both Frederick and
C. P. E. Bach.)

*Christmas Oratorio* (BWV 248). John Eliot Gardiner with the English Baroque
Soloists and Monteverdi Choir. Archiv, 1987.

*C. P. E. Bach: 8 Symphonies.* Christopher Hogwood with the Academy of
Ancient Music. Decca, 1997 (2 CDs).

*C. P. E. Bach: Flute Concertos.* Feinstein Ensemble. Black Box Classics, 2000.

*Flötenkonzerte & Sinfonien, Friedrich "der Grosse."* Hartmut Haenchen with
the Carl Philipp Emanuel Bach Chamber Orchestra. Capriccio, 1994.

*F Major Duetto* from *Clavierübung III.* Christopher Herrick on a CD titled
*Organ Miniatures.* Hyperion, 1996. (Includes his six-part ricercar from the
*Musical Offering.*)

*Frederick the Great, Bach and Benda.* Peter Schrier with Patrick Gallois, Klaus
Kirbach, *et al.* Polygram Records, 1995. (Includes works by all three.)

*Gloria in Excelsis Deo* (BWV 191). Ludwig Güttler with Virtuosi Saxoniae and
Concentus Vocalis Wien. Berlin Classics, 1995. (Includes Güttler's version
of the *Christmas Oratorio.*)

*Goldberg Variations* (BWV 998). Glenn Gould, the recordings of his very
different 1955 and 1981 performances. Reissued by Sony Classical, 2002.
After listening to this you can join the love-him-or-hate-him debate (I'm
with the former) and, along with the Schiff version (see the *Well-Tempered
Clavier*), comprehend what an extraordinary range of interpretation a work
like this inspires.

*Gott ist mein König* (BWV 71). Ton Koopman, Complete Cantatas Vol. 1.
Erato, 1995. (Vol. 1 also includes *Gottes Zeit ist die allerbeste Zeit,* or
*Actus Tragicus,* BWV 106.)

*Hercules at the Crossroads* (BWV 213). Gustav Leonhardt with the Orchestra
and Choir of the Age of Enlightenment. Philips, 1994. (Includes the
Coffee Cantata.)

*J. S. Bach: The Ultimate Organ Collection.* Anthony Newman. Excelsior, 1994.

*Magnificat in D-Major.* Philip Ledger with the Academy of St. Martin in the Fields. London Jubilee, 1976. (Pairs the father's version with C. P. E.'s very different one, which he seems to have used as his audition piece in making a bid for his father's job in 1749.)

*Mass in B Minor.* John Eliot Gardiner and the English Baroque Soloists and Monteverdi Choir. Deutsche Grammophon, 1990.

*Musical Offering* (BWV 1079). Neville Marriner with the Academy of St. Martin in the Fields. Philips, 1974–1978. (Includes his Art of the Fugue.) For an "authentic" performance, listen to the Hänssler Bachakademie version (1999), which includes wonderful interpretations of other Bach canons as well.

*Passion According to St. John* (BWV 245). John Eliot Gardiner with the English Baroque Soloists and Monteverdi Choir. Archiv, 1986.

*Passion According to St. Matthew* (BWV 244). Herbert von Karajan and the Berlin Philharmonic. Deutsche Grammophon, recorded 1972, reissued 1990.

*Six Suites for Unaccompanied Cello.* Yo-Yo Ma. Sony Classical, 1994–1997.

*Sonatas and Partitas for Unaccompanied Violin.* Nathan Milstein. Deutsche Grammophon, recorded in 1975, reissued in 1998.

*The Great Contest: Bach, Scarlatti, Handel.* David Yearsley, organist. Loft Recordings, 2001. (An imaginary play-off among the three great composers, all born in the same year, which demonstrates the range of Baroque composition for organ.)

*The Well-Tempered Clavier, Books I and II* (BWV 846–893). Andras Schiff. Decca, recorded 1983–1993, issued in 1996 in a twelve-CD boxed set entitled *Bach: Solo Keyboard Works.* (Includes his *Goldberg Variations,* the six Partitas, the French and English suites, the *Italian Concerto,* and other works.) Schiff's readings of Bach are original, profound, and unsurpassed.

*Twentieth-Century Bach: Virtuoso Orchestral Transcriptions.* Seiji Ozawa with the Boston Symphony Orchestra. Philips, 1992. (Includes Webern's transcription of the six-part ricercar on the Royal Theme, Stravinsky's arrangement of *Vom Himmel hoch* [BWV 769], and Schoenberg's transcription of the *Prelude and Fugue in E-flat* [BWV 552].)

*Vor deinen Thron* (BWV 668). Gustav Leonhardt on the Christian Müller Organ at the Waalse Kerk, Amsterdam. Seon-Sony, 1972–1973. (Includes his *Canonic Variations on Vom Himmel hoch.*)

**Affection**   In Baroque music theory, the emotion or idea that a work or passage of music aims to evoke.

**Ambitus**   The natural scope of keys for a given work, derived from the term that described the tonal range of *Gregorian chant*.

**Augmentation**   The statement of a canon subject in notes double the length of those in a previous statement.

**Cadenza**   Usually a brilliant passage by a solo instrument toward the close of a concerto.

**Canon**   The most rigorous form of *counterpoint*, in which a single musical phrase is imitated in various ways by successive voices at varying intervals of time and pitch (see *augmentation, inversion, crab canon*, etc.).

**Canonic imitation**   The variation of a *canon* subject (see *augmentation, inversion, crab canon*, etc.).

**Canon per tonos**   A *canon* whose subject is such that each iteration of the canon begins one whole tone higher; also known as a spiral canon.

**Cantata**   A vocal and instrumental work, usually in multiple movements, that may include arias, *recitatives*, duets, and chorus, and is based on a lyrical, dramatic, or religious text.

**Cantus firmus**   A melody from a *chorale, plainsong,* or folk tune that becomes the basis for a work of *polyphony*.

**Catabasis**   One of the *musical-rhetorical figures*, a descending musical passage that expresses negative affections.

**Chorale**   A hymn of the German Protestant church.

**Chorale prelude**   A composition for organ based on a *chorale*.

**Chromatic/chromaticism**   Terms referring to the introduction of harmonic or melodic complexity through the use of notes not common to the "normal" major scale (what would happen, for example, if the black keys of the piano were introduced into a C-major scale), turning the six whole tones in an octave into twelve semitones.

**Collegium musicum**   A society of musical amateurs, formed for the performance of music, often drawn from a university.

**Continuo**   The accompaniment part in a vocal and/or instrumental work, often for harpsichord or organ and a viola da gamba or cello.

**Contrapuntist**   A composer of *counterpoint*.

**Counterpoint**   A method of composition in which two or more related but independent lines play together according to a fixed set of rules developed in numerous treatises of the fourteenth through eighteenth centuries (see *polyphony*).

**Countersubject**   A subsidiary passage used to complement or comment on the subject of a *fugue* or *canon*.

**Crab canon**   A *canon* in which the subject is varied by playing it in reverse, also known as *retrograde*.

**Da capo aria**   A song consisting of two sections followed by a repeat of the first, resulting in the form A-B-A.

**Descensus**   See *Catabasis*.

**Diminution**   The statement of a *canon* subject in notes half the length of those in a previous statement.

**Dramma per musica**   The earliest name for Italian opera, used by Bach for certain of his secular *cantatas*.

**Fugue**   A work of *counterpoint* in which the subject is stated and/or imitated two or more times in close succession and reappears throughout the work, in combination with secondary material.

*Galant*   The light, elegant style of the rococo period, associated with the evolution from *counterpoint* to accompanied melody.

**Gematria**   The simple substitution of a number for a letter in the alphabet, as in A = 1, B = 2, etc., used to encode meaning.

**Gregorian chant**   The unharmonized, single-voiced music of the Roman Catholic liturgy, thought to have been introduced by Pope Gregory I at the end of the sixth century A.D. (see *monophony*).

**Homophony**   Music that consists of a melody and a supporting accompaniment, as opposed to the coequal voices of *counterpoint* (*polyphony*) or the single voice of *monophony*.

**Inversion**   The variation of a *canon* subject by changing each interval to the same interval in the opposite direction, so that an ascending interval is changed to a descending one and vice versa. Also known as a canon in "contrary motion."

**Mirror canon**  The *canon* that would result if you played a canon with the page turned upside down—in other words, a canon inverted and in *retrograde* motion (though sometimes also used as a synonym for *crab canon*).

**Monophony**  Music consisting of a single line or voice, sometimes also called monody (see *Gregorian chant* and *plainsong*).

**Musical-rhetorical figures**  Passages meant to evoke specific positive or negative emotional responses or to carry specific meanings (see, for example, *catabasis*).

**Oratorio**  A choral and instrumental composition that supports a long, usually religious text but without costumes or other staging.

**Passus duriusculus**  Literally "hard passage," a musical-rhetorical figure in which chromatic variation is introduced into a melodic line, a form of *pathopoeia*. See *chromatic/chromaticism*.

**Pathopoeia**  A general term for a musical passage meant to evoke a passionate affection through various means (for example, chromatic variation).

**Perpetual canon**  A *canon* whose subject leads back to its beginning and so permits the canon no natural ending. Rounds like *Frère Jacques* are simple examples of perpetual canon.

**Plainsong**  See *monophony*. Also used as a synonym for *Gregorian chant*.

**Polyphony**  Music that consists of two or more individual voice parts, as opposed to *homophony* and *monophony*, a term virtually synonymous with *counterpoint*.

**Puzzle canon**  A *canon* written in enigmatic notation, leaving the reader to "solve" the riddle of which intervals of time and pitch and which sorts of variation will work; also known as a riddle canon.

**Quodlibet**  A humorous form of *polyphony* in which well-known melodies and texts are combined to comment on one another.

**Recitative**  A free vocal style or form that follows the natural rhythms and dynamics of a piece of text, usually with only minimal accompaniment.

**Retrograde**  See *crab canon*.

**Saltus duriusculus**  Literally "hard leap," a *musical-rhetorical figure* meant to express something harshly negative.

**Subject**  A melodic passage that forms the basis of a composition, such as a *fugue* or *canon*.

## *A C K N O W L E D G M E N T S*

Attempting to write an interpretive essay about Bach's *Musical Offering* that involves the lives of two men as outsize as Bach and Frederick involves more than the usual hazards of biography. Both men have large, scholarly canons, but while the works on Frederick add up to a single person, there are virtually as many Sebastians as he has students. Bach was too little inclined and too busy writing and performing music to leave much record of himself, and that has resulted in a body of scholarship that is enormous and conflicted. Choices among sources must be made. I have been living with all these Bachs ever since I began playing his music as a child, and one of the reasons I wrote this book was to find out who he was, which really meant to find out which choices in the literature made sense to me. Bach could not have been both a radically secular composer forced by his times into the costume of a Lutheran cantor (an old East German interpretation, admittedly) and the "fifth Evangelist" whose feet barely touched ground (the opinion of a substantially larger group).

With deep gratitude and deference to all Bach scholars, without whose work I could hardly have undertaken this book, I found myself having to proceed according to the premise that no man with twenty children, a temper, and an engulfing life's work could have been anything but a very tough nut. My favorite representation of him, unlike the usual portraits of a rotund, bewigged, serious burgher, is a statue by Bernd Göbel in the market square of Arnstadt, the town that gave him his first full-time job as a musician. Something of a sensation when it was installed in the 1980s, it depicts a lithe young man in tight pants and an open shirt, with large hands and a steady gaze, a vivid Bach with blood in his veins and a little lust in his heart. There is no doubt that Bach was a deeply religious man—the many *NB*s and exclamation marks in the margins of his Bible leave no doubt of that—but spirituality and a hard edge do not of course represent a contradiction. Martin Luther was no saint either.

In any case, I am acutely conscious of having added yet another Sebastian to the literature that draws on a huge amount of scholarly research and scant information. In particular, Bach's silence left a great deal of room for subjectivity and speculation about the "extra-musical" meanings embedded in his work, which are central to this book. Albert Schweitzer, among others, has been accused of finding somewhat more meanings in Bach's music than there are. My prejudice has been that, on balance and within sensible limits, this was the right mistake to make, since finding too little meaning in his work risked a greater disservice to his command as a composer than finding too much. In approaching the ambiguities of interpretation, I tried to keep in mind both the injunction about Freudian dream interpretation, that "sometimes a cigar is just a cigar," and the fact that Freud, a cigar smoker, died of jaw cancer. This is why I have shied away from some of the woollier areas of Bach scholarship (all the intellectual mischief associated with the fact that there are numerological meanings in his music, for instance), and why I have not strayed beyond good current scholarship without making plain that I have done so.

§

CHIEF AMONG THOSE to whom I owe thanks for help in the making of this book is Courtney Hodell, without whose editorial acuity and hard work it would be very much poorer. She is every writer's best friend, a very painstaking and exacting reader, the sort of book editor who is said not to be around much anymore. Her partner at Fourth Estate, Christopher Potter, also demonstrated a quality of support that many writers are not lucky enough to get from their publishers. Also at Fourth Estate I must thank Amy Baker for her staunch and effective advocacy of this book as it made its way into the world, and Rachel Safko for her work on the book's behalf and for her gracious forbearance. Susan Bolotin gave me the initial push to write this book, and Liz Darhansoff gave me the support, both material and moral, that was needed to pursue it. She and several other friends, including Lee Aitken, Andras Fejer, and James Graff, made valuable observations at various stages. Dan Okrent, who was the recipient of several e-mail attachments in the course of this work, has given me lots of invariably sound advice and years of great friendship.

Many ingenious and devoted research librarians are the bulwark of this book. I thank especially the staffs of the New York Public Library at Forty-second Street and at Lincoln Center, where this book was first conceived, and the staff of the Bibliothèque Nationale in Paris, particularly the librarians at L'Opéra and those in the rare books collection at the Mitterrand center, custodians of Frederick's *Oeuvres*. For research help in Germany I am indebted to Dr. Ursula Sautter. I wish also to thank all the teachers who educated my understanding of Bach, music, and the subtleties of biography (in order of appearance): Donald Hageman, Julian DeGray, Donald Rock, McNeil Robinson, Anthony Newman, and Richard Gartner.

The substance of this book owes everything to the people listed in the notes and bibliography, and the ones from whom I have learned the most are cited in the text as well. One of these is the Bach scholar and organist David Yearsley, who made the foolhardy offer to read this book in an early draft. The benefit of his scholarship and of his generosity with it are everywhere on the pages of this book. So too is the work of Michael Marissen, whose essay on the *Musical Offering* in *Bach Studies 2* inspired and provides an underpinning for this book. Neither of them, I hasten to add, would agree entirely with what I have written. I have always found it odd when authors find it necessary to declare their sources and influences innocent of their errors, something that has always seemed to go without saying. I see now that it does not, that they have worked too carefully and too hard for too long to have their work used without some immunity from its misuse, and so I hereby absolve them, the teachers listed above, and the many other scholars on whose work I have drawn of any responsibility for whatever errors of fact and interpretation I may have made.

Finally and most important, I must acknowledge more than gratitude to the incomparable Karen Gaines, whose patience, love, support, and a certain amount of benign neglect during some very difficult years made writing this book at least marginally compatible with the wonderful and very lived life that she inspires in me and the terrific children to whom this book is dedicated.

—Paris
May 2004

family deaths and, 39–40,
43–44, 45, 135, 137, 138, 163,
187–88, 190
as father, 7, 11, 40, 112, 113,
135, 138, 162, 166–67,
187–91, 214, 221
on fortepiano development, 223
Frederick II's meetings with, 5,
6, 8–10, 222–24, 227–28, 238
improvisational skills of,
226–27, 238
income of, 78, 79, 92, 126, 162,
171–72, 174, 175, 216
independence of, 241–42
Leipzig home of, 167–68
marriages of, 7, 79, 89, 91–92,
112, 135, 165–66
musical influences on, 40–42,
45, 55–56, 58–59, 89–91, 98,
125–26, 129, 176, 263
as organist, 91, 114–15, 127–28,
163, 217, 228, 253
productivity of, 113, 127, 165,
168–69, 190
religious belief of, 7–8, 19, 44,
96–97, 136, 169, 188, 221,
237–38, 239, 241, 272
as representative of tradition,
5–6, 7–8, 124, 191, 220
Romantic aesthetic theory and,
186, 241
sightreading skills of, 114
spirituality joined with secular
life of, 135–37, 272
students of, 87–88, 113, 173–74,
180–81, 192

temperament of, 88, 130, 217,
237–38, 241
theological library of, 169–70
title obtained by, 177, 180, 187
Bach, Johann Sebastian, music of:
canons, 115, 116–22, 124, 215,
216, 230, 248–49
civic events marked by, 95
consistory prescriptions on,
91
critics of, 162–64, 173, 186–87,
191–92, 216
dedicatees of, 86, 117, 133–34,
177–78, 209, 228, 232, 249
final masterpiece of, 249
five annual cycles of, 168–69
Frederick II's challenge and,
9–12, 124, 221, 223–39
funeral cantatas, 92–95, 184–85
German cultural espousal of,
265–67
"Great Eighteen" organ
chorales of, 251
humor in, 216
ineffability of, 240
instrumental hierarchy
overturned by, 129, 130–31,
132–33
JSB's work process and, 11–12,
168, 229, 232, 241, 251, 252
librettists of, 184–85
lost works of, 113
mixture of styles in, 129–30,
134, 185
Mozart's work compared with,
256–57

Bismarck, Otto von, 267
"Blasphemy of Talking Politics
    During Bach Year, The"
    (McClary), 132–33
Boethius, Ancius Manlius
    Severinus, 48, 116
Böhm, Georg, 251
Boileau, Nicolas, 58
Bokemeyer, Heinrich, 46, 124
Boyd, Malcolm, 231
Boyle, Robert, 14
Brahe, Tycho, 14
Brahms, Johannes, 239
Brandenburg, 28–30, 33–34, 35,
    188
*Brandenburg Concertos* (Bach), 95,
    129–31, 132–33, 134
bubonic plague, 19
Burney, Charles, 218, 220, 262
Buxtehude, Dietrich, 55–56,
    88–91, 95, 249, 251

cadenza, 311
Calov, Abraham, 169, 170, 175,
    221
Calvinism, 23, 34, 44, 66, 134
*Candide* (Voltaire), 156, 258, 259
canon, 7, 115–16
    crab, 236, 248, 312
    critics of, 122–23, 124, 218–20
    defined, 311
    fugue vs., 116, 118, 224
    in *Goldberg Variations,* 215, 216,
        248–49
    of *Musical Offering,* 230, 232,
        234–35, 236–37

perpetual, 52, 117, 121, 122, 236,
    249, 313
puzzle, 117–21, 234, 236, 313
on Royal Theme, 230, 236
canonic imitation, 311
canon per tonos (spiral canon), 311
cantatas, 92–96, 97, 168–69, 311
*cantus firmus,* 94, 226, 311
*Capriccio on the Departure of the
    Beloved Brother* (Bach),
    86–87, 138, 233, 240
Carlyle, Thomas, 27–28, 64, 152,
    160, 268
*catabasis (descensus),* 82, 311
Catt, Henri de, 109
celestial music, 7, 48, 49, 250
Celle, dukedom of, 56
Chafe, Eric, 235
Charles VI, Holy Roman
    Emperor, 197, 198
Charles VII, Holy Roman
    Emperor, 207
Charles XII, king of Sweden, 86
chorales, 80–81, 94, 311
choral prelude, 311
Christiane Eberhardine, electress,
    184
Christianity:
    Anabaptist, 23, 44, 96, 241
    Calvinist, 23, 34, 44, 66, 134
    on crucifixion of Jesus, 183
    Pietist, 44, 96–97, 169, 260
    predestination doctrine of, 66,
        142, 242
    as target of Enlightenment, 154
    *see also* Lutheranism

## About the author

## About the book

## Read on

Insights,
Interviews
& More...

# A Conversation with
# James R. Gaines

*How did you end up in Paris and how long have you been there?*

We've been here for three years. When I left Time Inc. (having lived and worked in New York for thirty years) we moved to Boulder, Colorado—partly because my wife is a skier, partly because we have little kids, and partly because of the mountains. But we missed the life of a large city and (since we didn't want to go back to New York) settled on Paris. We might have moved to Italy, but it is so seductively enticing and my experiences there have been so thoroughly self-indulgent, I was worried it could feel too much like retirement.

*How does it feel to be an American living in Paris?*

Well, during the Iraq war I stayed in a lot! The thing that was most striking during that period was that many French people who knew I was American wanted me to know that Chirac did not speak for all the French. I never got the opposite—but then I was working very hard at the time. On the other hand, my American friends kept asking "Why are you living in that terrible country? They can't stand us!" It was as if I was being disloyal for living in Paris.

*What do you miss about America?*

Friends mainly—and being able to speak English all the time. For someone who cares a lot about words it's difficult to be anything

**We might have moved to Italy, but it is so seductively enticing . . . I was worried it could feel too much like retirement.**

2

less than fluent, and my French is far from that. And things are easier in America—though not always. At least people there think the customer is always right. . . . It's very different here.

*What do you love about Paris?*

It's so beautiful—the markets, the restaurants, the bread, and life in general is just . . . wonderful. Living inside history is also stimulating. In the States there isn't any. It's not our fault—we're young. I'm living in the places that I'm writing about in my next book, and in a sense I feel the history I'm writing every day.

*You've been a journalist and an editor—now you're a writer: What did you want to be when you grew up?*

I actually wanted to be a magazine editor. I remember telling my father when I was eleven that I could edit *Life* magazine and he looked at me as if I was crazy.

*How did you know what an editor was at age eleven?*

I have no idea. It wasn't from my parents. My father was a cash register repairman who rose through the ranks to become a corporate honcho. My mother stayed at home to raise us.

*What did you like about magazine editing when you finally got there?*

Being *an* editor was a slog, but being *the* editor—which is what I really wanted—is a bit like being an orchestra conductor. You ▶

❝ I remember telling my father when I was eleven that I could edit *Life* magazine and he looked at me as if I was crazy. ❞

## A Conversation with James R. Gaines
*(continued)*

don't write any stories, you don't take any pictures, but you bring out a little flute here and a little cello there and try to present the face and spirit of the publication in a way that is consonant with its mission and the expectations of the audience and that tries to make a difference in the world.

*Did you ever miss the writing once you were the editor?*

No. I didn't miss magazine writing—but I did miss book writing. I wrote *Wit's End* (about the Algonquin Round Table) in 1977 and I take comfort in the idea that a book can always be read. The issues of *Time* magazine that I edited stopped being read the week they were on sale, and that's the idea. If they aren't an expression of the moment they were published they aren't doing their job.

*What was your route to the editorship?*

I was a writer at *Newsweek,* at *Saturday Review,* and at *People.* I started in the editorial ranks at *People* (and finally wound up as the editor), then became the editor of *Life,* and then the editor of *Time*—which is kind of a natural progression.

*The competition between fathers and sons is one of the themes in Bach's* Musical Offering. *Were you ever spurred on by such competition yourself?*

Absolutely. I am a second son. There are real advantages to that because the expectations

66 I am a second son. There are real advantages to that because the expectations are not nearly as high. 99

are not nearly as high. Sometimes you can resent the fact that they are not as high, or wonder why. On the other hand, my parents told me I could be whatever would make me happy, and they told my brother that he was going to be a doctor. Period.

*When did you start learning to play the piano?*

When I was eight. That's when I discovered another great thing about having an older brother: they spur you on. My brother has perfect pitch and can improvise really well, but I knew I could play classical music better than he could. I just knew it—and I think that kept me going sometimes. When you're a kid, practicing can seem like the last thing you need to do, and I think the competition kept me at it. Not that he competed, really. He still improvises better than I do and I still play Bach better than he does.

*The book is a masterly musical education for those who know little about music. Did you have formal musical training?*

I studied hard in high school and was admitted to the music school at the University of Michigan. I realized almost instantly that I was not good enough to become a performing pianist (and I didn't think I would be a good teacher) so I transferred into liberal arts and majored in English. I continued to take piano lessons all through college and even for a couple of years after, but I would never try to pass myself off as a musicologist. I learned ▶

## A Conversation with James R. Gaines
*(continued)*

most of what I know about Bach doing research for the book.

*At the beginning of the book you describe what music is for Bach and for Frederick. What is it for you?*

It's a means of expression (as writing is)—it's consolation when things are going badly, and it's a great intellectual and physical challenge. Whatever the activity, there's something pretty terrific about finally doing something that you didn't think you could do. In music it's all about practicing and more practicing until that wonderful moment when you hear yourself doing it. There's also the ego appeal of performance, though I must say my nerves and fear of mistakes were always stronger than that—probably because I didn't practice enough. Music is certainly not calming for me. I know people who listen to music when they work or when they want to go to sleep, but it wakes me up. The last thing I would do on an insomniac night is listen to music.

*The defining moment of Frederick's life is Katte's execution and his own captivity; for Bach it is the death of his first wife. You write of their tragedies with great empathy. Is there such a defining moment in your life?*

Not like that, no. But the ending of the book reminded me of one defining experience. It was the very last thing I wrote. I had the entire book written and I could not think how to finish it. Eventually I wrote about the two contrasting views of the world that Bach and

> 66 For me, music is a means of expression (as writing is)—it's consolation when things are going badly. 99

Frederick represent. Bach's world can't quite be explained by reason—it's a world where things are fundamentally mysterious. The world in which Frederick lived (a machine—all cause and effect) was what I called at the end of the book a world of "something unremittingly solid." When I was proofreading the book I came across that phrase and suddenly thought: uh-oh, I think I've read that somewhere. Of course this is a nightmare for a nonfiction book. How was I ever going to find a three-word phrase in my library or notes? If I couldn't, I would have to take it out—and for a variety of reasons I really did not want to.

A couple of days later I realized that I had written that phrase thirty-five years before, when I had just left college and was trying to figure out what to do with my life. I had decided by that time that I wasn't good enough to be a pianist—and though I wrote poetry and short stories I felt I wasn't good enough to write fiction either. I decided I would go into journalism, because I'd done a bit of it in college and knew I was good at explicative declaratory prose. I was writing a short story at the time which was autobiographical. All my stories were autobiographical then, which is probably why I became a journalist. I had written a hyperdramatic paragraph about a young man standing at a fork in the road, remembering a time when he lived in a world of great overwhelming passion. He saw that that was gone and he was left alone in a heartbreaking world of unrelenting solids. That is where the phrase came from. Realizing that was a ▶

66 I wrote about the two contrasting views of the world that Bach and Frederick represent. Bach's world can't quite be explained by reason—it's a world where things are fundamentally mysterious. The world in which Frederick lived (a machine—all cause and effect) was 'something unremittingly solid.' 99

**A Conversation with James R. Gaines**
*(continued)*

relief, of course, but it also reminded me that the question this book is about (Which kind of world do we live in?) is one that I've been wrestling with all my adult life—and one I have yet to resolve.

*You write that in the Romantic period "The ultimate task of finding a source of meaning in the world would belong to the artist." Where do you find meaning in your own life?*

My kids; the family. I also think a lot. At various times in my life people have asked with some apparent irritation what I could possibly be thinking about all the time. I don't know if I think about the questions that I raise in this book more than other people do, but I think about them a great deal. For me, reflecting on large questions is one source of meaning.

*Do you find Paris more conducive to thinking than the States?*

In a way, yes. I think it would have been more difficult for me to write this book had I stayed in Boulder because the mountains constantly beckon. It's hard to feel good about sitting inside when it's so beautiful out there. During winter in Paris you definitely do not feel that way.

*Do you have a favorite work by Bach?*

I've said before that my desert-island Bach would be the cello suites—but I would really hate to have to make that choice. ∽

# How I Came to Write *Evening in the Palace of Reason*

SEVERAL YEARS AGO a friend at a publishing house called me with a proposition. She and I had worked together, and she knew I had always wanted to write a book about Bach. Her boss was looking for a Bach book, and she wondered if I would be interested in working up a proposal.

I was thrilled. From the time I started playing the piano I felt drawn toward the music of Bach. As I got older he became my great musical passion. In high school I thought I would be the next Glenn Gould— my piano teacher did not. When I got to music school I discovered there were a lot of kids more talented and driven to perform than I was, so I switched to liberal arts and went into journalism after college. There I spent the next thirty years of my life. I kept playing and thinking about Bach during those years, but careers and children have a way of pushing youthful passions to one side.

When my friend called I had retired from the magazine business and was spending my time learning to fly airplanes. This was something I had always wanted to do—as did every kid who grew up in Dayton, Ohio ("home of the Wright Brothers"). Her phone call reminded me of something else I had been wanting to do for the past few decades: find some excuse to bury myself completely in Bach for a while and apply real concentration to an area in which I had great enthusiasm for the work but very little knowledge of the man. I had read quite a bit about him—but I didn't ▶

> 66 In high school I thought I would be the next Glenn Gould— my piano teacher did not. 99

9

## How I Came to Write *Evening in the Palace of Reason* (continued)

" Do the book *you* want to write and we'll find a good place for it. "

know what to make of what I had read. He seemed to have sprung on the stage full-grown, having had no youth or growing up at all—a great man without dimension.

My friend's boss wanted a different sort of Bach book than the one I wanted to do. It was a wonderful idea in its own right, but it was not what I had come to care about. I called my agent, whose advice was immediate and clear: "Do the book *you* want to write and we'll find a good place for it."

By that time I had become interested in Bach's meeting with Frederick—in part because Frederick was just such an irresistible character. Not only was he the perfect foil for Bach (and vice versa), but their meeting also opened the door to a story even bigger than the one I had been thinking about. This was the story of a moment in history which raised a question that has been resonating ever since: What is the place for belief in the logical, post-Enlightenment, post-mythical world—a world where individual growth and justice are in the human rather than the divine province, and a world governed (with notable exceptions) by reason? This is a question that had bothered me ever since I was old enough to doubt.

Frederick was more than instrumental in this part of the story. In a way he is the poster boy for his own opposition. Beaten into submission by a mad father, Frederick (predictably) adopted a view of life as chaotic, accidental, and wholly without meaning—a kind of clockwork in which every person was just a witless cog. In his fifties he wrote to a friend, wondering aloud why he had waged wars, drained marshes to encourage agriculture, and promoted Prussian trade: "We are a poor race, which is very restless during the little time it vegetates on this atom of mud called the earth. Whoever passes his days in quietness and repose until his machine decomposes, is perhaps more sensible than they who, by so many torturous circles, spiked with thorns, descend to the grave. In spite of that, I am obliged to go round like the wheel of a water mill, because one is dragged by one's fate." Frederick loved the inventions of a fraud named Jacques Vaucanson, who built a mechanical shepherd that could play the flute and later constructed a duck that Vaucanson said could actually fart (the duck is one of my favorite characters, but the flatulence was rigged). Frederick was a convinced, hard-core materialist—the acolyte and patron of Julian La Mettrie, author of the scandalous *Man a Machine*. And yet even Frederick thought—needed to think—he had a soul. As much as he tried he could not wean himself from the idea.

I wrote this book because I have always loved Bach's music and always wanted to know the man who made it. But I was also drawn to investigate the opposition of reason and faith. This issue was outlined in high relief by the confrontation of Bach and Frederick and by the music that resulted from their meeting—Bach's *Musical Offering*. I don't pretend to have arrived at a definitive answer, but I do think the book asserts a provocative refinement of the question: If there were no place in this world for belief and no such thing as transcendence, how could we react as we do to the music of Bach? Or, to put it another way, if this is all there is how could there have been a Bach? ∽

> " Frederick loved the inventions of a fraud named Jacques Vaucanson, who built a mechanical shepherd that could play the flute. "

> " If there were no place in this world for belief and no such thing as transcendence, how could we react as we do to the music of Bach? "

# Author's Picks

### *Johann Sebastian Bach: The Learned Musician,* Christoph Wolff

A classical and highly respected biography.

### *The New Bach Reader: A Life of Johann Sebastian Bach in Letters and Documents,* ed. by David Theodor Hans, Arthur Mendel, Hans T. David, and Christoph Wolff

A collection of Bach's letters and articles about the composer, which offers an enlightening and entertaining insight into his character.

### *The Aesthetics of Music,* Roger Scruton

A philosophical discussion of what music is and means for humanity—both in terms of significance and enjoyment.

### *The Essential Bach Choir,* Andrew Parrott

A professional chorister investigates the history and practices of Bach's choirs in order to better understand how the composer constructed his many choral pieces.

### *Frederick the Great,* Theodor Schieder

A highly regarded series of essays about the king which throws light both on his personality and country.

### *Music and Silence,* Rose Tremain

In seventeenth-century Denmark, King Christian IV turns to music as the solace and solution to all the problems of his court and marriage—but his wife hates music. Told by four different narrators, the novel constructs a world that is at once gentle and violent, honest and deceitful, and good and evil.

### *Amsterdam,* Ian McEwan

The Booker Prize–winning novel in which two old friends, a composer and an editor, make a euthanasia pact—with disastrous results.

### *The Piano Shop on the Left Bank: The Hidden World of a Paris Atelier,* T. E. Carhart

A love letter to the piano and to Paris, written by an expat who describes his life with both.

# The Ten Best Books about Bach

The following books, selected by James R. Gaines, are alphabetized by author.

*The Cambridge Companion to Bach,* ed. by John Butt

*Bach and the Patterns of Invention,* Laurence Dreyfus

*The Social and Religious Designs of Bach's Brandenburg Concertos,* Michael Marissen

*Bach Studies 2,* ed. by Daniel Melamed

*Bach Among the Theologians,* Jaroslav Pelikan

*Bach: The Conflict between the Sacred and the Secular,* Leo Schrade

*Johann Sebastian Bach: His Work and Influence on the Music of Germany, 1684–1750,* Philipp Spitta

*Johann Sebastian Bach: The Learned Musician,* Christoph Wolff

*The New Bach Reader,* ed. by Christoph Wolff

*Bach and the Meanings of Counterpoint,* David Yearsley

# Have You Read?

## More by James R. Gaines

*Wit's End: Days and Nights of the Algonquin Round Table,* James R. Gaines (Harcourt Brace Jovanovich, 1977)

A biography of a literary group in New York City in the 1920s, including Dorothy Parker, Robert Benchley, and Alexander Woolcott.

*The Lives of the Piano,* ed. by James R. Gaines (Holt, Rinehart & Winston, 1981)

A collection of essays on the history, repertoire, pedagogy, and social meaning of the quintessential nineteenth-century instrument and a consideration of its future.

# The Web Detective

### www.jsbach.org

This Web site, set up in 1995, offers an extensive biography, bibliography, and catalogue of Bach's works as well as a useful tourist guide and map detailing sites worth visiting. Recordings and works are catalogued in several different ways, including by instrument, year, and (where relevant) recording label.

### www.baroquemusic.org/bqxjsbach.html

Detailed information about Bach's life and works presented against a rather-too-detailed bright blue background.

### www.pianosociety.com

Listen to free MP3 downloads of Bach's music played by both amateurs and professionals.

### http://jan.ucc.nau.edu/~tas3/bachindex.html

Tim Smith's Web site on the Bach canons is a great resource in itself, but is also fantastically well connected to other Bach Web sites and materials.

Don't miss the next book by your favorite author. Sign up now for AuthorTracker by visiting www.AuthorTracker.com.